MEDIEVAL TOTAL WAR™

OFFICIAL STRATEGY GUIDE

by Rick Barba

MEDIEVAL: TOTAL WAR™

OFFICIAL STRATEGY GUIDE

by Rick Barba

BradyGAMES Publishing
An Imprint of Pearson Education
201 West 103rd Street
Indianapolis, Indiana 46290

ISBN: 0-7440-0182-X

Library of Congress Catalog No.: 2002109607

Printing Code: The rightmost double-digit number is the year of the book's printing; the rightmost single-digit number is the number of the book's printing. For example, 02-1 shows that the first printing of the book occurred in 2002.

05 04 03 02 4 3 2 1

Manufactured in the United States of America.

BradyGAMES Staff

Publisher
David Waybright

Editor-In-Chief
H. Leigh Davis

Marketing Manager
Janet Eshenour

Creative Director
Robin Lasek

Licensing Manager
Mike Degler

Assistant Marketing Manager
Susie Nieman

Credits

Title Manager
Tim Fitzpatrick

Copy Editor
Sean Medlock

Screenshot Editor
Michael Owen

Book Designer
Chris Luckenbill

Production Designer
Bob Klunder

ACKNOWLEDGEMENTS

The author would like to acknowledge the folks at both The Creative Assembly and Activision for their extensive input on this project. Thanks also to copy editor Sean Medlock and book designer Chris Luckenbill for making the book read so cleanly and look so great, and to title manager Tim Fitzpatrick for his patient guidance and good humor despite the usual insane deadlines. Finally, thanks to Leigh Davis for yet another opportunity to work with such a professional crew.

Table of Contents

Chapter 1: Getting Started

Welcome to the official strategy guide to one of the most anticipated PC game titles in recent years, *Medieval: Total War*. After *Shogun: Total War* took the gaming world by storm a couple of years ago, the crew at The The Creative Assembly chose not to rest on their laurels (which always hurts). Instead, they launched production of the Next Great Thing. Previews over the past year have merely confirmed that something truly special was in the making. Indeed, the wait has been almost excruciating for people with discriminating tastes (like you) who know a true-quality original when they see one.

And now it's here. *Medieval: Total War* is rich, clever, and deep—a more-than-worthy follow-up to its remarkable predecessor. Considering its stunning depth of gameplay, the game is quite easy to learn. However, just knowing which buttons to push is a far cry from outmaneuvering the wily Khan and his Golden Horde at the Kalka River bridges of 1223 AD.

That's where *we* come in.

Our guide gives you the tools you need to achieve strategic and tactical mastery of this great historical simulation. Best of all, the book was written with the extensive participation of the most-expert experts on *Medieval: Total War*—the game's design and testing teams! Without their generous and voluminous input, this guide would be merely illuminating. Instead, thanks to the folks at The Creative Assembly and Activision, this guide is essential and downright indispensable.

Look for the special "Designer Notes" and "Tips from the Testers" sections throughout the book for some direct inside knowledge and advice about the game.

PLAY THE TUTORIALS!

There's no substitute for hands-on experience, and this particularly applies to a game like *Medieval: Total War*. Fortunately, the wizards at The Creative Assembly have designed a masterful (and entertaining) pair of step-by-step tutorials for the Campaign Map and the Battle Map. Play through these right away to get a feel for both the game's controls and its uniquely British sensibility (and we mean that in the best way).

READ THE MANUAL!

Read carefully here: *This book is not a replacement for the game manual.* The excellent in-box documentation that comes with *Medieval: Total War* is your first step to a fundamental understanding of the game and its controls. This strategy guide assumes you've read that documentation and know which buttons to click, and when.

Trust us, the *Medieval: Total War* manual is deep, thorough, well-organized, and chock-full of tips and tactics for achieving a basic mastery of the game. Best of all, it was written by an English guy with that great, cheeky sense of humor (or, rather, *humour*).

So if you haven't already done so, read the manual right now. Go ahead, it's okay. We'll wait for you right here until you get back.

HOW TO USE THIS BOOK

Really, this book couldn't be any easier to use. Here's a quick breakdown:

Chapter 2: Campaign Map Strategy features numerous insider tips and strategies for success in the turn-based Campaign Map component of *Medieval: Total War*.

Chapter 3: Battle Map Tactics gives you extensive tips and expert advice on deploying your troops across the fabulous, undulating 3-D Battle Map, where the vast scope of medieval warfare comes alive before your very eyes. It also includes an in-depth, brain-bending look at the game's elegant combat system.

Chapter 4: Units gives you a stat-by-stat rundown on all of the infantry and cavalry units in *Medieval: Total War*. (For stats on Artillery and Ships, see Appendix 4.) The game's development team offers an enlightening overview of each unit class—Mounted Knight, Heavy Cavalry, Light Cavalry, Archer, Spearman, and so on.

Chapter 5: The Full Campaign provides some optimal strategies for each faction in the game's sprawling and historically accurate Single Player Full Campaign (again, courtesy of the designers).

Chapter 6: Historical Campaigns gives you sound tactical advice for all of the battles in the Historical Campaigns. In particular, we urge you to read the detailed, step-by-step walkthroughs for both the French and English in the Hundred Years' War campaigns. These form a sort of advanced battle tutorial, and once again, they come right from the gentlemen who designed the Historical Campaign scenarios.

Chapter 2: Campaign Map Strategy

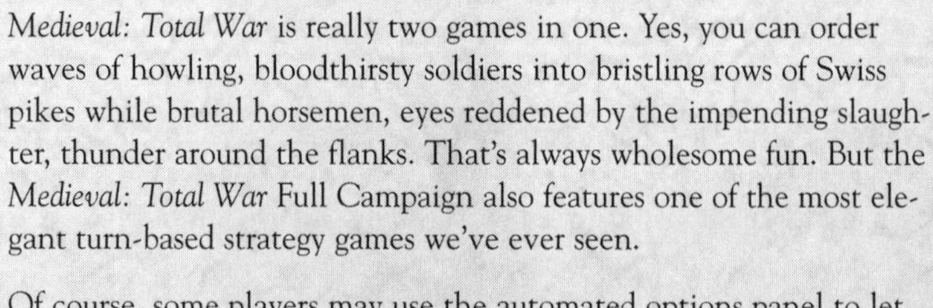

Medieval: Total War is really two games in one. Yes, you can order waves of howling, bloodthirsty soldiers into bristling rows of Swiss pikes while brutal horsemen, eyes reddened by the impending slaughter, thunder around the flanks. That's always wholesome fun. But the *Medieval: Total War* Full Campaign also features one of the most elegant turn-based strategy games we've ever seen.

Of course, some players may use the automated options panel to let the game take care of many (or all) of the strategy elements. But that would be a shame because the strategy map is a blast, presenting challenges that we find downright exhilarating.

The Campaign's strategy map offers an entirely separate layer of fun.

Note that a few of the tips in this chapter are derived from familiar sources, such as the manual and in-game tutorials. We include those here to give you one central source for help. However, most of this chapter's advice is freshly hatched from the minds of the game's creators, as well as the ace testers at both The Creative Assembly and Activision.

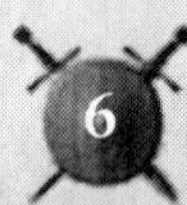

BUILDING & TRAINING

Half the fun of the *Medieval: Total War* strategy map lies in developing your own technology and economy, making your own troop training decisions, and assembling your own armies. The following tips should help you make better decisions about these topics.

FIRST, UNDERSTAND THE TECHNOLOGY TREE

Check out the cool Technology Tree chart that came with the game. (It's reproduced in Appendix 1 of this book as well.) If you look down the left side of the chart, you see five levels of castles, ranging from the simple Fort to the imposing Fortress. Each castle has its own individual characteristics and upgrades. But more importantly, each castle makes an entirely different level of technology and construction available in the castle's province.

Note that each castle is associated with a level number. The Fort is Level One, the Keep is Level Two, the Castle is Level Three, the Citadel is Level Four, and the Fortress is Level Five. If you trace a horizontal line across the chart from any of these five castle types, you find an entire array of buildings associated with each castle's level.

Buildings associated with the Keep, for example, are lined up in the shaded area designated as Level Two—Gunsmith, Church, Shipwright, Horse Breeder, and so on. Important: No matter how many Level One buildings you've constructed, you cannot build *any* of these Level Two buildings until you first build a Keep. This is true of all levels on the Technology Tree. Until you build the castle type for a particular level, you cannot build *any* of the buildings associated with that level.

Now look across the top of the chart at the Level One buildings—Royal Palace, Horse Farmer, Spearmaker, and so on. Flow chart arrows start at these buildings and run vertically down the chart, connecting an entire sequence of buildings. These arrows indicate the order in which you can build, from top to bottom. For example, once a province has a Fort, you can build a Bowyer, which lets you train Archers. A downward arrow connects the Bowyer to the next building in the sequence, the Bowyers' Workshop. This is a Level Two building, so you cannot construct it until you first build a Keep.

Tips from the Testers

Upgrade for Effect!

Cover up weaknesses, or enhance strengths, with armor and weapon upgrades. Build and upgrade Metalsmiths and Armorers to make sure your units have either enough armor to survive or weapons good enough to slay the enemy as fast as possible.

The Developers

But suppose you build a Keep and then immediately build the next-higher level, the Castle. The Level Three archery-related building is the Bowyers' Guild, which lets you train powerful Longbowmen and Arbalests. Now that you have the Level Three castle, can you skip over the Level Two Bowyers' Workshop and immediately build the Bowyers' Guild? The answer is no. You must build structures from top to bottom on the chart. You can't build the Level Four Shipbuilder's Guild until you build the ship-related buildings from the previous three levels—the Port (Level One), the Shipwright (Level Two), and the Dockyard (Level Three). And again, you must first build the castle associated with each of those levels before you can build the buildings.

Build Castles Soon, and in the Right Places

Once again: Castles not only provide defensive shelter, but are necessary for military and economic upgrades. As the manual suggests, you should build your first castles where they will bring the maximum benefit: provinces rich in agriculture that needs protection, or regions with special benefits, such as trade goods, mineral deposits, or special types of local troops. (For example, Switzerland produces the finest pikemen in the world.)

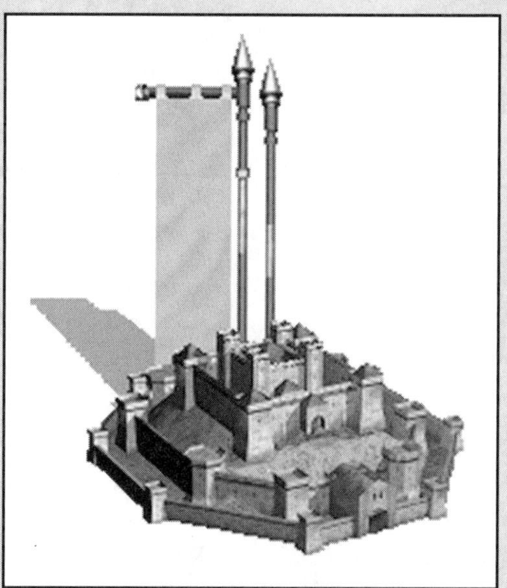

Castles provide defense… and the basis for your economic and technological development.

Defend High-Level Castles with Blind Ferocity

You expend *far* too many precious resources when building higher-level castles and facilities to risk losing them. Keep your "high-tech sectors" well-patrolled and well-garrisoned! Do not let them fall into enemy hands and be destroyed or used against you.

Try the "Three Region" Approach

Obviously, you want to produce the highest-level troops, agents, and income-producing facilities as possible, and as *quickly* as possible. But it takes a lot of time and money to build your way up to the top of the Technology Tree. You just cannot afford to cover all facets of development in every province you control. So we suggest you divide your provinces into three regions—military, strategic agent, and income-production.

In your military region, build everything you need to train and outfit troops for your armies: Spearmaker, Bowyer, Swordsmith, Armorer, Horse Farmer and Breeder, Town Watch and Guard, Gunsmith (after gunpowder is discovered in 1260 AD!), and Siege Engineering facilities. Ultimately, you want a Chapter House to produce the orders of knights (such as the Knights Templar), and Royal or Baronial Estates for the more powerful elite knight units.

In your *strategic agent region*, build everything required to conduct diplomacy and intrigue of all kinds. You want a Royal Palace for Emissaries, a religious facility (Church or Mosque) for holy men to spread the word, and then a Chapter House or Ribat to fire up the countryside with a Crusade or Jihad. You want a Tavern to attract mercenaries and recruit Assassins, plus a Brothel to produce Spies. Other establishments, such as a Chancellery or Admiralty, can raise the level of leadership in your faction.

In your *income-production region*, build facilities that improve your trade, merchant, mining, and farmland activities. Every time you step up a level in each area, it increases your treasury funds and thus your power and influence.

Provinces in all three regions, of course, require a regular upgrade of your castle type. Try to keep at least one province from each area working on a higher-level castle at all times.

Tips from the Testers

Combination Units Are Powerful!

Remember, some units have multiple abilities and uses. Boyars are cavalry with bows, and they have a powerful charge attack as well! Use their charge as well as skirmishing with bows for maximum effect.

The Developers

Tips from the Testers

Look for the "Provincial Specials"

Each province has its own strengths and weaknesses that you should exploit fully. Carefully select which areas will specialize in each type of troop, upgrade, or moneymaking activity. Don't try to build every building in every province.

The Developers

Center Your Military Region Around Provinces with Iron and Other Special Bonuses

Note that some provinces gain a bonus for producing a particular troop type that the region is famous for. For example, Wales was famous for its Longbowmen, so any Longbowman unit produced there will have a +1 Valor bonus. These "special-unit" provinces are certainly good bases for military production.

Also, some provinces have iron as a natural resource. Having iron allows the building of Metalsmiths, which gives a weapon bonus to all troops produced there due to their superior weapons.

Iron-producing provinces are great for military production. Build Metalsmiths there for weapon upgrades.

Subdivide Your Military Region by Troop Focus

Armies need balance and flexibility to deal with various threats. (See the next section for more on this.) In other words, you must train a variety of troops if you want solid armies. Getting a good mix of units takes time, however. You have to build your way up the Technology Tree to get facilities that produce higher-level troops, and each troop type (spearmen, cavalry, swordsmen, archers, and so on) has its own path up that tree.

So it's a good idea to have provinces within your military region specialize in different unit types. One province can focus on Archers, adding (in order) the Bowyer, Bowyers Workshop, Bowyers Guild, and Master Bowyer, while training the associated missile troops at each level. Another can focus on the cavalry tree of Horse Farmer, Horse Breeder, Horse Breeders Guild, and Master Horse Breeder. Still others can expand capabilities for Spearmen, Militia, Swordsmen, and Siege Machines.

Train a Balanced Army

As provinces develop various troop specialties, you should move their newly trained units across borders, mixing and matching so that every provincial army has a good variety of troop types. After all, every battle can be like a round of Rock, Paper, Scissors—Cavalry beat Swordsmen, Swordsmen beat Spearmen, Spearmen beat Cavalry. So you can't load up on just one kind of unit. Your swarm of Teutonic Knights may seem invincible, sweeping away lowly infantry with apparent ease. But just wait until they run into a bristling, 5-deep formation of Swiss Armored Pikemen. Ouch!

Our troop training suggestions for the early going: Start by producing Archers and Spearmen in even numbers. Once you get a Town Watch or two, add a unit of Urban Militia for every two Spearmen units you have. Their shorter polearms don't have the same anti-cavalry effect as spears, but they do have better armor-piercing ability and are quite useful against enemy infantry.

Build Spearmaker Workshops so stronger spear units become available, such as Feudal Sergeants or Saracen Infantry. Now produce those units instead standard Spearmen. As soon as you can, get a Town Guard and start building Militia Sergeants instead of Urban Militia. When cavalry is finally available, by all means add some horsemen to your provincial armies.

A well-balanced army consists of the following:

- 4 Archer units
- 5 Spearmen units
- 4 Men-at-arms units
- 3 Cavalry units

Tips from the Testers

Don't Forget to Train a Few Peasants!

Weak units are quite useful for setting up other attacks. They can guard or delay an enemy assault long enough for you to set up a counterattack. For example, Spearmen might hold off another unit until cavalry can flank, or Peasants might keep a more powerful unit in place so Naptha Throwers can get into range.

The Developers

PRE-INVASION TIPS

Medieval: Total War is certainly all about conquest. But before you rush off in an acquisitive frenzy, there are a few things to keep in mind. Let's start by reiterating a tip made in the manual.

Determine Your Key Provinces

Provinces, and provinces alone, provide your income. So you'd better protect them. Keep an army in every province that borders enemy lands. Undefended provinces are an open invitation to invaders—and to internal rebellion, for that matter. Of course, some provinces are barely worth defending. Know when to withdraw gracefully in the face of an invasion force. But keep your wealthy provinces well garrisoned, and defend them tooth and nail if necessary.

As the manual points out: "**Land** *equals* **Money** *equals* **Army Pay**!" What could be more medieval than that equation?

Always Spy First

Never invade a province blindly. Plan ahead! Drop a Spy, Emissary, Princess, or Holy Man into a province targeted for invasion and take a good look at the enemy's troop composition. From a distance, his armies (as indicated by the army battle flag) may seem small. But your agent might reveal that the army you outnumber 2 to 1 is composed entirely of powerful mounted knights.

Note how many Archers and Gunners the enemy has in comparison to your invasion force. If he has numerous missile troops and you don't, you want to attack through wooded areas or wait until the weather is rainy. Both of these situations will decrease the effectiveness of missile troops.

Make Careful Note of Terrain Features on the Campaign Map

Another reminder from the manual: "In the full campaign game, the battlefield used is directly related to the terrain in the province or along its borders. If, for example, your army invades over a mountainous border, you'll have to fight a battle in mountainous terrain. This could well favor the defender and be highly unsuitable for cavalry."

So choose a border with terrain that best suits your invading army or that most hampers the enemy. (That is, if you know his troop composition. See the previous tip and the "Knowledge Is Power!" sidebar). For example, hot desert terrain is brutal to armored knights, and mountainous terrain can be a terrible disadvantage for any sort of mounted troops.

TIPS FROM THE TESTERS

Knowledge Is Power!

Use various agents and Watchtowers to gather information from nearby enemy provinces. If a huge hostile army is building up on your border, check what kind of troops it contains. A thousand Peasants might look scary from far away, but up close they're not tough at all!

The Developers

Watchtowers give you a valuable peek into neighboring provinces.

EXPANDING YOUR EMPIRE

You can't conquer the known world without a healthy income and some good, trustworthy local leadership. Keep the following tips in mind as you bring new provinces into the fold.

Keep an Eye on Your Treasury

Sure, this seems like obvious advice. But you'd be surprised how easy it is to run out of money when you're engaged in *Medieval: Total War*. As the manual states, there's a *lot* to spend your money on—troop maintenance costs, new buildings, new units, bribes, ransoms, and Crusades.

Appoint Governors with Good Acumen

Assign your provincial governance to generals with good Acumen (or check the Auto Assign Titles option in the Automation Settings box) to increase the income from your provinces. If you don't, you may run out of money rather quickly.

Examine each of your unit leaders on your very first turn, and bestow titles to the men with the highest Acumen ratings. When you find a suitable general, pull his unit out the Review Panel and set it down on the strategy map as a single-unit army. Then drop the title you want to assign on this army. This assures that the right man gets the title.

Again, a governor with high Acumen boosts the income from his province, and you need all the cash you can get at the start of play.

Governors need High Acumen ratings to wring the most income out of their provinces.

In the early going, your governors don't need to be strong combat commanders. If necessary, you can strip them of their titles later. Or, as the manual so brazenly suggests, you can assassinate a weak commander and give his title to a high-ranking general whose loyalty is important.

Be Flexible About Taxation

Low taxes cripple your war machinery. High taxes put undue stress on provincial loyalties and can cause general unrest. But each province is unique. Other factors, such as a governor with special, loyalty-inspiring virtues, may boost loyalty so much that you can levy high taxes and still have happy subjects. So don't just set a uniform tax rate across your entire kingdom. As the manual sagely suggests: "Use taxes to keep people just loyal enough that they won't revolt."

Minimize Your Border Exposure When Invading Other Provinces

The more borders you share with enemies, the more you can expect to repel invasions on a regular basis. Try to expand your empire in such a way that it borders on as few regions as possible. This can be tricky, of course, but it ensures a minimum number of places from which an enemy attack can be launched.

Here's an example of intelligent expansion, courtesy of one of the game's developers: "Whenever you invade an enemy-controlled province, you want the biggest invasion force possible. But if you take too many troops out of your province for the attack, you might leave it too weakly defended to stave off a counterattack if another enemy province borders it too. So if possible, you want to launch attacks from provinces that border *only one* enemy province."

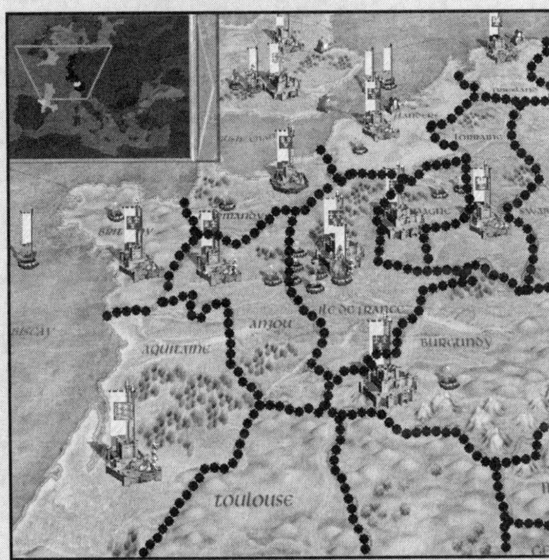

Try to launch invasions from provinces that border only one enemy province to prevent easy counter-invasions of your launch province.

For example, suppose you control the French faction and you have armies in Brittany, Normandy, Flanders, Champagne, Ile de France, Anjou and Aquitaine. Your army in Anjou could attack one of two regions, Toulouse to the south or Burgundy to the east. But invading Toulouse would leave Anjou open for a counter-invasion from Burgundy, and vice versa. In the same manner, your army in Flanders could attack either Friesland or Lorraine, but doing so would leave Flanders open for reprisal.

However, your army in Champagne borders only one enemy province, Lorraine. This should be your first choice for invasion. Once you capture Lorraine, Flanders borders only on Friesland and the Ile de France borders only on Burgundy. You can then move those armies in to attack without leaving yourself exposed. Finally, you can move the army in Anjou into Toulouse. Now you have taken four provinces without exposing yourself to counterattack, advancing your empire a step further to the east.

In summary, then: By attacking from a province that borders only one enemy province, you won't need to split your forces and reduce your invasion force just to make sure the province you're attacking from is defended.

If Your Army Is Not Strong Enough to Capture the Region You Invade, Weaken the Opposing Army Instead

Fight a quick battle and cause as much damage to their key units as possible while minimizing your own loses. This will prevent them from attacking you and give you time to build up a stronger force for subsequent invasion.

Feign a Secondary Invasion to Forestall Enemy Counterattacks

If you move your army out of a province to invade an enemy province and leave your own region very lightly defended, this often encourages the enemy to counter-invade from a second bordering region. You can prevent this by splitting off some of your forces and invading the threatening second region with a small army, even if you don't intend to fight for it. This often discourages the enemy's counter-invasion and allows you to commit the bulk of your forces to conquering the first territory. Then, when the pre-battle window comes up for your second invasion, cancel it. Just withdraw your second army, and your general won't suffer any loss of rating due to a military loss.

Leave Enemy Kings Alive but Crippled to Prevent an Unpleasant Reemergence

When you're invading enemy lands with a view to wiping them off the map, it can be more prudent to leave the faction leader alive with one province remaining. Keep an eye on him, and feel free to occasionally raid his borders to wipe out any buildings he may be constructing.

Otherwise, if you totally eradicate him, his faction will reemerge unexpectedly at a later date (at least once!) with a large number of crack troops. This is *not* what you want to see if you have only Peasants or other low-level troops garrisoning his former provinces.

Slash and Burn When Necessary

If you take an enemy region and you don't think you can hold it, destroy all the buildings. Indeed, it can be quite profitable to conquer an enemy province, loot and pillage and raise merry hell until nothing remains standing, and then scamper away, abandoning the province before the enemy returns for some payback.

Often, the previous owner will move back in and start rebuilding. Guess what you do next? That's right: Invade again! The English designers of *Medieval: Total War* seem quite proud of the fact that their countrymen specialized in this tactic—called a *Chevauchée*—during the Hundred Years War against France.

Disband Useless Units

Troops cost money—sometimes a *lot* of money—for upkeep and support. Some are worth every florin. But as time goes by and more advanced soldiers take the field, your older, outmoded units become a drain on the treasury. As you upgrade your facilities and gain the ability to field higher-level troops, consider disbanding Peasants and other low-level units. Direct the money you save into training better troops.

But Think Twice Before Disbanding "High-Valor" Units

Remember that although any unit you disband no longer costs you upkeep money, it hasn't completely disappeared from the game. It becomes a company of mercenaries and is available for hire by anyone with the cash. Be careful if you decide to get rid of any unit with a high Valor rating—it could end up working for your enemies!

> **Tips from the Testers**
>
> **Retrain Troops for Maximum Effect**
>
> Instead of disbanding a unit and training an entirely new one, consider retraining your troops. This can upgrade a unit's Valor rating, armor, and weapons, and it can bring in new recruits for full unit strength!
>
> The Developers

LOYALTY

Loyalty is quite important in *Medieval: Total War*. Disloyal commanders or subjects can ruin a perfectly good autocracy. So a smart king keeps everyone happy (or scared) enough to toe the royal line. Here are a few suggestions.

After a Battle, Release the Rebels You Capture

A merciful king is a popular king, and a popular king is one who inspires loyalty in his vassals and subjects.

Keep Provinces Happy or Scared

Keep an eye on the loyalty of your subjects or they may revolt. Simply hold down one of the Shift keys for a quick check. Green provinces are loyal, yellow provinces are wavering, and red provinces are distinctly disloyal and ready for a rebellion.

Lower a province's tax rate to inspire a bit more loyalty. Remember that moving troops or Spies into a disloyal province can be very "inspirational" too. Watchtowers and Border Forts keep a Big Brotherly eye on the populace, enforcing loyalty via watchful control. Finally, you can appoint a governor with a high Dread rating. His renowned brutality will keep the locals in line.

> Tips from the Testers
>
> **Keep the Peace with Secret Police!**
>
> Spies can be used as secret police to keep your own population under control, as well as defend against enemy agents. Keep a few Spies in every province. They'll make sure everyone stays loyal, and they'll help to catch enemy Spies or Assassins passing through.
>
> The Developers

Buy Loyalty with Titles and Offices

One way to ensure loyalty in your generals is to give them a stake in your kingdom. When you bestow a title such as Duke or Earl of a particular province, the recipient's Loyalty always increases. Offices of State (such as Chancellor or Vizier) increase Loyalty and, usually, some other trait such as Command or Acumen.

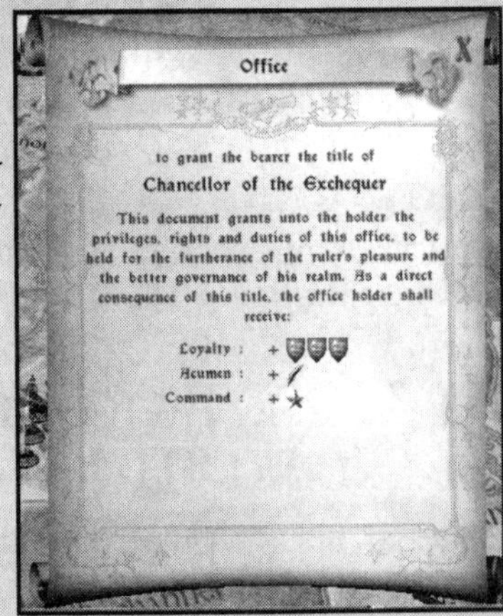

Titles and offices give generals more reason to be loyal to your cause.

> Designer Notes
>
> **On Promoting Non-Nobility**
>
> The auto-assign function in the automated options panel will not give titles or offices to generals of the lower caste. But nothing stops you from making a lowly peasant into a duke if he has the right stuff. Keep in mind that your other nobles may not be so happy about this, though.
>
> The Developers

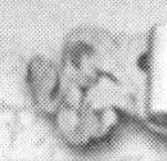

Watch Your Generals!

A disloyal general can be a royal nuisance. Keep an eye on them—*all* of them, every turn. This is especially important for generals with many troops, high command ratings, and/or royal blood. These are the men who can become ringleaders in a civil war if they aren't very loyal. Give your powerful generals provincial titles and offices of state, or drop a princess on them to offer them marriage into the royal family. All of these tactics help to keep them loyal.

Be Ruthless in Eliminating Disloyal Generals

If a general's loyalty drops despite marriage, titles, or other enticements… well, sometimes you have to be ruthless. Drop an Emissary on him to strip his titles. Or if you wish to embrace your dark side, send an Assassin or Inquisitor to remove him. When you drop an Inquisitor on a Catholic general with low Piety, the poor fellow likely will be tried for heresy and (if you're lucky) sent to the stake. Just remember to move any Bishops or Cardinals out of the province first, because they tend to get in the way of the Inquisitor's dirty work.

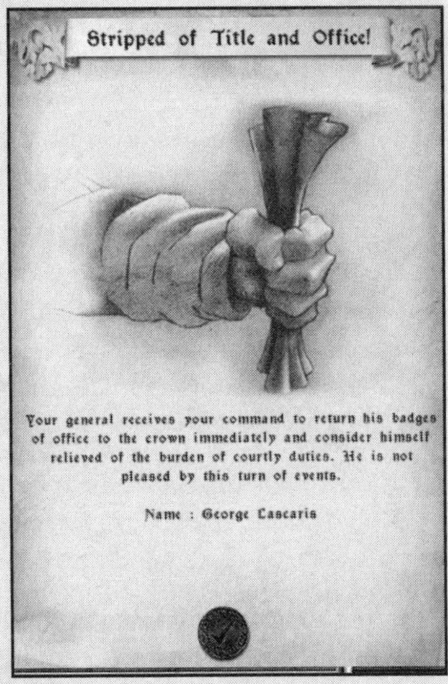

Strip any titles or offices from a disloyal general. Or drop an Assassin or Inquisitor on him to usher him out of the picture.

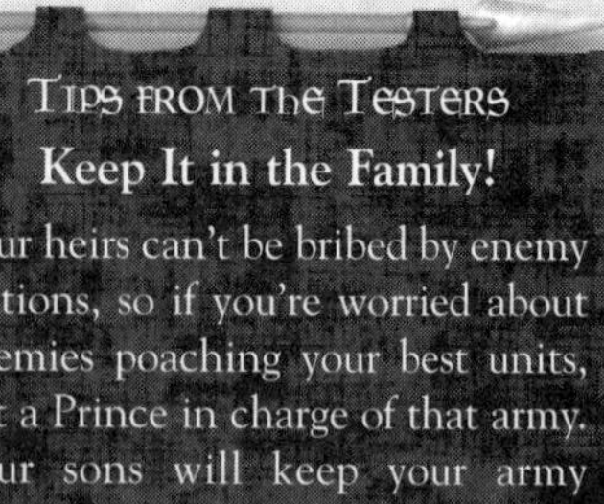

Tips from the Testers

Keep It in the Family!

Your heirs can't be bribed by enemy factions, so if you're worried about enemies poaching your best units, put a Prince in charge of that army. Your sons will keep your army secure!

The Developers

You can also get rid of a low-loyalty general by disbanding his unit. But before you do that, use his unit to "top off" other reduced-strength units—that is, drag and drop his unit on other units of the same troop class—until he is left nearly alone with only a small contingent of men. Then disband his unit, dumping him out of the game with only minimal troop loss. If there are no battle-damaged units hanging around, move him into an army led by a loyal general who outranks him.

Send Disloyal Generals on a Crusade

This is one of our favorite tricks. Place your problem generals in a Crusade army and send them to the other side of the map! Believe me, they will be *much* too busy fighting infidels to indulge traitorous thoughts or organize a civil war. Best of all, if the Crusade is successful, your faction leader enjoys a significant increase in his Influence rating… so all his generals' Loyalty increases! Those problem generals will return from their glorious Crusade with a whole new attitude about things.

Nurture the Virtues of Your Generals

The "vices and virtues" effect is one of the most important aspects of *Medieval: Total War*. Although generals acquire some of these personal traits randomly, most vices and virtues are gained directly as a result of doing something in the game. In other words, they are under *your* control! So you can nurture your generals by specializing them—that is, creating special roles for each one.

For example, always use the same generals for attacking so they will gain Command bonuses when attacking. (Command is particularly important because it affects the combat effectiveness of all your men.) Do the same for defensive and siege situations. Place specialist defenders in regions you think may be attacked.

Of course, once you painstakingly develop these special generals, you want to avoid *losing* them. If you think you're probably going to lose a battle, deploy a lesser general you don't mind throwing away.

It's worth making sure your general's unit always gets some kills in every battle. He'll gain a poor reputation if he never fights, which will give your whole army a Morale penalty. (Mowing down some routing Peasants usually does the job.) At all costs, avoid having your best general get routed off the field. He'll never live it down, and it will take a lot of work to compensate for the Morale penalty his army will suffer. If you find yourself losing, don't wait to be routed—withdraw!

Virtues and/or vices can affect a commander's combat and governing (and your fortunes) in very significant ways. Remember that you can control how they develop.

Understand How the Vices and Virtues of Your Leaders Affect Your Troops and Provinces

If an army commander has a vice or virtue that affects Morale or Command, the penalty or bonus applies to his entire army—that is, to each of the units in the army. If his vice/virtue affects only Valor, the penalty or bonus applies only to the general's own unit. Combat-oriented vices and virtues affect governors or your faction leader just as they would a normal general.

But governors and your faction leader can acquire certain vices and virtues that affect province-wide or kingdom-wide relations (Happiness, Dread, Acumen, Loyalty, Piety), as well as building, agriculture, or trade. If the King of France is a Great Trader, for example, this adds +10 Happiness in all provinces controlled by the French faction and boosts all French trade income by +20 percent. If a French provincial governor is a Great Trader, however, the effects apply only to his province. So if the Duke of Burgundy gains the Great Trader virtue, the same bonuses (+10 Happiness and +20 percent trade income) apply only to Burgundy.

When a provincial governor acquires a vice or virtue that has a province-wide effect, its bonus or penalty applies to his province no matter where he is or who is currently sitting in his province—the king, other governors, it doesn't matter. The Duke of Burgundy governs Burgundy even if he's off crusading in the Middle East.

The only person whose exact location does matter is the faction leader. The loyalty of his generals and provinces depends on their distance from the faction leader. The further away the leader is, the more their loyalty drops.

STRATEGIC AGENTS

Medieval: Total War features quite an array of non-military units that can exert a powerful influence on the course of a typical game. Proper management of your cadre of strategic agents can tilt the scales in your faction's favor. Here are a few good tips on how to manage some of the more influential agents in the game.

Send Emissaries Behind Enemy Lines

Sometimes your foes develop their major production regions behind the front lines, leaving them very lightly defended with just a few troops in the castle. If you can get an Emissary to bribe the castle's garrison commander, you can take over the region very quickly.

Of course, you probably can't hold the region for more than a turn. But in that turn, you can trash the region by destroying the buildings. This has the triple benefit of making you some cash, crippling your enemy's production, and forcing him to pull troops back from his forward provinces to retake the region in the next turn—which may give you a chance to attack his front lines.

> Tips from the Testers
>
> **Bribe Early, Bribe Often**
>
> Use your Emissaries for more than just treaties. Bribe enemy units, and you'll gain armies and conquer land at the same time!
>
> The Developers

Spies Don't Just "Spy"

Spies infiltrate. Of course, *any* agent (even a princess) can be used to gather information from enemy provinces. Even Watchtowers act as "spies" into neighboring provinces. But Spies have other, more nefarious uses. They can keep tabs on enemy Spies and Assassins and enforce loyalty in your own provinces.

They can reveal the vices and virtues of any general, unlock the gate of a castle you are besieging, and, when used in sufficient numbers, spark rebellion in enemy provinces. In short, espionage can be a very worthwhile activity.

Spies are very useful strategic pieces with several important functions.

Foment Unrest with Priests and Princesses, and Follow Up with Your Spies

If there is a large enemy army in a province, it is very difficult for your Spies to start a revolt. It requires a large number of them, and the enemy will no doubt quickly counter your efforts with Border Forts and his own Spies/Assassins. But if the targeted province does not practice your faction's religion, there is a better way.

Introduce holy men and princesses into the province. They can reduce the population's loyalty and are harder for the enemy to deal with. Once you have increased the percentage of the population who practices your religion to more than 75%, send in half a dozen spies. This will cause a revolt and will make the local populace friendly towards your faction.

Tips from the Testers

Spies Aren't Just for Gathering Information!

Using Spies to cause rebellions allows you to keep your treaties and take land at the same time. Place multiple Spies in an allied province to cause a rebellion. When the rebels overtake their current masters, buy the rebellion with an Emissary! This way you don't alienate your ally.

The Developers

Spy on Your Own Side

Keeping Spies in your own provinces has multiple benefits. First, they intercept and kill enemy agents. Second, they help suppress the population. Third, they increase the chance of you finding out about an impending civil war before it happens. If your faction leader's Influence is low and you have many disloyal generals, you'll get a warning before civil war breaks out. It may even reveal who the ringleader is.

Use Spies to Thwart Civil Wars

A civil war won't start unless a very competent general exists who can lead it. This brings us to another benefit of using spies at home—if you have a strong but disloyal general you want to get rid of, just drop a spy on him. He'll be framed for treason and executed, whether he's guilty or not. Fun!

Or, you may decide to manage your civil war by making it very one-sided. Once you think a civil war is inevitable, do everything you can to make it worse. Strip everyone of their titles, make sure the likely ringleader isn't in the same place as the king, and make sure any loyal generals are buried low in the command structure of armies commanded by disloyal generals. When the civil war comes, everyone will join the rebels, leaving the King all on his own. He'll be quietly killed, a new King will take the throne, and all your loyalty and influence problems will be over.

Spy on Your Enemies

Dropping a spy on an enemy general (particularly an older, more experienced one) can reveal his secret vices. Once these vices become public, the general may suffer crippling penalties.

A spy in the same region as an enemy king can give you reports on his plans. For example, you may learn that he's planning to invade you in three years. If nothing happens to change his mind, the invasion will proceed as planned—but you will be prepared for it.

Spy with Your Princesses

Princesses who are deployed to neutral and even enemy provinces receive the courtesy of the court she visits. Even if no one wants to marry a princess, remember that she acts as a spy in the province where she currently dwells. This can be very useful for picking an invasion route through someone else's kingdom!

Assassination

As the manual puts it, "A single knife in the hands of an assassin can do more damage than a thousand swords—when it is plunged into the right target!" Assassinating a general paralyzes his army. Assassinating a king paralyzes the whole country!

Train Assassins Quickly

The sooner you get a reliable contingent of Assassins at your service, the easier it is to rule with a firm, steady hand. For example, when the Inquisition appears, the Inquisitors will raise hell across your empire if they cannot be removed by judicious assassination attempts.

Assassins can be very powerful agents of your success. Get a Tavern and recruit some as soon as possible.

TIPS FROM THE TESTERS

Fear and Ignorance Are Key

Build Taverns and train Assassins early, and don't be shy about sending your killers out into the world. Attack every Emissary that you can, because they are easy prey until they gain a bit of Valor. Keep your Assassins in practice, because you never know when you'll need to remove a key target in a hurry. This will deny the enemy information about your provinces and keep them on their toes!

The Developers

RELIGION

Religion was a driving force in medieval times. Sometimes it was a stabilizing force, but at other times it was an engine of radical change for both good and ill. In *Medieval: Total War*, religion plays an important role in many aspects of the strategy game.

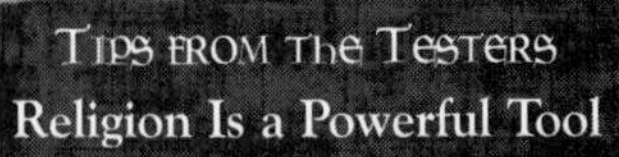

TIPS FROM THE TESTERS

Religion Is a Powerful Tool

Sending religious units into an area in advance of an invasion can help convert the population to your religion. Then, when you take over, the old faithful won't rebel as much. Remember, the will of the people can turn against you if not managed correctly.

The Developers

USE HOLY MEN TO KEEP THE PEACE IN YOUR PROVINCES

Holy men can act as powerful stabilizing forces in the lands you already control.

USE HOLY MEN TO INFILTRATE ENEMY PROVINCES

Sent into enemy provinces, holy men can act as spies and can start converting the population to your religion as well! This can increase the chances of a religious revolt.

AVOID EXCOMMUNICATION AT ALL COSTS!

If you control a Catholic faction and you attack another Catholic faction in a bullying manner, you may get excommunicated. Excommunication usually prompts other Catholic factions to break off alliances with you or even launch Crusades against your homelands. It also triggers regular uprisings within your provinces—Catholics don't like to be ruled by excommunicated heathens. So the first time the Pope warns you about excommunication because of such actions, take heed immediately!

Remember: Even trivial-seeming acts of piracy against fellow Catholics may trigger the excommunication cycle. Furthermore, sometimes simply defending yourself against an aggressive Catholic faction may get *you* excommunicated rather than them.

Excommunication by the Pope creates a dire situation for any Catholic king. Avoid it at all costs!

FIGHT FAST WARS AGAINST FELLOW CATHOLICS, IF POSSIBLE

Playing as a Catholic faction, try to fight short, annihilating wars against your fellow Catholics. If you can completely wipe out a faction in a year or two, the Pope never gets round to excommunicating you.

PULL OUT ALL STOPS TO GET YOUR EXCOMMUNICATION RESCINDED

To get yourself back in the Pope's good graces after excommunication, you can offer alliance to the Papal States or arrange for the untimely demise of your own faction leader (while keeping his heirs safe, of course).

But keep in mind that when the Pope dies, all of his previous excommunications are forgotten. And it doesn't matter *how* the Pope dies... if you catch our meaning. (Nudge, wink.) So if you go to war against another Catholic faction, it's always worthwhile to keep an Assassin or two near Rome, just in case you need the Pope to have an "accident." Of course, you can drop an Inquisitor on the Pope and have him tried for heresy.

Burn Your Way to Victory

Inquisitors, as the manual points out, are *very* scary guys. When dropped on any Catholic general (particularly one with a low Piety rating), an Inquisitor is likely to root out some form of heresy and put the unfortunate commander to the stake. This remarkable skill can be used to eliminate Catholic foes.

Remember that an Inquisitor has the best chance of success against a low-piety target, and that the presence of a Bishop or Cardinal (even one from his own faction!) in the province will significantly reduce the Inquisitor's chances of success. The presence of a faction leader also makes an Inquisitor's job harder, so it's very difficult to send a King (or the Pope) to the purifying flames.

On the other hand, used in conjunction with an Assassin or two to wipe out any nearby religious fellows, an Inquisitor can be an excellent way of burning through an enemy Catholic faction.

Crusades and Jihads

One phenomenon of the historical period depicted in *Medieval: Total War* is the zeal of the Catholic military campaigns known as the Crusades, as well as the Muslim response of holy war, or Jihad. A Crusade or Jihad can have a powerful effect on the course of a game and can create advantages for the smart player.

Prepare Fertile Ground for Your Crusades

A province's religious zeal determines how many soldiers join a Crusade as it moves through on its way to its target. So before you send a Crusade marching off across the country, lace its route with Inquisitors to raise the zeal of those provinces. Using Inquisitors in this way ensures two things: One, the Crusade army will be bigger, and two, your rival factions will have troops stripped from their armies and there's little they can do about it!

Tips from the Testers

Don't Underestimate the Papacy!

The Pope has an enormous amount of power. If you're playing a Catholic faction, being excommunicated will turn your entire populace against you! Avoid it at all costs, unless you know you can quickly "convince" the Pope to change his mind.

The Developers

Designer Notes

On Bishops, Inquisitors, and the AI

I've seen the AI do some sneaky things with Bishops and Inquisitors. (It's alive, I tell you!) For example, once I was playing the Byzantines and was allied to the French. The French sent a Catholic Bishop into one of my provinces and left him there for a while to make converts. Then they followed up with an Inquisitor. By then, my province had enough Catholic converts to start an Inquisition, which went rampant.

The population was very unhappy about this, and a huge rebellion forced me to withdraw. A French Emissary then bribed the rebels. So the French effectively took a province off me while we were allied. Neat trick! Believe me, I learned from it.

The Developers

Ch.2

Launching a Crusade carries great risk, but it can reap great rewards for victorious faction leaders.

Be Patient

When a Crusade begins, it may not be strong enough to take its target. In the early going, Crusades are made up of many ragtag units and a lot of Peasants. If you can, add a few units of Spearmen, Archers, and Men-at-Arms to give the crusading army more flexibility.

Send a Capable Commanding General

A Crusade needs a strong leader. A general with a Command rank of 2 or 3 stars will be fine, but a 4-star general is preferred. If you have several heirs, send the eldest. Try to avoid sending a Duke, unless he is a very high-ranking general or you wish to dispose of him. It can be difficult to find suitable replacements for governors with high Acumen.

Don't send your King or heirs on a Crusade unless your provinces are in great shape and you're feeling particularly gung ho. Once a commander has taken up the cross, there's no turning back. He stays with the Crusade until it succeeds or is destroyed, and sending a King a long way from home without any route back is a recipe for rebellion.

Move Inexorably Toward Your Target Province

When the Crusade army is on the move, make sure it does not remain in a region for more than one turn. As it moves, it picks up new recruits from provinces it passes through, while some of its current troops die from disease. When a Crusade first enters a province, it will gain more men than it loses. But if the Crusade hangs around for too long, it starts losing more and more men until it eventually disbands.

Use Crusades for Selfish Strategic Advantages

Crusades can be useful for creating large armies quickly. If you find yourself at war with someone and they have the upper hand, a well-timed Crusade can swing the balance back to your side. Wait until you have just repulsed an attack and inflicted heavy casualties on your foe, and then send in the Crusade to attract more troops away from him.

Don't Lose!

Always make sure your victory is assured. If a Crusade fails, it will cost your King a lot of influence. This can be dangerous because it reduces the loyalty of your generals and thus makes civil wars more likely.

TRADE AND FLEETS

As the manual points out, the prospect of trade makes a province with a coastline more valuable than an equivalent landlocked one. Once you construct a Port and a Shipwright, start building boats. Send your ships out to control a chain of sea regions that link you to the ports of other provinces. Traders there can sell their goods to you, and vice versa. This trade can be extremely profitable.

Here are a few tips on trading and sailing. Thanks to the developers for their notes on these matters.

Keep One Cheap Boat in Each Region to Maintain Trade Through It

Use fleets of 3 to 4 warships to roam around and take care of any enemy ships.

Place Seagoing Vessels in the Central Sea Regions

Trade routes run along the coastlines of the map, naturally. After all, the idea is to control sea regions that connect your ports to those of other provinces. But it's a good idea to gain control of the two big central sea regions, the Atlantic Ocean and the Western Mediterranean. That way, if a boat is lost through war or storm in one of your coastal regions, there won't be a gap in your trade network.

Trade via ports and sea regions can bring untold riches to an industrious faction.

Tips from the Testers

Use Trading for Maximum Advantage!

Remember, trading is a great way to earn lots of florins for funding your wars. As soon as possible, set up Ports, Trading Posts, and a fleet of ships along the coastline to export all your goods.

The Developers

Make Sure Your Trade Returns Are Worth the Ship's Support Cost!

The farther away a boat sails from its home region, the higher its support costs. After a boat reaches a certain distance, it can cost you more money to support the ship than you gain in extra income from your trade exports. For example, Pomerania gains 38 florins per turn for each port it trades with. If you place a Pomeranian ship in the English Channel, its support costs are 80 florins per turn. So if only one port exists in the English Channel region, Pomerania loses 42 florins per turn! You would need more than two ports in that sea region before you'd have a positive cash flow from the trade.

Dump Slow Boats from Your Attack Fleets!

The speed of your fleet is equal to its slowest boat. If an enemy fleet keeps moving between regions and evading your attack, make sure you remove boats that are slower than your enemy's fleet.

Split Up Strong Fleets When Chasing a Weak Fleet

Given fleets of equal speed, a chaser fleet has a 50% chance each turn of catching a target fleet before it moves out of a region. So when you're pursuing an enemy fleet and you lack ships that are faster than theirs, consider splitting up your ships into several fleets to have a better chance of catching the enemy. Of course, that means you reduce your odds of winning the battle later on because you have fewer ships.

Split Up Weak Fleets When Being Pursued by a Strong Warship

A single strong warship can defeat an entire fleet of inferior ships in a single turn. However, you can use the inferior fleet to engage the strong warship for *many* turns if you split up your boats into many individual, single-ship "fleets." The enemy warship will need a full turn to destroy each one of these one-ship fleets. This can buy you a lot of time to upgrade your shipbuilding facilities to produce your own high-level warships.

OTHER STRATEGIES

We conclude this chapter with a grab bag of tips, tactics, and war stories. The first three appear in the manual. The others came to us via the helpful folks at The Creative Assembly.

Engineer a *Coup D'etat*

Civil wars need not be a bad thing. If you have a particularly weak faction leader with a poor collection of heirs (or no heirs at all), it is possible to drive down the loyalty of your most powerful general in the hope that he will start a civil war and lead others in a rebellion. Here's how: Drop an Emissary on the strong general to remove his offices and titles, give him an enormous army to command, and then wait for the revolution. If it happens, choose to back the rebels rather than the current king!

Keep Making Those Royal Babies

Good breeding tells, allegedly. But more important to a successful royal line is *fast* breeding. Make sure your heirs are married! If foreign princesses don't beat a path to your door, make sure you send emissaries to find them and propose marriage. That way, you have a much better chance of a king having the "heir and spare" when they are needed at his death.

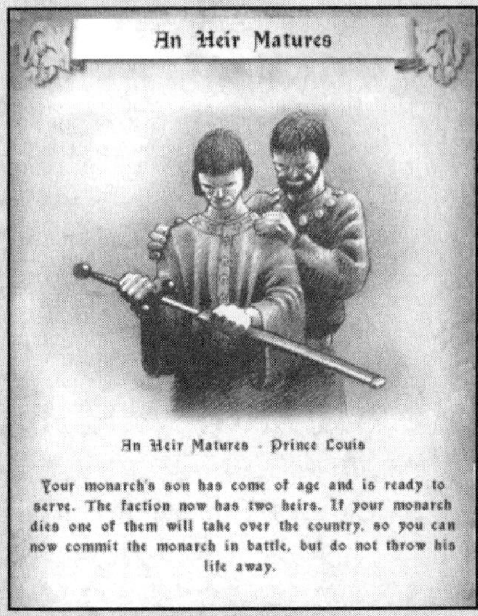

Every king should have at least two male heirs to his throne—an "heir and spare."

Be Provincial When Necessary

Some provinces on the map excel in producing certain types of units. For example, Switzerland produces very good Spearmen and Pikemen. The province descriptions will give you details. There are also a few units that can only be trained in specific provinces. Bulgarian Brigands come from Bulgaria and nowhere else—as you might just suspect from the name. Sometimes, it can be worth conquering a province just to train these specialized or superior troops.

The Endgame Scenario

When an opponent has only one province left, often he has the remnants of all his armies in it. These usually combine to be a very large force, especially if you attacked several of his regions at once in the previous turn and all of his troops retreated to the same place.

Attacking this last province may not be an option—his force may be too strong, and if you lose, the door is open for him to counterattack and reclaim his empire. On the other hand, most likely he will not attack you. If he loses, he's finished. An unfortunate stalemate develops.

However, time is on your side. As turns go by, the enemy will be losing money and growing eager to expand. Wait for him to attack someone else. This will divide his forces and provide an easier target for you to attack.

The Decisive Response

You've just successfully defended a region and inflicted heavy casualties. Your enemy is weakened and reeling. Seize this opportunity to attack on the very next turn, when he's at his most vulnerable! If successful, keep pushing forward. Often you can sweep through several provinces before the enemy can make a successful stand.

A Cunning Tactic

This testimonial is courtesy of one of the developers: "I was massing armies in Cyranacia, preparing to invade Tunisia, which at that time was held by the neutral Almohads. We both had fleets in the surrounding sea regions, and they were using these fleets to move troops into their region, anticipating my attack.

"However, they had left Algeria relatively undefended. I sent half a dozen of my spies there to create a revolt. Then I sat and waited for the right moment to attack. A large rebel force appeared and successfully captured the region. This cut off the Almohad army and left them with only one escape route—across the sea.

"A-ha! I declared war and attacked. My fleets blockaded theirs, leaving the Almohad army with nowhere to go. When the dust had settled and the battle was over, the shattered remains of the enemy had nowhere to retreat and were captured. In one move, I had destroyed over half of the Almohad's forces."

Chapter 3: Battle Map Tactics

The turn-based Campaign Map is certainly fun, but the real-time 3D Battle Map is the true heart of the game. With as many as 15,000 troops howling and swarming the battlefield at any one time… well, that's where things get *really* medieval.

Of course, you can't just hurl rows of bodies at the enemy and expect to win. Superior forces can lose their advantage on certain terrain, or can break and run when outflanked or facing an opponent with a morale advantage. Indeed, you may outman your enemy, but if you lose your general or you face a force led by a vastly superior general, your numbers advantage will do you little good.

The Battle Map tests your generalship.

This chapter gives you some solid tactical advice on how to deploy your troops before and during a live battle. First, it explores the various unit settings—the formations and engagement modes. Then, it lists a number of very helpful quick tips, including basic and advanced maneuvers for attacking and defending. Finally, it examines the amazing *Medieval: Total War* combat system and explain how battles work in the game.

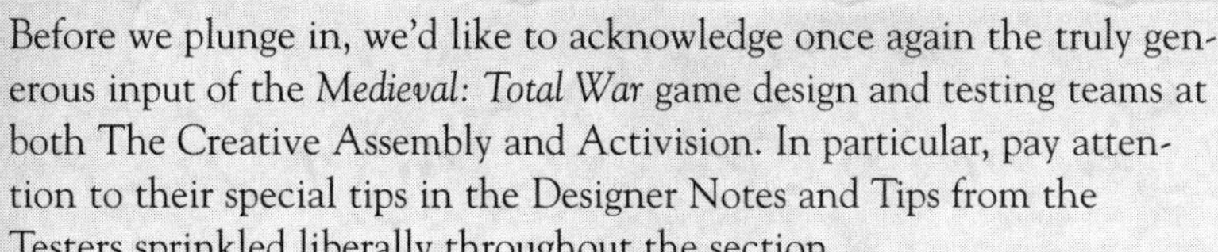

Before we plunge in, we'd like to acknowledge once again the truly generous input of the *Medieval: Total War* game design and testing teams at both The Creative Assembly and Activision. In particular, pay attention to their special tips in the Designer Notes and Tips from the Testers sprinkled liberally throughout the section.

UNIT FORMATIONS AND ENGAGEMENT MODES

Here's an overview of the Formations and Engagement Modes you can assign to your units, again courtesy of Bob Smith at The Creative Assembly. Read these carefully for some good advice on basic troop deployment.

FORMATIONS

The overall shape and dispersion of a unit's deployment can be a critically important component of its battlefield success. This section discusses the three standard formations available in the game. (Remember that you can also change a unit's formation manually by clicking and dragging from left to right on the battlefield, as described in the game manual.)

CLOSE

This is the basic default formation for all units. As the game manual points out, Close formation is useful for hand-to-hand combat, where getting the most men into action is important.

LOOSE

Loose formation should be used when you're under missile fire. Your troops are more spread out, so missiles that miss their target are more likely to fall harmlessly on the ground, rather than hitting another man. Each soldier in Loose formation also has more room to dodge arrows. The game gives them an extra point of armor to simulate this.

However, units should *never* enter melee combat in Loose formation. Enemy soldiers can penetrate Loose formations much more easily. The individual men in your unit try to keep their distance from each other, which means that each one of your men often must engage several enemies at once. Loose formation is especially bad for spear- and pike-armed units, because they're not able to present the wall of spear-points that they usually do. Even cavalry can defeat them.

Loose formation is good for dodging missile fire when troops aren't engaged in melee combat.

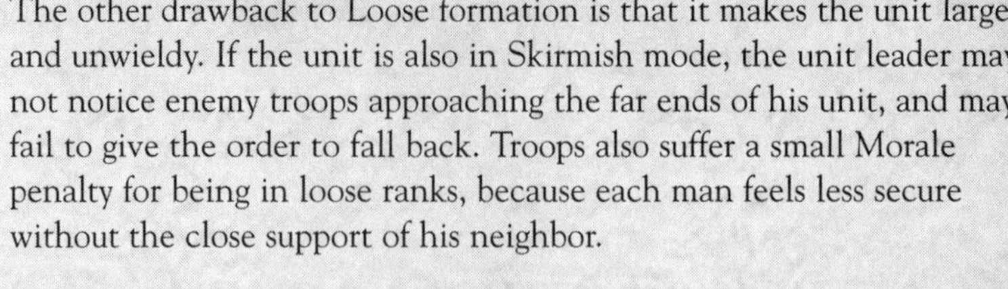

The other drawback to Loose formation is that it makes the unit large and unwieldy. If the unit is also in Skirmish mode, the unit leader may not notice enemy troops approaching the far ends of his unit, and may fail to give the order to fall back. Troops also suffer a small Morale penalty for being in loose ranks, because each man feels less secure without the close support of his neighbor.

Wedge

The Wedge is an aggressive formation, boosting Attack stats but lowering Defense.

Wedge is both a *formation* and an *attitude*. When Wedge is assigned to a unit, its troops form up in the distinctively tight, triangular formation. Moreover, in combat they behave more aggressively than normal. The combat engine models this by adding 3 to their Attack factor and deducting 3 from their Defense. Thus, ordering a unit into Wedge formation, even if it is already fighting, increases casualties all round. Obviously, you want to do this only if your unit is poised to attack enemies it can defeat or is already winning fairly easily.

Charging in Wedge formation is most useful when there is little space to engage, or when you wish to engage one enemy unit with several of your own. It can also be used if you need to punch through a thin line to engage a unit behind it. The disadvantage of Wedge formation is that only a few of your soldiers are engaged in the initial charge. In many instances, charging in a line rather than a wedge has a far greater impact on the enemy force, due to the greater numbers engaged.

Charging long, thin lines of cavalry while in Wedge formation is dangerous because the horsemen at the ends of the enemy formation can swing into the flanks of your unit. Leaving units deployed in Wedge formation when they're not attacking is not a good idea because they are vulnerable due to their reduced Defense factor.

Engagement Modes

Different troop types require different sets of operating orders from you, the commander. Some units fight better in tight, controlled formations, while others are more effective when given freer rein.

Engage At Will

In this mode, individual soldiers can break formation to find an enemy soldier to attack once their unit becomes engaged. Engage At Will is usually the best mode for attacking, except for the various spear and pike units that are most effective when in rank formation. Yet even pikemen and spearmen should switch to Engage At Will when fighting much weaker units or enemies that are few in number.

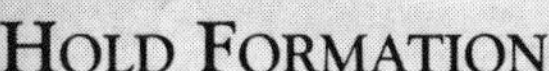

Hold Formation

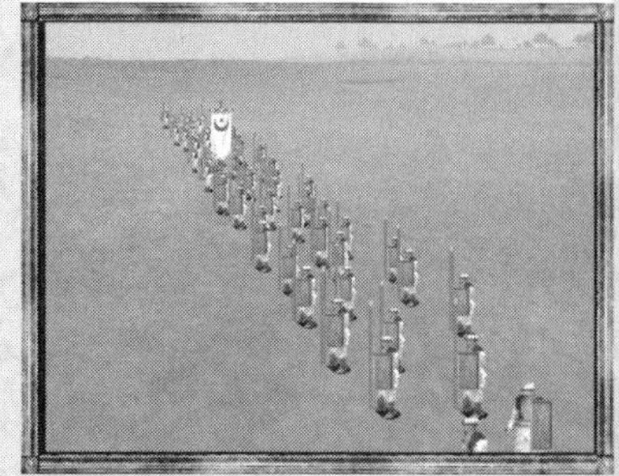

The Hold Formation engagement mode is most useful for spear and pike units who depend on supporting ranks for combat bonuses.

This mode instructs soldiers to stay in formation during combat. They may move a short way to support a comrade, but must otherwise stay in ranks. Soldiers fight defensively, which the combat system simulates by subtracting 2 from their Attack factor and adding 2 to their Defense. Spear- and pike-armed units get an additional Defense bonus due to the wall of spears they present.

In general, units fight less effectively in Hold Formation mode because many soldiers are forced to stand by idly. Use it only when holding the line is more important than inflicting casualties. One good tactic is to stall an enemy attack with a wall of defensive infantry in Hold Formation mode while you counterattack the enemy's flanks with more mobile units.

Hold Formation is especially useful for spear and pike units, even when attacking, because it keeps rear-rank soldiers in position to provide support (and thus combat bonuses) to those fighting in the front line. Otherwise, once combat is entered, the formation is soon lost and the men in the front rank are left to manage as best they can with their long, unwieldy weapons. You can tell when a rear-rank soldier is providing support to the front, because he will play his fighting animation.

Skirmish

Only units that are armed with missile weapons can use the Skirmish engagement mode. This mode instructs the unit to avoid melee combat altogether. If the leader of a unit that's set to Skirmish spots an enemy unit approaching, he automatically orders his troops to fall back. This works well if the unit is faster than the attacking enemy force, or if there is a friendly melee unit to withdraw behind. Skirmishing units stop moving forward if an enemy blocks the path, as well.

If a unit set to Skirmish is large or deployed in a long line, the unit leader may not notice when the enemy approaches from the flanks. You must be careful and observant. Conversely, attacking from the flank, or at an angle, is the best way to deal with a skirmishing unit that you are not fast enough to catch.

Since soldiers won't move to support each other in this mode, it's best to select another mode if melee combat is inevitable.

Hold Position

This state, which can be set to either On or Off, affects the behavior of the unit as a whole. This is in contrast to Hold Formation mode, which affects the behavior of the individual soldiers within the unit. This mode is most useful when troops must protect your army's flank or a narrow passage, such as a bridge or castle gate entrance.

When you order a unit to Hold Position, the following behaviors apply:

- The unit will not change its "facing direction" to shoot at targets, nor will it turn toward enemies attacking it.
- If firing missiles, the unit will not pursue targets that move out of range.
- If the unit is forced to move away from its last ordered position by an enemy advance, it will attempt to move back to that position afterward.
- If the unit is engaged in melee combat and its opponents run away or disengage, it will not pursue them unless its Morale is in the Impetuous state. Note that units that are disciplined (either by their innate characteristics or as the result of a discipline upgrade) are much less likely to become impetuous.

Fire At Will

This mode applies to missile troops only and is the default setting for non-artillery units. If a unit that's set to this mode hasn't been explicitly ordered to fire at a particular enemy, it will fire at the enemy unit closest to its front. Exception: Units set to Fire At Will won't automatically target an enemy unit if it is engaged in melee combat *and* shooting at it has previously resulted in friendly fire casualties.

It's usually best to leave your missile units in Fire At Will mode, unless you need to save ammunition. Just remember that clicking on an enemy unit to target it always overrides the automatic target selection of Fire At Will.

BATTLE TIPS AND TACTICS

Looking for quick help? Here it is—a veritable smorgasbord of Battle Map tips and tactics. We've divided them into general areas of interest—Pre-Battle, Troop Deployment, Terrain, Attacking, Defending, and Artillery and Siege Tactics—to make it easier to find the advice you seek. But we recommend that you sit down, grab a highly caffeinated soda beverage, and just read through the entire section.

Some of these tips reiterate points made in the game manual—you *did* read the manual, didn't you?—but most are fresh insights from the experts who created and tested *Medieval: Total War*. Check out all the Tips from the Testers for priceless nuggets of wisdom from the insiders who know the game best.

PRE-BATTLE TIPS

Some battles are won or lost in the preparation phase, before hostilities even begin. Here are a few tips for good generalship in the calm before the storm.

SURVEY THE FIELD BEFORE YOU FIGHT

Be sure to carefully examine the battleground and make a deployment plan *before* you click Continue and engage the enemy. Note the high ground, the hiding places for ambush, and any other geographical features that can affect the fighting.

Keep in mind, however, that you can't always see the enemy in the pre-battle deployment phase. His forces may be arrayed in an unusual or unexpected manner. So try to plan for various contingencies.

Sometimes rain is good for combat, such as when the enemy has rank after rank of archers and you don't.

CHECK THE WEATHER

Visibility is crucial for conducting effective tactical maneuvers. Fog, rain, snow, and sandstorms can limit visibility and hamper your deployment. Wet weather also has an adverse effect on the weapons used by archers and gunners. In fact, gunpowder weapons don't work *at all* when damp.

Finally, remember that every type of unit tires easily when operating in snow and cold. On the other hand, knights and other troops wearing heavy armor suffer terribly in hot desert conditions.

FIGHT ARCHER-LADEN ARMIES IN WET WEATHER

This is the obvious corollary of the previous tip. If you know that your enemy has a lot of missile troops and you don't, wait for rain before you attack. Wet bowstrings will cripple his ranged defenses, and your light cavalry or regular infantry can rout his archers with minimal losses.

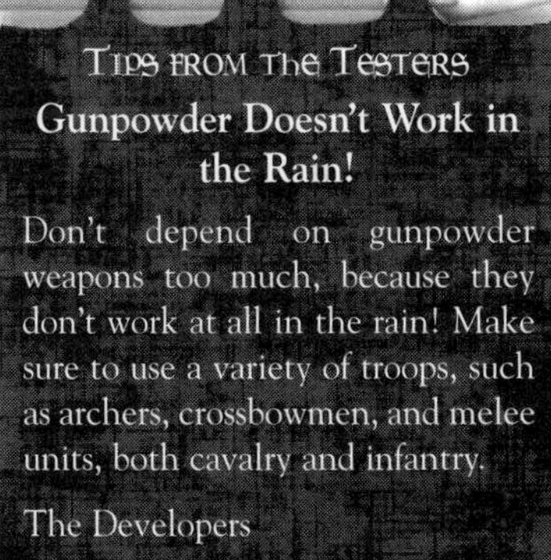

TIPS FROM THE TESTERS

Gunpowder Doesn't Work in the Rain!

Don't depend on gunpowder weapons too much, because they don't work at all in the rain! Make sure to use a variety of troops, such as archers, crossbowmen, and melee units, both cavalry and infantry.

The Developers

TROOP DEPLOYMENT

This section features the biggest batch of tips in the chapter—no surprise there. Here's where you learn the fundamentals of fighting: which units to deploy against other units, which formations work best, and other tricks of the battlefield.

Hit That Pause Key Frequently

Some people think it's cheating, or just lame, to pause the action when the flow of the battle gets mind-boggling. We, however, find the Pause button to be our best friend and have no problem admitting it. Stop the game and cruise around the landscape with the camera controls. Check out the status of all units. Who's winning? Who's losing? Are your flanks exposed? Who could benefit from reinforcement? Where should you redirect your missile fire? Don't be ashamed to take a cautious, systematic approach. Your men depend on you!

Protect Your General

The tester tip on this page makes this point, but it's so important that we want to reemphasize it here: *Do not let the unit that contains your army's commanding general get in serious trouble!* (Unless, of course, you *want* to get rid of him!) If he dies or his unit is routed, the overall Morale of your army plummets considerably.

On the other hand, the general's personal unit may be good fighters, such as Royal Knights. If so, you don't want to keep them completely out of combat. (And remember that a general can gain Command stars and occasional Virtues if he fights successfully in actual combat.) But consider holding them as a reserve unit. Use them to charge into weak lines, break stalemates, and mop up exhausted enemy units. Just be ready to pull them back out of harm's way at a moment's notice!

> Tips from the Testers
>
> **Morale Is Very Important!**
>
> Morale is very important in a battle! Protect your army's commanding general, because if you lose him your troops are likely to lose heart and flee. Many a battle has turned just from the loss of the general.
>
> The Developers

Hold Your Formation with Spears and Pikes, But Let Swordsmen Engage at Will

Always remember that spear and pike units gain their combat advantage from their supporting ranks' ability to engage the enemy at the same time as the front rank. This only works if the formation is deep, tight, and holds together. Set your spearmen and pikemen to Hold Formation, and be sure to deploy them deep enough to maximize the bonus—3 or 4 ranks for spearmen, 5 or 6 for pikemen.

Swordsmen can be deployed wider than pike or spear units, however, because they gain no rank support bonus. This wider formation can be good for outflanking foes in a frontal assault. Use Engage At Will mode to get the best effect. This way, swordsmen at the far ends of the formation line swing in and fall on their enemy's flanks.

Send Swift Cavalry to Flank Spear Formations

Spear units are much more vulnerable if struck in the flank or rear. This is the best way for light cavalry to defeat spearmen. Even if only a few horsemen contact the flank, avoiding the wall of spears means they can kill many men on the first impact, which may be enough to break the spear unit. If this first charge doesn't succeed and the spearmen turn on you, it's usually possible to disengage your horsemen with fairly minimal losses.

Pack a Six-Pack of Pikemen

Arrange pikemen in rows 5 or 6 deep to maximize their supporting ranks bonus.

Pikemen are most effective in formations at least 6 deep. Pikes are such long weapons that 4 full rows *behind* the front rank (that is, rows 2 through 5) can strike at the enemy. The sixth row is to provide fresh pikemen to fill in when front-row soldiers fall.

Counter Spear and Pike Units with Arrows

Pikemen are deadly opponents of most cavalry and infantry units in melee action. But their weapon requires two hands to use, so pikemen cannot carry shields. This leaves them vulnerable to missile fire. Don't charge into pikemen. Nail them from afar with your archers.

Also, many spear-armed units suffer from low Morale. Although a frontal assault against them may make slow progress, combining it with missile or artillery fire will send the spearmen running much more quickly.

Keep Swordsmen Deep Against Cavalry

Sword-armed foot soldiers tend to get swept away by enemy cavalry charges, particularly if their line is thin. We suggest you form a tight alignment, at least 4 or 5 soldiers deep, when your swordsmen face a mounted charge.

> TIPS FROM THE TESTERS
>
> **Charge Those Archers!**
>
> Deploy light cavalry to charge missile units, because a quickly moving target is more difficult to hit with arrows. Your horsemen can rush in past the hail of arrows or spears and remove a potential threat with great ease.
>
> The Developers

> TIPS FROM THE TESTERS
>
> **Use the Right Units and Formations.**
>
> Knowing the strengths and weaknesses of your units, and those of your enemy, can make the difference in a battle! For example, Halbediers are great against other melee units, including infantry and heavy cavalry. But they're too slow and are largely ineffective against missile-firing cavalry. A company of Horse Archers can decimate Halbedier units.
>
> Also, make sure that your units are in the proper formation for their weapon type. Any sort of spearmen unit should be kept in close formation, no more than 4 men deep, so that all their weapons can come to bear on the enemy. Archers should be strung out in lines no more than 2 deep so that as many as possible can get the attack bonus for being in the first couple of ranks.
>
> The Developers

Ch.3

Got Knights? Charge!

Mounted Knights gain a powerful bonus from their charge. Don't let them get bogged down in a melee stalemate. If their initial charge doesn't break and rout an enemy's line, consider pulling them out of the fray, regrouping, and charging again.

Spread Knights and Other Cavalry in a Wide Formation

Mounted Knights are built for the charge. Spread knight units wide enough to wrap around at least one flank of the enemy unit.

This is another version of the previous tip on deploying your swordsmen thin and wide. The mounted, fully armored frontal charge is always fearsome and hits home hard, but horsemen have another neat trick when attacking tight groups of enemy units. If you deploy your knights in a line that extends wider than the enemy's formation at either end, and you make sure they're set to Engage At Will, they will curl around the enemy formation at the sides and envelop it, falling fiercely on the enemy flank and even the rear.

Form Missile Units into 2 or 3 Lines

The front 2 ranks (3 in loose formation) of an archer unit can see their targets clearly and shoot with full accuracy. The archers behind them cannot see their targets and shoot at reduced accuracy. In practice, 3 ranks deep is a good compromise between getting the best shooting accuracy and keeping the unit formation from being too strung out.

Crossbow and arbalest units are best deployed in formations only 2 ranks deep (3 if in loose formation) because the men further back find it very hard to shoot over the heads of those in front.

Missile Units Can Shatter Enemy Morale

The effect of missile fire isn't just in the casualties it causes. It also reduces enemy morale—even more so if heavy casualties are inflicted—and can often be the decisive factor in making the enemy crack first in a hard-fought contest. Archers are particularly useful for dashing the enemy's spirit because arrows can arc over the heads of friendly troops and put down a *lot* of fire in a short time.

Set Most Archers to Skirmish Mode

Most archers are weak melee fighters, despite carrying melee weapons in addition to bows. When you set archers to Skirmish, they withdraw from enemy melee attackers, avoiding hand-to-hand contact while continuing to launch missile fire.

But Stand Your Ground with Short-Range Missile Troops

Short-range missile troops, such as Naptha Throwers or the javelin-tossing Murabitin Infantry, must hold steady until the enemy is close. Unlike your standard archer, they can cause *massive* damage from close range if they stand their ground. Order these troops to Hold Formation until they toss a few javelins or bombs, and then switch to Skirmish mode and let them withdraw to safety. Then repeat the cycle.

Tips from the Testers

Keep Everything Together!

Keep your units grouped together, arrayed with good depth and minimal gaps in the line. Troops can help each other out if needed, and they all are *much* happier when their flanks are protected.

The Developers

Be Careful When Firing Missiles into Melee Action

Firing into a massed melee runs the risk of shooting some of your own men in the back. As the manual points out, "Arrows and artillery fire are no respecters of loyalty." If you direct missile fire into a melee involving your own troops, expect to take casualties from friendly fire.

But this tactic is often worthwhile, especially if your melee units are more heavily armored than the enemy's, if the enemy troops are in a denser formation, or (this is cruel) if your melee fighters are mere peasants. After all, the common folk should be honored to take an arrow or two in the back for their king!

Tips from the Testers

Hold Troops in Reserve!

Fresh troops rushing into the fray can tilt the balance of power on a battlefield. Try to keep some troops in reserve—preferably units with decent speed and a strong Charge factor, such as light cavalry—and be ready to unleash them on the exhausted enemy.

The Developers

Send Mounted Archers Around the Flanks

Mounted archers fire less accurately than foot archers, so the best tactic is to use their speed to move into an advantageous position on the target's flank or rear. They can also move to close range against *non-missile* infantry targets (see the next tip) because their speed will keep them out of danger.

Keep Horse Archers Away from Foot Archers

Never engage your mounted missile troops in a stationary shooting match with infantry bow units. The mounted units will almost always lose because they fire less accurately, and their horses (or camels) present much bigger targets to the foot archers.

Turn Your Axemen Loose on Armored Foes

Big swipes with a good axe can penetrate even heavy armor. Remember that axemen feature a special armor-piercing bonus. Try to deploy them in your battle lines so they match up against armored enemy units.

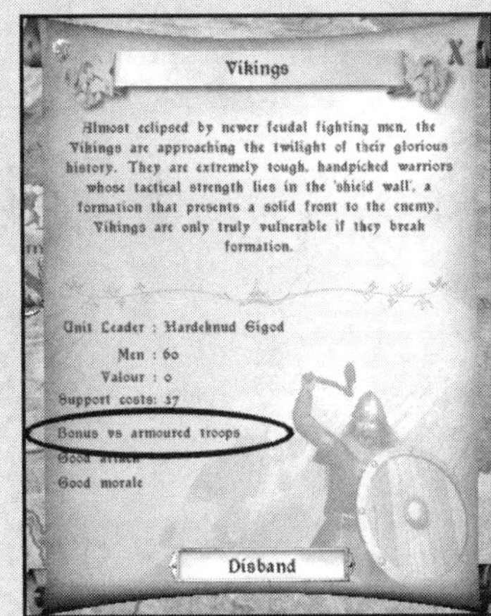

Don't forget that axes can pierce armor.

Ch.3

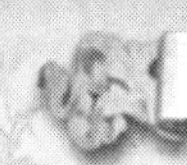

Never Underestimate the Ballista's Ability to Kill Your General

Ballistae are fearsome weapons that fire big projectiles hundreds of yards. When used against your commanding general's unit, the ballista stands a good chance of piercing your fearless leader with a spear-like bolt or stone missile. Immediately send foot troops to chase off ballista crews and destroy the weapon.

Remember: Horses Hate the Smell of Camels

Send any camel cavalry directly at enemy horse-mounted cavalry. Horses fear camels, and thus horsemen suffer a penalty when fighting camel units.

Terrain

The ground you fight on can play a critical role in the success or failure of your combat engagements.

Seize the High Ground

Height gives your troops a longer line of sight *and* a Morale bonus. If defending against a stronger enemy force, take a hill... and stay there! Do *not* chase enemies down if they rout, because if they rally you can find yourself out of position, fighting without the height advantage, and you'll be defeated.

Troops Get Tired Moving Uphill

Try to maneuver your troops so that the enemy is the one fighting the uphill battle. Your units will be less fatigued when fighting downhill and will fight much better.

Fighting from the high ground gives every troop type an advantage!

Tips from the Testers

Use Height for Fun and Profit

Remember, attacking downhill gives your troops a massive advantage. Two units that are otherwise identical will have completely different outcomes when one attacks uphill and the other attacks downhill!

The Developers

Height Gives Your Missile Units Greater Range

Archers gain considerable benefits from being uphill from the enemy. They gain extra range and power, plus they can see over intervening units and thus avoid any accuracy penalty for shooting overhead. Shooting uphill produces the inverse effect and is far less effective.

Note, however, that if a hill is *too* steep, it reduces the downhill effectiveness of missile weapons. Arrows flying down very steep hills can zoom over the heads of the enemy.

Trees Negate the Supporting Rank Bonus

Keep your spear and pike units out in the open ground! There are no rank support bonuses when fighting in the woods, so neither spearmen nor pikemen gain any advantage there.

Tactical Maneuvers: Attacking

Attacking is always fun, but it's also risky. Seizing the initiative with aggressive offensive tactics can let you dictate the course of a battle. But if you overextend your forces or send the wrong troops into the fray at the wrong time, your aggressiveness can lead to disaster. Here are a few good tips on attack maneuvers.

Spring an Ambush

A flank ambush by units hidden in trees is one of the most effective attacks in the game.

A surprise flank attack by a previously hidden unit inflicts a Morale penalty of –8 on the enemy being attacked. Add that to the normal bonuses you gain by hitting the enemy's flank, and you have all the makings of a quick rout.

Use Your Army as a Crab's Claw and Encircle the Enemy

When surrounded on all sides, the enemy is more likely to rout and will have nowhere to run. Trapped and panicked troops can be easy game, so this tactic can let you inflict truly demoralizing defeats on foes.

Tips from the Testers

Use Forests to Your Advantage!

Sneak some troops (especially weaker infantry units) into woods whenever possible. Remember, units hiding in trees can spring a nasty surprise on your enemy. Not only can you ambush nearby foes with a vicious charge into their unsuspecting flank, but your forest deployment also makes for a great defense against powerful cavalry, because mounted units don't fight well in the trees.

However, in the course of deploying troops into the woods, be careful not to split up your forces too much. If your hidden units are too isolated from the main body of your army, their sneaky ambush may turn into a deathtrap!

The Developers

Use Heavy and Light Cavalry in Tandem

Use your heavy cavalry to entice the enemy spearmen and cavalry away from the main body of their army to create a hole. Your light cavalry can then charge through this and slaughter the archers to the rear. Divide and conquer!

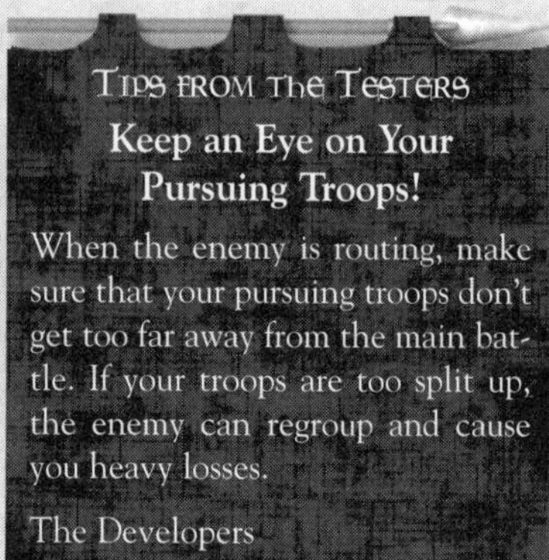

Tips from the Testers

Keep an Eye on Your Pursuing Troops!

When the enemy is routing, make sure that your pursuing troops don't get too far away from the main battle. If your troops are too split up, the enemy can regroup and cause you heavy losses.

The Developers

Use Artillery to Rip Holes in Enemy Ranks

Bombarding close-formation enemy troops with heavy artillery is a powerful tactic. Use multiple artillery pieces to increase the carnage and amplify the panic.

Flank and Rear Attacks Are More Effective Than Frontal Assaults

Where possible, try to charge your cavalry units into the flank or rear of an enemy unit. This eliminates the target unit's Shield bonus (if it has one) and maximizes the shock impact of the attacking cavalry's charge. It also means that the cavalry will not start to suffer heavy casualties until their target can reorganize itself. There's a good chance that the target unit won't recover from the shock of the initial impact, and thus will break and run.

Use Waypoints to Direct Flanking Maneuvers

Remember, you set waypoints by left-clicking on terrain while holding down the Shift key. Move units from waypoint to waypoint to get around and behind enemy troops.

Use a Feigned Retreat to Draw Out Well-Organized Enemies

Remember this one from the manual? (You *did* read the manual, didn't you?) This is the dangerous (but often effective) tactic of pretending to run away to draw the enemy out of a strong position. Start an attack on the position, and then use the Rout command for a feigned retreat. If enemy troops break out of the position and follow, rally and attack!

If it goes well, the enemy can become disorganized and you can cut them to pieces. However, if it goes wrong, there's little chance of recovering control of your army!

Tactical Maneuvers: Defending

Defense is never quite as much fun as attacking, unless you're a true student of military tactics. As the saying goes, offense wins games, defense wins championships. A solid defensive position can break the spirit of an overaggressive foe and set up the perfect conditions for a crushing counterattack.

Use Spearmen Primarily to Screen and Defend

Spearmen are best on defense, and thus they make excellent screens for keeping attackers away from your archers. But although their attack factors are generally low, the momentum of a formed body of spearmen is considerable, so spear units have offensive potential too.

However, if the first charge isn't successful, don't expect a quick breakthrough. Consider switching back to a more defensive posture.

Screen your archers with rows of spearmen at least 3 or 4 deep.

Use Peasants to Buy Time

Yes, peasants are worthless fodder as combat troops, but they do have their uses. Line peasants up against your enemy's strongest infantry units to keep them engaged while you wipe out the rest of his army. Even if your peasants break and run, they entice the enemy troops to chase them, keeping them tied up even longer or drawing them out of a strong position.

Of course, seeing your peasants routed can adversely affect the Morale of some of your other units. But elite and disciplined units won't be affected much, and if you're winning elsewhere on the field, you can make up any Morale deficit and maintain good order.

Use Light Cavalry to Protect Your Flanks

Light cavalry can't really slug it out with other kinds of troops, but they're highly mobile and most have a fairly lethal charge. Keep a light cavalry unit or two in a central position behind your main force. If you see hostile units trying to flank you, send horsemen galloping to protect the endangered flank until you can march fresh infantry to extend your line. Once the situation is under control, pull the light cavalry back to their central position.

> **Tips from the Testers**
>
> **Force the Attacker to Make the First Move!**
>
> When on the defense, keep in one place if you can, and make the enemy come to you. They'll be tired out by the time they get to you, and you'll have plenty of time to organize your troops.
>
> The Developers

Light cavalry makes an excellent rapid deployment force that can rush to hotspots and shore up fading units.

Rush Light Cavalry to Hotspots Where Morale Is Wavering

This corollary of the previous tip uses light cavalry as a rapid deployment force. As you survey the battlefield with your cursor, monitor which troops are losing or have Morale that's dipping into Uncertain or Wavering. When you find troops in trouble, rush your light cavalry reserve right to that spot at full speed.

The shock of a cavalry charge can often turn the tide of battle almost immediately. At the very least, you can shore up the Morale of units in your line and keep them from routing.

> TIPS FROM THE TESTERS
>
> **Always Protect Your Missile Troops!**
>
> Your missile troops can be a great asset against all enemies, but you must protect them. Keep a unit of strong melee troops in front of your archers to make sure they stay safe while peppering the enemy with arrows!
>
> The Developers

Artillery and Siege Tactics

Artillery pieces in *Medieval: Total War* can be brutally effective war machines, if deployed and used properly. The following section is a comprehensive list of insider tips on artillery usage and some other siege tactics. The first two tips reiterate points made in the manual, but the rest come directly from the game's designers. Thanks, once again, to the folks at The Creative Assembly and Activision.

Place Your Artillery So It Can Hit Stuff

You'd be surprised how easy it is to forget this basic tip. When deploying your army, pay attention to where you place artillery, both mechanical and gunpowder units. Once these are in place they can't be moved, so you need to make sure that they're in the right place from the start of the battle. When besieging a castle, make sure your artillery is close enough to actually hit the walls!

Artillery placement should be done carefully and methodically. Make sure you can actually hit your targets!

Create Effective "Killing Zones"

Artillery units should be set up to cover the likely attack routes of the enemy. Ideally, the enemy should have to approach your army through a killing zone of artillery fire. Even on the attack, you can use light cavalry and horse archers to tempt the defenders to moving into artillery range.

Send Any Pavise Units in Close

Pavise Crossbowmen and Pavise Arbalesters are very useful in castle assault situations. Their pavises—huge wooden shields they can set on the ground for protection—let them make a close approach to the castle without taking too many casualties from its defenses. Pavise units are slow, but this doesn't matter in a siege because enemy units remain inside their castle.

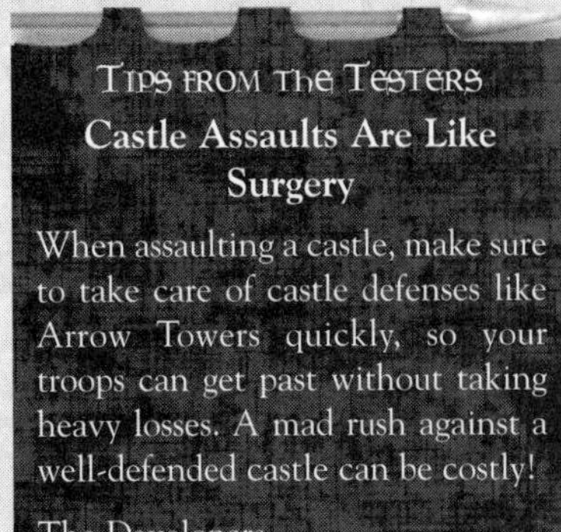

Tips from the Testers

Castle Assaults Are Like Surgery

When assaulting a castle, make sure to take care of castle defenses like Arrow Towers quickly, so your troops can get past without taking heavy losses. A mad rush against a well-defended castle can be costly!

The Developers

Fire from the High Ground

When deploying artillery, you should look for a height advantage. This will give your artillery greater range, reduce the effective range of incoming missile fire, and slow down any enemy unit charging up the hill toward it. The mouse pointer will indicate whether an artillery piece has a clear shot at a given target, even during deployment. You should take a few seconds to advantageously position your artillery, especially when besieging a castle.

Determine Range and Firing Arc

Some types of artillery can rotate their base in a full 360 degree arc, but some of the larger types can't. Generally, the big, immobile pieces have a longer range to compensate. They also have a wider *firing cone*, or the narrow angle within which the crew can swivel the piece's aim to either side of its set facing. Most artillery has a minimum firing range as well as a maximum one. Some types of artillery simply cannot be brought to bear on a target at close range.

Again, use the mouse pointer's red/green shooting indicator to determine your best deployment positions. Since even artillery that can rotate can't be moved to any other position on the map once the deployment phase has ended, you need to assess the parts of the map you can see to figure out your best fields of fire.

Know How Your Crews Fire Accurately

Artillery becomes increasingly accurate the more shots you take at the same target, as the crew ranges in on it. If the artillery has to turn, your accuracy is lost and the crew will start ranging in again. Of course, there's no guarantee that a crew's first shot will be on target, or in the case of a rookie crew firing at long range, anywhere near it!

You can't influence a crew's accuracy except by shooting at nearer targets. But if a crew scores kills on the enemy, its Valor rating increases and its ability to range in improves. High-Valor artillery crews can put their first shot within a couple of meters of the target.

Artillery projectiles can tear gaping holes in close-formation troops.

Artillery will try to *lead* a moving target. If the target moves out of the firing cone, the artillery piece will rotate (if it can) until it's perfectly lined up with the target before firing again. This gives the piece the best chance of taking several shots before the target moves out of the firing cone again. If it can't rotate, the artillery will have to stop firing.

Target Close Formation Troops

We mentioned this earlier, but it's worth expounding on. Artillery projectiles are *big*, and most of them bounce a few times when they land. This gives you several chances to kill enemy troops! The smallest projectile is fired by the mortar, and even this will kill any man it hits. The larger rocks and cannonballs wreak mayhem if they land in the middle of an enemy unit—which will suffer not only casualties, but also an enormous Morale penalty.

For this reason, bombarding close-formation enemy troops with heavy artillery is a powerful tactic. If you can, use multiple artillery pieces to amplify the panic.

Tips from the Testers

Siege Weapons Intimidate the Enemy!

If you have siege weapons, place them so the enemy has a *lot* of time to approach them. They'll take heavy losses! Oncoming foes will often be scared off by the amazing firepower of your siege engines.

The Developers

Know Your Artillery Crews

The bigger the artillery piece, the more men are required to make it work. A crew has a minimum strength and a maximum effective strength. If enough crewmen are killed to bring the total below the maximum effective strength, the surviving crew are not as efficient when reloading between shots. If the crew level falls below the minimum strength, the artillery piece becomes unusable.

Some types of artillery come with "spare" crew who are there to replace casualties. But the larger artillery pieces do not, so you should guard them fanatically or their effectiveness will drop the moment they lose a man.

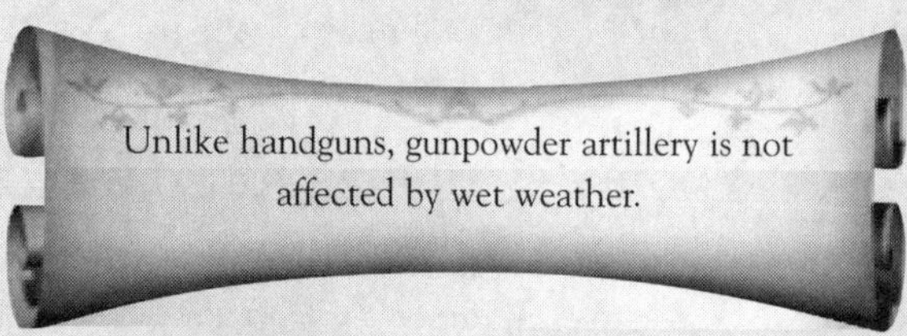

Unlike handguns, gunpowder artillery is not affected by wet weather.

Artillery crews are naturally timid, and if they are in Skirmish mode (their default setting), they will abandon their artillery if threatened. Once the area around their weapon seems relatively safe, they will automatically return to it.

Tips from the Testers

Use Siege Weapons to Their Fullest Against Castles!

Make sure that you're fully using your siege weapons in a castle assault. Don't just destroy one wall and rush in. Use up all the ammo possible so that the castle defenses are severely weakened. Destroying more than one wall is also very useful because you can attack the castle from more than one side at once!

The Developers

Knock Out Enemy Artillery Right Away

You can destroy artillery pieces by shooting at them with your own artillery (especially effective when defending a castle), or by physically attacking them like you would a castle gate or other building. It pays to send a fast cavalry unit to scare off the crews and demolish the artillery.

Don't let enemy field pieces shred your positions. Deploy fast troops to scatter artillery crews and destroy their pieces.

Beware the Instability of Some Artillery Pieces

Some artillery is unsafe. Early gunpowder weapons were prone to self-destructing in their crews' faces! Be particularly cautious about relying on the Bombard, Siege-Cannon, or Demi-Cannon. Each one is guaranteed to fire a minimum number of shots without danger, but thereafter each shot has a chance of blowing up in the barrel, destroying the gun and setting off an explosion that can affect nearby units. The Bombard is the worst offender. Each shot after the third has a 10 percent chance of making the piece self-destruct!

Remember that you can enjoy an exciting "projectile-eye view" by right-clicking a single piece of artillery and selecting Follow Projectiles from the context menu. This will make your battlefield camera "ride" each projectile fired by that piece of artillery. Repeat the procedure to go back to the normal camera.

HOW THE COMBAT SYSTEM WORKS

Okay, let's be perfectly honest. Many of you could care less about how *Medieval: Total War* makes its geekazoid calculations to determine the outcome of battles. Those of us who limped through college as humanities majors prefer combat engines to be transparent.

Medieval: Total War features clashes of mighty armies, but combat is made up of individual soldiers fighting individual battles.

But true *Medieval: Total War* fans get a charge out of understanding the underlying math of combat. Not only that, but they gain an edge, too. Mastery is always much easier if you can glimpse how the game "thinks."

The following discussion comes to you courtesy of the programmer who created the game's brilliant combat system.

The Kill Chance

In *Medieval: Total War*, all combat occurs between individual soldiers. When opposing units engage, each soldier in each unit can make one strike per animation cycle (which lasts about one second) against one enemy soldier. Note, however, that a soldier may have to defend *several* strikes against him during that cycle, because several opponents may have targeted him.

In Medieval: Total War, an "animation cycle" lasts approximately one second. Thus, individual soldiers can make about one strike per second. Although strikes are processed in a strict order, they are effectively simultaneous within each cycle. That is, even if Soldier A strikes and kills Soldier B, Soldier B gets to make his strike for that cycle before he expires.

So it is entirely possible for Soldiers A and B to kill each other simultaneously!

When a soldier makes a strike, the combat engine adds up various factors to calculate a number that determines the probability of killing the targeted foe—the Kill Chance. Specifically, that Kill Chance number is determined by taking the striker's Attack value, subtracting his target's Defense value, and then modifying the difference by a number of situational factors.

We'll examine these situational factors in a moment. But first, let's take a look at the importance of the Charge bonus in the initial phase of combat.

Charge Bonus

Once you select a unit, you can order it to attack an enemy by clicking on the target unit. As your unit approaches the target, it automatically *charges*—that is, breaks into a full running attack. A charging soldier makes immediate strikes against all opponents he contacts, and a special Charge bonus applies to each strike. (You can find the Charge bonus for each unit in Chapter 4, "Units.") His opponents are also given a chance to strike back against him. How long the soldier's charge continues (and the Charge bonus applies) is a factor of winning and momentum.

In a charge, the amount of momentum a soldier gains depends on how long he was charging before contact with the enemy. Only 2 or 3 seconds of charging is required to get the maximum momentum allowed.

The soldier builds up *momentum* while charging. Each time he fights, a little momentum is lost. As long as the charging soldier keeps killing or pushing back foes and has sufficient momentum, he can move forward and strike new opponents. When sufficient momentum is lost, the charge ends and the soldier loses the Charge bonus.

THE "PUSH BACK" EFFECT

In an attack, the striker may not score a kill, but he may force his target to move back a step. This "push back" gives a strong bonus to the striker in subsequent strikes. After all, troops falling back have "negative momentum" and thus are more vulnerable to their onrushing enemy's blows.

The chances of pushing back an enemy depend partly on the Kill Chance, but also on other factors. For example, a charging striker often forces his target to step back, an advantage in supporting ranks can force a pushback on the target, and a mounted man can push back a footman with ease. Indeed, one of the things that makes cavalry so dangerous to infantry is that a charging cavalryman will *always* push back any foot soldier who is not facing him with a spear, pike, or polearm.

KILL CHANCE FACTORS

Numerous factors are used to determine the Kill Chance of any strike. These factors are calculated *in the current animation cycle* as follows.

BASIC FACTORS

First, the engine sums the values derived from the basic stats of both units (striker and target). The Attack and Defense values here include modifications for each unit's Valor rating, general's rank, general's vices and virtues, bonuses versus cavalry units, and weapon and armor upgrades.

ADD the striker's Attack value

SUBTRACT the target's Defense value

ADD the striker's Charge bonus if charging

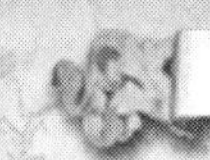

Troop Type Factors

ADD the Armor piercing bonus if the striker has an Armor piercing weapon.

The value of the striker's Armor piercing bonus is calculated as follows:

(Target's Armor value - 2) / 2

However, the target's Armor value is modified to subtract the contribution of his shield and horse to his Armor rating.

SUBTRACT 4 if the striker is afraid of the target

The only case where this applies is when horse units fight camel units. Horses fear camels!

OR

ADD 2 if the target is afraid of the striker (same as above)

Positional Factors

Strikers gain additional bonuses if attacking targets from the flank or rear.

ADD 5 if striking target from the flank

OR

ADD 7 if striking target from the rear

ADD 2 additional bonus for charging into target's flank or rear

If the target has a shield, a Shield bonus was included in the target's initial Defense factor. But if you strike the defender from the rear, he can't use his shield. So the Shield bonus gets plucked out of the equation.

If striker hits target from the rear:

ADD 2 if target is a footman with a large shield

OR

ADD 1 if the target is mounted or has a small shield

Supporting Ranks

Only spearmen and pikemen can claim supporting ranks. Spearmen can have up to 2 supporting ranks, and pikemen can have up to 4 supporting ranks. Other units always count as 0 supporting ranks. *Remember, there are no rank support bonuses or penalties when fighting in woods.*

ADD number of striker's supporting ranks if charging

OR

ADD half the number of striker's supporting ranks if not charging

SUBTRACT the number of target's supporting ranks

Terrain Factors

Still with us? Good. Now the combat system takes into account the advantages and disadvantages of the terrain at the point of the strike.

ADD bonus for the striker being higher than the target (amount depends on height difference)

OR

SUBTRACT penalty for the target being higher than the striker (amount depends on height difference)

SUBTRACT 2 if the striker is a mounted troop in the woods

OR

ADD 2 if the target is a mounted troop in the woods

ADD 1 if the striker is camel-mounted and fighting in a sandy desert

SUBTRACT 1 if the striker is camel-mounted and fighting in lush or temperate terrain

Fatigue Factors

Fatigue factors are *not* cumulative. Thus, if the soldier's fatigue state changes, the previous value disappears and is replaced in the calculation by the value associated with the new state.

So the striker's Fatigue level calculation uses only one of the following:

SUBTRACT 2 if striker is quite tired

SUBTRACT 3 if striker is very tired

SUBTRACT 4 if striker is exhausted

The Fatigue level that's displayed in the Unit Information Panel is the average for the entire unit. Each soldier has an individual fatigue rating. Thus, men fighting in the front rank get more tired than those behind them.

SUBTRACT 6 if striker is totally exhausted

ADD 1 if target is very tired

ADD 2 if target is exhausted

ADD 3 if target is totally exhausted

Formation and Combat Mode Modifiers

Soldiers gain striking power (and lose some defensive prowess) if deployed in a tight wedge formation. On the other hand, units *lose* striking power (and gain defensive strength) if deployed in the Hold Formation engagement mode:

ADD 3 if striker's unit is in wedge formation

ADD 3 if target's unit is in wedge formation

SUBTRACT 2 if striker's unit is in Hold Formation mode

SUBTRACT 2 if target's unit is in Hold Formation mode

Miscellaneous Factors

Hang in there, you're almost home. Now you just have a few miscellaneous values to add in for some special circumstances.

ADD 6 if the target is falling back as a result of a previous strike (see "The 'Push Back' Effect" earlier in this section)

OR

ADD 4 if the target is routing

OR

SUBTRACT 8 if the striker is routing

ADD 5 if the target has insufficient space to fight (for example, in the crush coming through a gate or over a bridge)

Maximum/Minimum Factor

Here's your last step. The Kill Chance factor cannot be any greater than 20 or any lower than –20. So if the number is greater than 20, the combat system rounds it down to 20. If the number is any lower than –20, the system rounds it up to –20.

Ch.3

Calculating the Kill Chance

Ha! You made it! You've got the Kill Chance factor of the strike. If that factor is 0, the chance of making a kill is 1.9 percent. For each factor above 0, the chance to make a kill is increased by 20 percent, and it's reduced by 20 percent for each factor less than 0.

This gives you the following Kill Chance percentages:

COMBAT FACTOR	KILL CHANCE PERCENT
-20	0.05
-10	0.31
-5	0.76
-4	0.92
-3	1.10
-2	1.32
-1	1.58
0	1.90
1	2.28
2	2.74
3	3.28
4	3.94
5	4.73
10	11.76
20	72.84

Again, whatever your combat factor, increasing it by 1 always increases your chance to kill by 20 percent. Also, increasing it 4 factors approximately doubles the chance of a kill.

Once the Kill Chance percentage is finally calculated, the engine "rolls" a random number using the percentage to determine if the strike kills the target or not. And then it's on to the next strike!

How Valor Affects Troops

As units fight battles and gain combat experience in *Medieval: Total War*, they become more *valorous*—that is, their Valor point rating increases. Valor points have the following effects on combat stats:

+1 Attack per Valor point gained

+1 Defense per Valor point gained

+2 Morale per Valor point gained

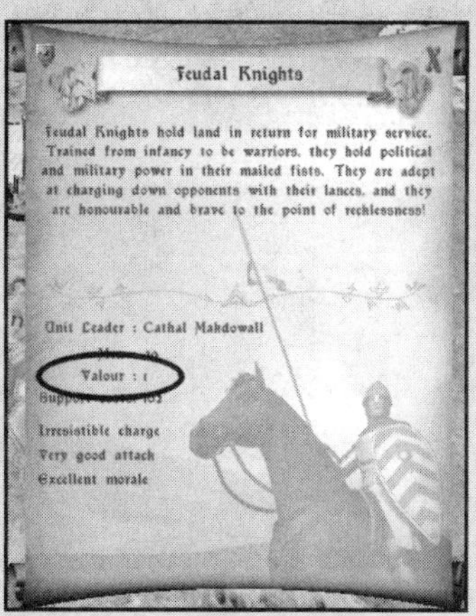

Each Valor point earned by a unit adds +1 Attack, +1 Defense, and +2 Morale to its stats.

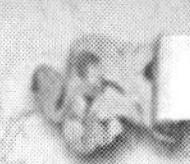

How Morale Affects Troops

Morale affects the behavior and performance of every unit in tactical combat. Each unit's morale is continuously evaluated moment by moment during a battle, producing a numeric Morale rating that translates into one of five "Morale states"—*Impetuous*, *Steady*, *Uncertain*, *Wavering*, and *Routing*.

Generally speaking, a unit's Morale state is determined by various factors that apply at that particular instant—factors such as Fatigue, Winning or Losing, Threats to Flank, and so on. But some units "remember" other factors (such as a general's death) that continue to effect them for a few seconds.

Units with low Morale are likely to break and run away.

The combat system evaluates each of these factors that affect Morale as either a positive or negative number. These are summed together and added to the base Morale value for the unit type, and then modified by Valor and Morale upgrades. The resulting value falls into one of the five ranges that correspond to each Morale state. If a unit's total Morale value drops lower than the lowest value for its current Morale state, that unit's Morale will drop to the next lowest state. If the unit's total Morale value rises higher than the highest value allowed for the current state, the unit's Morale rises to the next higher state.

Important: The ranges for Morale states *overlap*, as you can see in the following table. So if a unit's Morale has fallen to a lower state, a considerable increase in Morale is needed to bring it to a higher state.

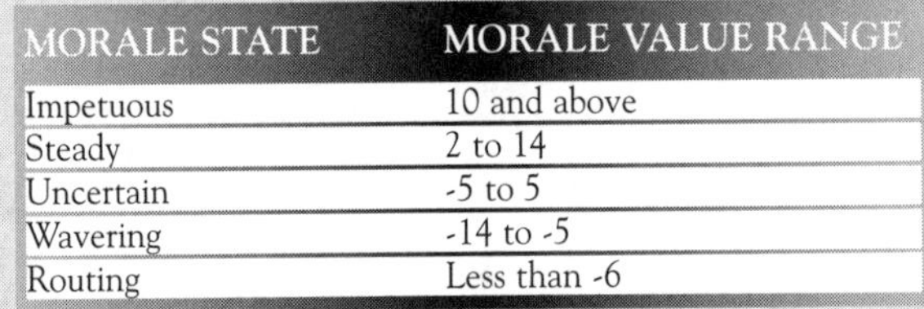

MORALE STATE	MORALE VALUE RANGE
Impetuous	10 and above
Steady	2 to 14
Uncertain	-5 to 5
Wavering	-14 to -5
Routing	Less than -6

The Five Morale States

Here's a quick look at how a unit's Morale state affects its behavior:

Units that are *Impetuous* will pursue enemies for longer and may disregard orders to hold position. Some troop types may charge without orders.

Steady is the normal Morale state.

Mainly, the *Uncertain* and *Wavering* states inform the player that morale is getting low. However, in combat, Uncertain or Wavering men who aren't currently fighting are less likely to charge, and those who are fighting are more likely to fall back.

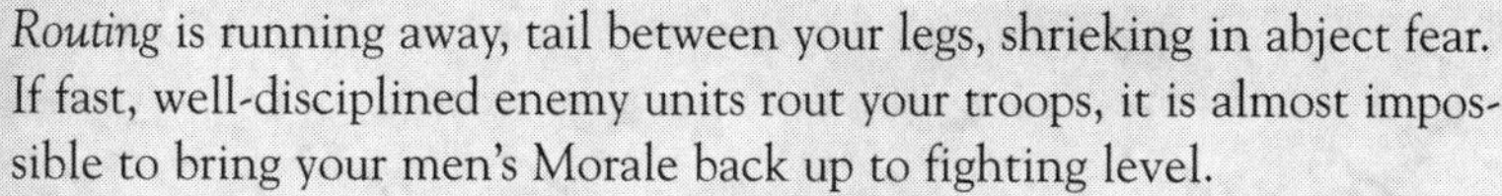

Routing is running away, tail between your legs, shrieking in abject fear. If fast, well-disciplined enemy units rout your troops, it is almost impossible to bring your men's Morale back up to fighting level.

Penalty Factors

Here's a list of selected factors or combat situations that negatively affect a unit's Morale rating.

Disordered or Loose Formation

No troops, not even peasants, like to maneuver or fight in a disorganized mob. And as any medieval military tactician knows, tight formations help soldiers perform better in combat. Suffering from disordered ranks or loose formations costs a –2 Morale penalty.

Outnumbered by Enemy Forces

Units suffer a -4 Morale penalty when outnumbered 2 to 1. This penalty can be as large as -12 when outnumbered 10 to 1. This particular factor takes into account the quality and speed of the enemy, too. So in essence, Morale suffers when the unit is outnumbered *or* outclassed.

Threats to Flanks

Units get very disconsolate when enemies approach them from the side or rear. Morale suffers -2 if one flank is threatened. Morale suffers -6 if two flanks, or one flank and the rear, are threatened. Being charged in the flank inflicts a –4 Morale penalty. Infantry units charged by cavalry in the flank, or while disordered, suffer a –6 Morale loss. Finally, if a previously hidden unit suddenly charges into your unit's flank, you suffer a major Morale loss of –8.

A surprise ambush from the woods into an enemy's flank inflicts a major Morale penalty in the target unit.

General's Death

Leadership is an important factor in combat, particularly for undisciplined units. The loss of an army's commanding general lowers Morale considerably in the first moments of chaos after his death. (This penalty doesn't apply to highly disciplined units.) Units in the general's army suffer a -8 Morale penalty in the first few seconds after he dies. After that, the penalty is –2.

Routing Friends

The sight of friendly troops broken and fleeing in chaos puts a real damper on Morale, as you can imagine. A unit can suffer up to –12 Morale at the sight of two units that it cares about—that is, units of an equal or higher level—being routed by foes.

Note that for this calculation, elite and disciplined units consider lesser unit types to be only half a unit. So if Royal Knights see a pack of peasants routing to the rear, they won't find this quite as demoralizing as if the fleeing friendlies were fellow knights or noblemen.

Casualties

For some reason, troops also find it kind of discouraging to see their ranks slaughtered. Unit Morale drops -2 for a 10 percent casualty rate, -8 for a 50 percent rate, and –12 for an 80-percent decimation.

Taking Enemy Fire

Simply being shot at by missile weapons drops Morale by –2, plus an additional –4 penalty if shot at by weapons that cause fear, such as gunpowder weapons.

Skirmishing

If your missile units are skirmishing and being pursued a long distance by an enemy as fast as they are, Morale sinks by –6. If they're skirmishing and they run out of ammo, Morale drops by another –6.

Fatigue

Fatigue can lower Morale considerably, as you might expect. Very Tired units lose –3 Morale, Exhausted units drop –6 Morale, and Completely Exhausted units suffer a –8 Morale loss.

Losing

There's nothing quite as Morale-shattering as the knowledge that you're losing a battle. Units can lose up to –8 Morale, depending on how badly the fight is going. For infantry losing to cavalry, however, an *additional* Morale loss of –6 is possible. Thus, when cavalry charges infantry, the infantrymen either stand firm and repel the cavalry… or they fold very quickly.

Positive Factors

Okay, the bad stuff is out of the way. Now let's examine the factors that *boost* Morale in your troops, inspiring them to jump wholeheartedly into the fray and then stand their ground and fight hard.

Protected Flanks

When both of a unit's flanks, or one flank and its rear, are protected, those troops gain a +4 Morale bonus for the duration.

No Retreat Possible

When troops fight in a province from which there is no possibility of retreat, they are highly motivated to fight hard, as you might expect. In fact, units in that situation get a nice +8 Morale boost.

Rally/No Enemy Nearby

Routing troops suffer from plummeting Morale. But a quick click of the Rally button gives a +8 infusion of Morale to your running men. In most cases, that's enough to bump them up a level to the next highest Morale state and get them back under your control.

Redeploy them carefully, however, because their Morale is still fragile. If possible, move them away from the fray for a few minutes. Troops gain an automatic +4 Morale bonus when no enemy units are nearby. Another suggestion: Put low-Morale troops in a support position on a strong unit's flank or rear until their Morale climbs back into Steady territory.

Enemy Routing

Seeing your foes break and run from the field of battle is truly an uplifting sight. Your troops can gain up to +8 Morale (when two enemy units are routed) if this happens. Add +4 for outnumbering nearby enemy (see the previous section), and you have a truly invigorating boost of Morale.

Uphill Position

Any good medieval general knows the value of terrain, and in particular the benefits of attacking downhill. Men not only fight more effectively with gravity on their side, but they also enjoy a general raising of spirits. Being uphill of all nearby enemy gives a +2 Morale bonus to your forces.

Winning

When the tide of combat goes your way, adrenalin pushes your men to that wonderful state of aggressive optimism so essential to victory. If a unit is winning a battle, its Morale can rise by as much as +6.

Impetuous Charge!

Some proud units, such as Mounted Knights, are particularly impetuous and aggressive, occasionally operating with minds of their own. Making an unordered charge can create a warlike giddiness in these fellows and raise their Morale by +4.

Troops near your commanding general's unit (indicated by the big square flag) get a Morale boost from his presence.

Outnumber Nearby Enemy

A 3:1 advantage in numbers over nearby enemy forces gives any of your units in that area a +4 Morale boost.

Valor

As mentioned earlier in "How Valor Affects Troops," units gain a +2 Morale bonus for every Valor point they've gained.

Proximity to General

The presence of a competent commanding general always inspires and uplifts soldiers. Indeed, the higher his Command rating, the greater the Morale boost. Units close to the commanding general (within 50 meters) gain +1 Morale per every star of the general's Command rating. Troops farther away (more than 50 meters away) gain +1 Morale per every 2 stars of the commanding general's rank. The commanding general's own unit always gains an additional +2 Morale, regardless of his rank.

Easier Game Settings

The last and easiest way to boost the Morale of your units is to play *Medieval: Total War* in its Easy mode. This automatically raises the Morale of all units by +4. Or, if you want a different gameplay experience that's preferred by some *Medieval: Total War* gamers, you can go into the Options menu, select Game, and then uncheck Morale in the Realism Settings. This automatically raises Morale by +12 per unit.

Chapter 4: Units

CHAPTER 4: UNITS

Medieval: Total War features more than 100 individual units, each with its own capabilities. In this chapter, the game's design team helps us delineate the strengths and weaknesses of the various unit classes—mounted knights, heavy cavalry, archers, and so on. Under each class, we review each individual unit type using a table that lists basic stats and such key attributes as weapon, armor, and shield types. These tables also include the full in-game description of each unit.

Special thanks to R.T. Smith, the game's AI programmer, for putting together the illuminating discussions of *Medieval*'s unit classes. Thanks also to Ian Roxburgh of The Creative Assembly for facilitating the flow of insider information from the design team to us, and thus, ultimately, to you.

QUICK REFERENCE: UNITS BY CLASS

If you're not sure of a particular unit's class ("Are Byzantine Cavalry heavy or light cavalry?"), you can look it up in the following table. All available *Medieval* units are listed in alphabetical order, with each one's class indicated. This way, it's easy to find the detailed information in the corresponding section.

Some units fall under more than one class. The first class listed in the following table is that unit's primary class, indicating the section where you'll find the unit listed with its stats and info.

ALPHABETICAL UNIT REFERENCE LIST

UNIT	UNIT CLASS
Abyssinian Guard	Axeman
Alan Mercenary Cavalry	Light Cavalry
Almohad Urban Militia	Militia
Almughavar	Spearman, Javelin Thrower
Arbalester	Arbalester
Archer	Archer
Armenian Heavy Cavalry	Heavy Cavalry
Arquebusier	Arquebusier
Bedouin Camel Warrior	Camel
Berber Camel	Camel, Mounted Missile
Billman	Polearm
Boyar	Heavy Cavalry, Mounted Missile
Bulgarian Brigand	Archer
Byzantine Cavalry	Heavy Cavalry, Mounted Missile
Byzantine Infantry	Swordsman
Chivalric Foot Knight	Polearm
Chivalric Knight	Mounted Knight
Chivalric Man-At-Arms	Swordsman
Chivalric Sergeant	Spearman
Crossbowman	Crossbow
Desert Archer	Archer
Fanatic	Fanatic
Feudal Foot Knight	Swordsman
Feudal Knight	Mounted Knight
Feudal Man-at-Arms	Swordsman
Feudal Sergeant	Spearman
Futuwwa	Fanatic, Archer
Gallowglass	Barbarian
Gendarme	Heavy Cavalry
Genoese Sailor	Archer
Ghazi Infantryman	Fanatic, Axeman
Ghulam Bodyguard (Early, High, Late)	Heavy Cavalry
Ghulam Cavalryman	Heavy Cavalry
Golden Horde Heavy Cavalryman	Heavy Cavalry
Golden Horde Horse Archer	Mounted Missile
Golden Horde Warrior	Archer
Gothic Foot Knight	Swordsman
Gothic Knight	Mounted Knight
Gothic Man-At-Arms	Swordsman
Gothic Sergeant	Spearman
Halberdier	Polearm
Handgunner	Handgunner
Hashishin	Archer
Highland Clansman	Barbarian
Hobilar	Light Cavalry
Horse Archer	Mounted Missile
Hospitaller Foot Knight	Swordsmen

UNIT	UNIT CLASS
Italian Infantry	Spearmen
Janissary Archer	Archer
Janissary Heavy Infantry	Polearm
Janissary Infantry	Archer
Kataphraktoi	Heavy Cavalry
Kern	Barbarian, Javelin Thrower
Khwarazmian Cavalry	Heavy Cavalry
Knight Hospitaller	Mounted Knight
Knight of Santiago	Mounted Knight
Knight Templar	Mounted Knight
Lancer	Heavy Cavalry
Lithuanian Cavalry	Light Cavalry
Longbowman	Longbow
Mamluk Cavalry	Heavy Cavalry
Mamluk Handgunner	Handgunner
Mamluk Horse Archer	Mounted Missile
Militia Sergeant	Militia
Mounted Crossbowman	Crossbow, Mounted Missile
Mounted Sergeant	Light Cavalry
Murabitin Infantry	Javelin Thrower
Muslim Peasant	Peasant
Muwahid Foot Soldier	Spearmen
Naptha Thrower	Naptha Thrower
Nizari	Fanatic, Archer
Nubian Spearman	Spearmen
Order Foot Soldier	Spearmen
Ottoman Infantryman	Archer
Ottoman Sipahi	Heavy Cavalry
Pavise Arbalester	Arbalest

UNIT	UNIT CLASS
Pavise Crossbowman	Crossbow
Peasant	Peasant
Pikeman	Pikeman
Polish Retainer	Light Cavalry
Pronoiai Allagion	Heavy Cavalry
Royal Knight (Early, High, Late)	Mounted Knight
Saharan Cavalry	Light Cavalry
Saracen Infantry	Spearmen
Sipahi of the Porte	Heavy Cavalry (Mounted Missile)
Spanish Jinete	Mounted Missile (Javelin Thrower)
Spearman	Spearmen
Steppe Cavalry	Light Cavalry
Swiss Armored Pikeman	Pikeman
Swiss Halberdier	Polearm
Swiss Pikeman	Pikeman
Trebizond Archer	Archer
Turcoman Foot Soldier	Archer
Turcoman Horseman	Mounted Missile
Turcopole	Mounted Missile
Teutonic Knight	Mounted Knight
Teutonic Sergeant	Heavy Cavalry
Urban Militia	Militia (Polearm)
Varangian Guard	Axeman
Viking	Axeman (Barbarian)
Woodsman	Axeman (Peasant)

A QUICK NOTE ABOUT STATS

According to a programmer, the values listed in our unit tables take into account all basic combat factors, including the protection provided by the unit's shield. Keep in mind, however, that any unit's Shield bonus doesn't apply if that unit is attacked from behind.

Also remember how each unit's Valor rating affects its statistics. As mentioned in Chapter 3, for every increase of 1 point in a unit's Valor, its Attack and Defense values improve by 1 point and its Morale value increases by 2 points.

Finally, use the listed Speed values to compare how fast *Medieval*'s units march, run, and charge in relation to each other. Of course, some of you (and you know who you are) will be thrilled to know that you can calculate each unit's exact speed in meters per second by multiplying the Speed value by 0.28. From that, you can extrapolate that the average infantry unit (marching speed of 6) marches at 3.72 miles per hour.

Get out your calculator and get to work. This kind of information really impresses girls.

MELEE UNITS: MOUNTED

The introduction of the stirrup to Europe between 700-800AD transformed warfare in early medieval times, eventually melding man and horse into a swift yet powerful fighting unit. Indeed, mounted shock troops inevitably became the dominant force on the medieval battlefield.

Many of the finest mounted units of that era are available for your command in *Medieval: Total War*.

Mounted Knights

Knights are the lords of the battlefield in *Medieval: Total War*. With their ferocious mounted charge, mobility, heavy armor, and good combat ability, they can defeat almost any opponent. And their high morale means they'll keep fighting to the last. A charge from a fresh knight will drive back any other cavalry and completely sweep away most infantry.

The knights' Achilles heel is their reckless and arrogant nature, which often leads them to charge without specific orders from you. Once a knight unit begins an advance toward enemy positions, a wild charge is almost inevitable. Knights can charge right into disaster—an ambush, for example. But more often they'll carry the day, or at least hold their own, letting you focus your attention elsewhere on the battlefield.

The only infantry that can stand against a knightly charge are those armed with spears, pikes, or polearms. Polearms in particular can be deadly to any mounted unit, but knights needn't be too shy of tackling spearmen. The thunder of their charge may cause wavering troops to flee, and if a few mounted knights can make their way around the flanks of the foot formation, they may bring victory.

Even if things go badly, the defense-oriented nature of spear formations, coupled with the knight's heavy armor, mean that your knight casualties are usually light. If stymied by spears or pikes, the knight unit can withdraw to try its luck elsewhere. (There's no shame in withdrawing, if it's only to charge harder next time!)

Designer Notes

On Knight Impetuosity

Knights prefer to fight against their social equals, so they may ignore a target you've ordered them to attack in favor of opponents they consider more worthy of their mettle. Their impetuous nature can also lead them to pursue fleeing (and faster) lighter cavalry for longer than is prudent—exhausting themselves so that they cannot resist a counterattack.

The various military order knights are better disciplined and won't charge without orders (except for the notoriously reckless Teutonic Knights).

The Developers

Beware the Woods, Good Sir Knight

Forested areas can be dangerous for any mounted unit, including knights. But even though he's disadvantaged in the trees, a knight's raw combat power can carry him to victory over lighter infantry units.

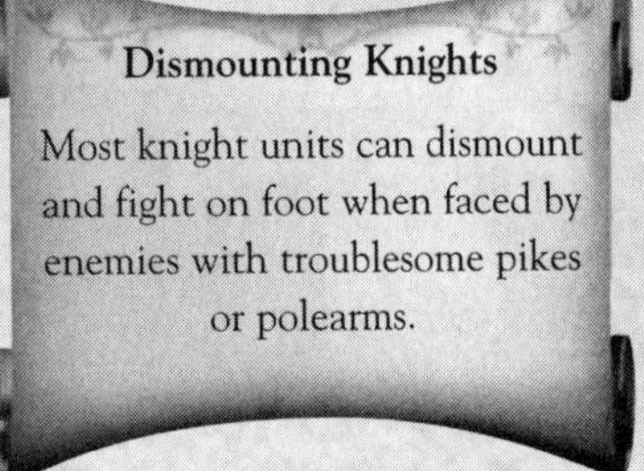

Dismounting Knights

Most knight units can dismount and fight on foot when faced by enemies with troublesome pikes or polearms.

The knight's heavy armor protects him from ordinary bowfire, but as the game progresses, longbows and crossbows are capable of piercing armor. Heavy armor can also be a drawback in both the desert heat and very cold weather, causing men to tire quickly and succumb to more lightly armored troops.

Although the knight is deadly in any combat situation, its most powerful tactic is its charge. One contemporary historian described Frankish (western European) knights as "able to charge through the walls of Babylon." Try not to let your knights be caught stationary. If they're immersed in a pitched battle, consider making them gallop away and then turn to charge again. As a programmer puts it, "The best knightly tactics are *attack*, *attack*, and *attack*."

Mounted Knights

Feudal Knights

Charge	8	Weapon	LANCE
Attack	4	Shield	LARGE
Defense	4	Horse Armor	NONE
Morale	8	March Speed	9
Armor (Value)	MAIL (5)	Run Speed	20
		Charge Speed	22

Feudal Knights hold land in return for military service. Trained from infancy to be warriors, they hold political and military power in their mailed fists. They are adept at charging down opponents with their lances, and they are honorable and brave to the point of recklessness!

Chivalric Knights

Charge	8	Weapon	LANCE
Attack	5	Shield	LARGE
Defense	5	Horse Armor	BARDED
Morale	8	March Speed	9
Armor (Value)	HALF PLATE (7)	Run Speed	20
		Charge Speed	22

Chivalric Knights are a considerable improvement in arms and armor. They and their horses are well-protected by plate mail and barding, their lances give them an advantage in the charge, and they are trained to fight from childhood. They are a true elite, but they can be impetuous in battle!

Gothic Knights

Charge	4	Weapon	MACE
Attack	4 (ARMOR PIERCING)	Shield	NONE
Defense	7	Horse Armor	FULL
Morale	8	March Speed	9
Armor (Value)	FULL PLATE (9)	Run Speed	12
		Charge Speed	16

Protected by superb armor, Gothic Knights fear little, although archers and pikemen still have to be treated with respect. Complete with heavily armored horses, these are fearsome warriors. Their personal armor reaches a peak of practicality and beauty, and their heavy cavalry tactics have been perfected.

Knights Hospitaller

Charge	8	Weapon	LANCE
Attack	5	Shield	LARGE
Defense	5	Horse Armor	BARDED
Morale	8	March Speed	9
Armor (Value)	HALF PLATE (7)	Run Speed	20
		Charge Speed	22

The Knights of St. John were established to protect pilgrims and a hospital in the Holy Land, and they are a powerful fighting order. The Hospitallers are superb heavy knights, armed with lances and able to charge in devastating fashion on the battlefield. In battle, they are completely reliable.

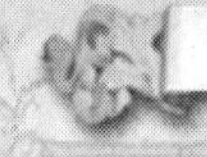

Knights of Santiago

Charge	8	Weapon	LANCE
Attack	5	Shield	LARGE
Defense	5	Horse Armor	BARDED
Morale	8	March Speed	9
Armor (Value)	HALF PLATE (7)	Run Speed	20
		Charge Speed	22

Originally guards for Christian pilgrims in Spain, the Knights of Santiago are a fighting order organized along semi-monastic lines. They are excellent and reliable heavy cavalry, able to break many enemies when they charge, and are without the impetuous folly often shown by secular western knights.

Knights Templar

Charge	4	Weapon	SWORD
Attack	5	Shield	LARGE
Defense	5	Horse Armor	BARDED
Morale	8	March Speed	9
Armor (Value)	HALF PLATE (7)	Run Speed	20
		Charge Speed	22

The Knights Templar are a warrior elite, more fearsome than many other knights in Christendom. On the battlefield, they may be the finest cavalry trained in Europe, able to charge home against tremendous odds and still triumph! But while they are brave, some people express doubts about their religious purity.

Royal Knights (Early)

Charge	8	Weapon	LANCE
Attack	5	Shield	LARGE
Defense	7	Horse Armor	NONE
Morale	8	March Speed	9
Armor (Value)	MAIL (7)	Run Speed	20
		Charge Speed	22

Royal Knights are an elite royal household guard. The combination of mail and lances makes them formidable enough, but their dedication to serving their King makes them fearsome indeed! The King and Royal Princes command small groups of these knights. Raising extra Royal Knights is possible, but costly.

Royal Knights (High)

Charge	8	Weapon	LANCE
Attack	5	Shield	LARGE
Defense	7	Horse Armor	BARDED
Morale	8	March Speed	9
Armor (Value)	HALF PLATE (8)	Run Speed	20
		Charge Speed	22

Royal Knights of the High Period added plate mail and barded horses to their powerful battlefield presence.

Royal Knights (Late)

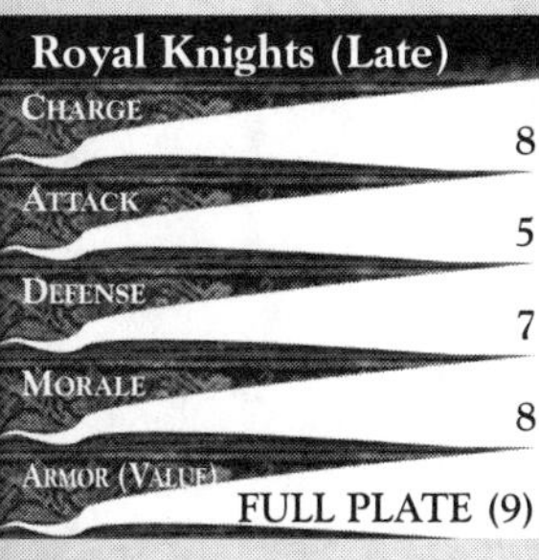
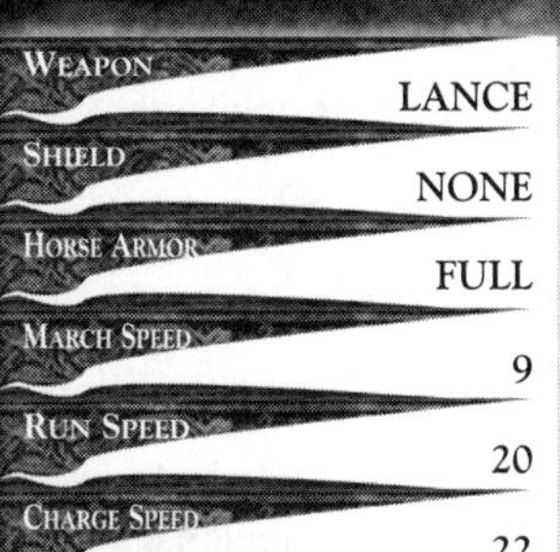

Stat	Value	Stat	Value
Charge	8	Weapon	LANCE
Attack	5	Shield	NONE
Defense	7	Horse Armor	FULL
Morale	8	March Speed	9
Armor (Value)	FULL PLATE (9)	Run Speed	20
		Charge Speed	22

The combination of full-plate body armor and a fully armored horse makes the Royal Knights of the Late Period the most formidable shock troops in the world.

Teutonic Knights

Stat	Value	Stat	Value
Charge	8	Weapon	LANCE
Attack	5	Shield	ORDER
Defense	5	Horse Armor	BARDED
Morale	8	March Speed	9
Armor (Value)	HALF PLATE (7)	Run Speed	20
		Charge Speed	22

The Teutonic Knights are an order of German warriors, committed to fighting against infidels and pagans alike. They are easily the equal in combat of the other Orders of Knighthood, if not quite so disciplined. This lack of discipline is of no comfort to anyone facing the Teutonic Knights!

Heavy Cavalry

Many nations have heavy cavalry of their own. Although they don't quite have the power and élan of knights, heavy cavalry units are nevertheless very powerful. They're perfectly capable of defeating knights if they can attack from a flank, or if the knights are tired. Lacking knightly arrogance, they are more controllable too. Heavy cavalry can easily sweep away lighter types of infantry, or those armed only with swords.

Armenian Heavy Cavalry

Stat	Value	Stat	Value
Charge	8	Weapon	LANCE
Attack	3	Shield	LARGE ROUND
Defense	4	Horse Armor	BARDED
Morale	4	March Speed	9
Armor (Value)	MAIL (5)	Run Speed	20
		Charge Speed	22

Even in Roman times, Armenian cavalrymen were often given a position of honor in an army. The Byzantines and others still know that the Armenians are disciplined, aggressive, and capable. Armed with lances, their initial charge is powerful, and they are steady and reliable when compared to feudal cavalry.

Gendarmes

Stat	Value	Stat	Value
Charge	4	Weapon	SWORD
Attack	3	Shield	LARGE
Defense	5	Horse Armor	BARDED
Morale	4	March Speed	9
Armor (Value)	HALF PLATE (7)	Run Speed	20
		Charge Speed	22

Gendarmes are high-quality militia cavalry, raised in the growing towns. They often have superb equipment, and unlike most part-time soldiers, they're rather disciplined. The Gendarmes lack the dashing bravery and valor of real knights. Wealthy French provinces can excel at producing Gendarmes, thanks to their growing regional pride.

Ghulam Bodyguards (Early/High)

Stat	Value	Stat	Value
Charge	6	Weapon	LANCE
Attack	3	Shield	LARGE
Defense	7	Horse Armor	NONE
Morale	6	March Speed	9
Armor (Value)	MAIL (6)	Run Speed	20
		Charge Speed	22

Ghulam (the word means "slave") cavalry are the best troops available to the Sultan and form his bodyguard. In heavy mail and armed with lances, they are at least as good as other cavalry. The Sultan (and every Prince) leads Ghulams. Additional units can be trained at high cost.

Ghulam Bodyguards (Late)

Stat	Value	Stat	Value
Charge	6	Weapon	LANCE
Attack	3	Shield	LARGE
Defense	7	Horse Armor	NONE
Morale	6	March Speed	9
Armor (Value)	FULL PLATE (7)	Run Speed	20
		Charge Speed	22

The addition of full plate armor in the Late Period makes the Sultan's Ghulam Bodyguards better than most other cavalry units in the field of battle.

Ghulam Cavalry

Stat	Value	Stat	Value
Charge	6	Weapon	SPEAR
Attack	3	Shield	SMALL ROUND
Defense	4	Horse Armor	NONE
Morale	4	March Speed	9
Armor (Value)	MAIL (5)	Run Speed	20
		Charge Speed	22

Ghulam Cavalry are useful heavy attacking units for any desert general. With mail armor and light lances, they can charge into an attack and can fight well against other cavalry, but they need to take care when engaging spearmen. Against missile troops, their best option is a swift attack.

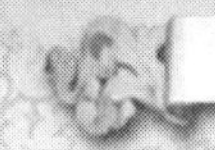

Golden Horde Heavy Cavalry

Stat	Value	Stat	Value
Charge	6	Weapon	LANCE
Attack	3	Shield	LARGE ROUND
Defense	7	Horse Armor	FULL
Morale	6	March Speed	9
Armor (Value)	HEAVY MAIL (8)	Run Speed	20
		Charge Speed	22

These warriors have the traditional role of all "nobility": the breaking of lesser troops through shock impact. All superb horsemen, these cavalrymen are heavily armed with spears and well-protected by plentiful armor and shields. They are best at attacking infantry and riding down units that are about to break.

Kataphraktoi

Stat	Value	Stat	Value
Charge	8	Weapon	LANCE
Attack	3	Shield	NONE
Defense	5	Horse Armor	FULL
Morale	4	March Speed	9
Armor (Value)	HEAVY MAIL (7)	Run Speed	12
		Charge Speed	16

The fearsome, disciplined Kataphraktoi trace their origins to Roman times. Both man and horse are so massively armored that they are almost unstoppable shock troops. This power comes at a price—the Kataphraktoi are slow and expensive compared to other cavalry—but this is of little comfort to their enemies!

Khwarazmian Cavalry

Stat	Value	Stat	Value
Charge	6	Weapon	SPEAR
Attack	3	Shield	NONE
Defense	5	Horse Armor	FULL
Morale	4	March Speed	9
Armor (Value)	HEAVY MAIL (7)	Run Speed	20
		Charge Speed	22

Unusual for Islamic cavalry, both Khwarazmian cavalrymen and their horses are heavily armored. This makes them very effective when charging lighter opponents, but it means they are far from nimble. As shock troops, they are the equals of western knights but with more discipline—some would say more common sense!

Lancers

Stat	Value	Stat	Value
Charge	8	Weapon	LANCE
Attack	5	Shield	NONE
Defense	7	Horse Armor	FULL
Morale	8	March Speed	9
Armor (Value)	FULL PLATE (9)	Run Speed	20
		Charge Speed	22

Lancers are very heavy cavalry, used primarily to charge into and break the enemy. Their plate armor is cunningly designed so extra pieces can be added. The shock value of their charge should not be underestimated, but against spearmen they should attack the flank or rear for best effect.

Mamluk Cavalry

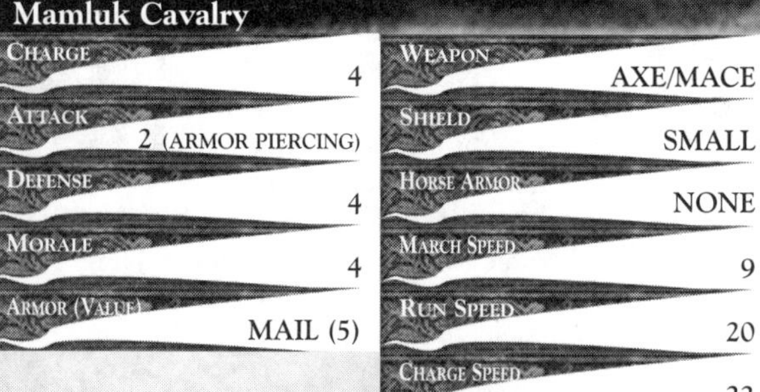

Stat	Value
Charge	4
Attack	2 (ARMOR PIERCING)
Defense	4
Morale	4
Armor (Value)	MAIL (5)

Stat	Value
Weapon	AXE/MACE
Shield	SMALL
Horse Armor	NONE
March Speed	9
Run Speed	20
Charge Speed	22

The Mamluks are warrior slaves with superb military skills. Their cavalry are well-armed and armored, highly disciplined, and particularly good against armored opponents thanks to the armor-piercing maces they wield. These medium cavalry can be used for many tasks on the battlefield and can give heavier cavalry a nasty surprise!

Ottoman Sipahi

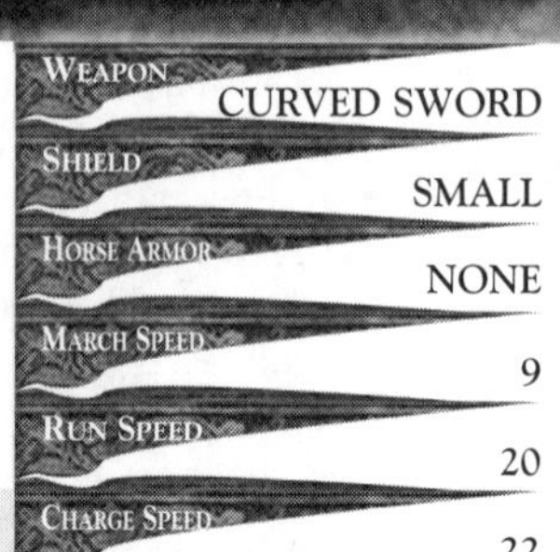

Stat	Value
Charge	4
Attack	2
Defense	4
Morale	2
Armor (Value)	MAIL (5)

Stat	Value
Weapon	CURVED SWORD
Shield	SMALL
Horse Armor	NONE
March Speed	9
Run Speed	20
Charge Speed	22

Turkish Sipahi differ from many European troops in one important respect—discipline. They are professionals who can be relied on to obey orders. Deployed correctly, the only units the Sipahi need to fear are spearmen or pikemen. Their equipment is fully the equal of any other heavy cavalry.

Pronoiai Allagion

Stat	Value
Charge	6
Attack	4
Defense	4
Morale	8
Armor (Value)	MAIL (6)

Stat	Value
Weapon	SPEAR
Shield	LARGE
Horse Armor	BARDED
March Speed	9
Run Speed	20
Charge Speed	22

Even the coffers of Byzantium are not bottomless, so the mercenary Pronoiai Allagion are paid in land instead of money. These men are the Byzantine equivalent of heavy knights: part soldiers, part local rulers. With mail armor, lances, and horse barding, they are as good as many western knights.

Teutonic Sergeants

Stat	Value
Charge	4
Attack	3
Defense	5
Morale	4
Armor (Value)	HALF PLATE (6)

Stat	Value
Weapon	SWORD
Shield	LARGE
Horse Armor	NONE
March Speed	9
Run Speed	20
Charge Speed	22

The fighting Orders are socially exclusive, not taking men from the lower ranks of society into an Order itself. The Teutonic Sergeants are socially inferior men trained as heavy cavalry, but without the dash and valor of true knights. In battle, they are almost as effective as the Order's Knights.

Heavy Cavalry (Missile-Armed)

The following three unit types are horseback missile troops, but they are primarily considered Heavy Cavalry units. So we list their information here rather than in the "Mounted Missile Units" section later in this chapter.

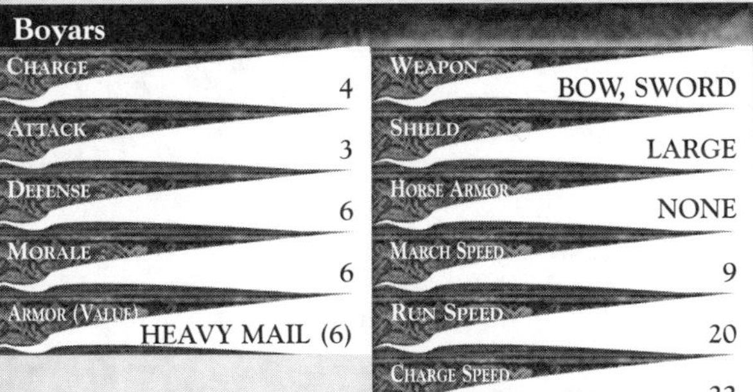

Boyars

Stat	Value	Stat	Value
Charge	4	Weapon	BOW, SWORD
Attack	3	Shield	LARGE
Defense	6	Horse Armor	NONE
Morale	6	March Speed	9
Armor (Value)	HEAVY MAIL (6)	Run Speed	20
		Charge Speed	22

Boyars are the landed, social elite in Russia. They are trained to fight as a heavy cavalry bodyguard. Heavy mail and a combination of sword and bow make them powerful, and combined with rigorous practice for war, they are a very effective force indeed!

Byzantine Cavalry

Stat	Value	Stat	Value
Charge	2	Weapon	BOW, CURVED SWORD
Attack	3	Shield	NONE
Defense	3	Horse Armor	NONE
Morale	4	March Speed	9
Armor (Value)	MAIL (4)	Run Speed	20
		Charge Speed	22

The Byzantines have a state army as well as mercenaries. These cavalry are the disciplined, armored successors to the Roman legions, armed with bows and swords. Although they're not as fleet as steppe mercenaries, they can be relied on to give a good account of themselves in any battle.

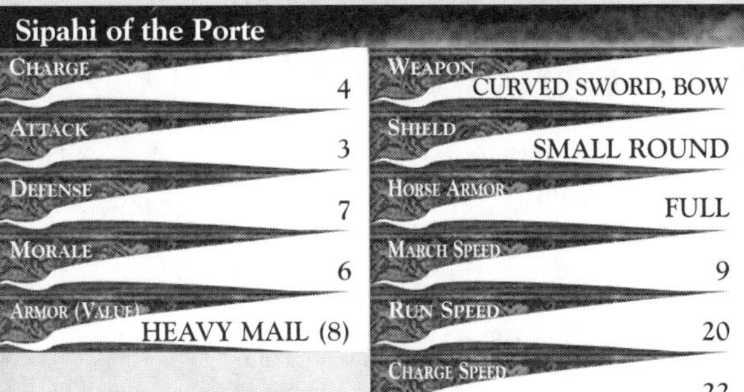

Sipahi of the Porte

Stat	Value	Stat	Value
Charge	4	Weapon	CURVED SWORD, BOW
Attack	3	Shield	SMALL ROUND
Defense	7	Horse Armor	FULL
Morale	6	March Speed	9
Armor (Value)	HEAVY MAIL (8)	Run Speed	20
		Charge Speed	22

The Sipahi of the Porte are the elite Turkish royal bodyguards. Their combination of heavy mail, armored horses, sword, and bow make them formidable enough, but their vigorous training makes them fearsome indeed! The Sultan and Royal Princes all command small Sipahi units. Raising extra Sipahi of the Porte is expensive.

Light Cavalry

The advantages of light cavalry are speed, cheapness, and initial hitting power. These swift mounted units don't have the stamina for a long fight, so the best way to use them is to attack from the flank or rear. Light cavalry has a powerful initial charge and can damage even the strongest units. But if your opponent does not break quickly, the best thing is to withdraw your light cavalry from the melee.

Light cavalry units use no horse armor. Also, several light cavalry types are not listed here because they're armed with missile weapons. Missile-armed light cavalry units—also called horse archers—are discussed in the "Mounted Missile Units" section later in this chapter.

Remember: Light cavalry units have the speed to get away from heavier cavalry, and they can lead impetuous enemy units such as knights on long and tiring goose chases. They make good reserves too, because their speed and good charge help them make timely and decisive interventions. They can also be used to drive off pesky enemy horse archers.

Alan Mercenary Cavalry

Charge	6	Weapon	SPEAR
Attack	3	Shield	NONE
Defense	1	March Speed	9
Morale	4	Run Speed	24
Armor (Value)	LIGHT (3)	Charge Speed	26

The Alans are excellent steppe horsemen—almost as if they were born in the saddle! The Byzantines consider them the best light cavalry mercenaries available. They can be used to skirmish, ambush, and act as a swift covering force for the flanks of heavier cavalry.

Hobilars

Charge	6	Weapon	SPEAR
Attack	2	Shield	NONE
Defense	2	March Speed	9
Morale	2	Run Speed	20
Armor (Value)	LIGHT MAIL (3)	Charge Speed	22

Hobilars ride small horses and are useful as scouts and pursuit troops. They come into their own when an enemy must be driven from the field or captured for later ransom. They are not heavily armed or armored and can't put up much of a fight against nobility.

Lithuanian Cavalry

Charge	6	Weapon	SPEAR
Attack	2	Shield	LARGE
Defense	4	March Speed	9
Morale	2	Run Speed	20
Armor (Value)	MAIL (5)	Charge Speed	22

These light cavalry are drawn from Lithuania's minor nobility, and they wear light mail and carry lances and bows. They are excellent horsemen, but they also have the ability to dismount before battle and fight as foot archers. Although they are noblemen, they are no match for knights.

Mounted Sergeants

Charge	8	Weapon	LANCE
Attack	2	Shield	SMALL
Defense	3	March Speed	9
Morale	2	Run Speed	20
Armor (Value)	LIGHT MAIL (4)	Charge Speed	22

These cavalry are more lightly equipped than knights, but they are fast and their lances can be devastating when charging opponents. They are best used to charge home (to an enemy flank or rear, preferably) to cause maximum casualties. Their speed can help them disengage and evade pursuit.

Polish Retainers

Charge	8	Weapon	LANCE
Attack	3	Shield	LARGE
Defense	4	March Speed	9
Morale	4	Run Speed	20
Armor (Value)	MAIL (5)	Charge Speed	22

These minor Polish nobility are good medium cavalry, with both mail armor for protection and heavy lances to provide a real punch when charging enemies. Although they're good attackers, they are not the equals of knights and will have trouble holding their ground when committed against such powerful foes.

Saharan Cavalry

Charge	4	Weapon	SWORD
Attack	2	Shield	SMALL
Defense	1	March Speed	9
Morale	0	Run Speed	24
Armor (Value)	NONE (3)	Charge Speed	26

In a desert, beneath the merciless sun, speed is better protection than armor that roasts its wearer! Saharan Cavalry are fast "skirmishers" used to protect an army's flanks, keep archers away, and chase down enemies. Even armed with their swords and shields, they are not suited to prolonged melees.

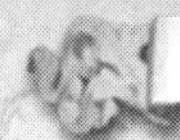

Steppe Cavalry

Stat	Value	Stat	Value
Charge	6	Weapon	SPEAR
Attack	2	Shield	SMALL
Defense	2	March Speed	9
Morale	0	Run Speed	24
Armor (Value)	LIGHT (4)	Charge Speed	26

The men of the steppes learn to ride as soon as they can walk. Along with hunting, it is a necessary survival skill of life and war. They are superb, almost matchless light horsemen and masters of wide variety of weapons. They are best when used to harass and pursue the enemy.

Camel Units

Most cavalry units rode horses in medieval times, of course. But camels were sometimes used in desert areas. Their strange smell and appearance easily spook horses, so camel-mounted fighters gain an advantage against horse-mounted cavalry. Nevertheless, given their light weapons and armor, camel units have little hope of standing up to knights or other heavy cavalry, although they can be effective against lighter units.

Although camels are slower than horses, they enjoy the same advantages as horse cavalry against foot troops. Just keep in mind that low combat factors make frontal assaults inadvisable. Camels make very large targets for missile fire, so try to keep them out of the firing line.

Camel Tips

Camel-mounted units enjoy an extra combat bonus in sandy desert terrain. However, camels do not thrive in wet climates, so they suffer a penalty in lush and temperate terrain types.

Also, camel-mounted warriors can dismount before battle and fight on foot against pikemen and tough spearmen.

Bedouin Camel Warriors

Stat	Value	Stat	Value
Charge	6	Weapon	LANCE
Attack	2	Shield	SMALL
Defense	1	March Speed	9
Morale	0	Run Speed	14
Armor (Value)	NONE (3)	Charge Speed	16

The Bedouin are hardy warriors but are sometimes a little undisciplined when fighting in a group. Their shock value against troops who are unused to camels is considerable, particularly when charging home, but they are vulnerable to spearmen in the same way as other cavalry. Horses usually hate the smell of camels.

Berber Camels

Stat	Value	Stat	Value
Charge	2	Weapon	BOW, SWORD
Attack	0	Shield	SMALL
Defense	1	March Speed	9
Morale	0	Run Speed	14
Armor (Value)	NONE (3)	Charge Speed	16

The Berbers are hardy desert warriors and are at their best when used as light cavalry archers to disrupt enemies. They are capable in hand-to-hand combat against similar light cavalry, and their camels are an advantage because many horses are unwilling to go too close because of the smell!

Mounted Archers

Because mounted archers fight and behave differently than mounted melee troops, they're discussed in the "Mounted Missile Units" section later in this chapter.

MELEE UNITS: INFANTRY

Although mounted shock troops, particularly knights, were the elite units of the age, medieval armies still relied on a backbone of infantry. Waves of old-fashioned swordsmen and spearmen can still carry the day in *Medieval: Total War*, if deployed properly and in sufficient numbers. And pikemen in tight, well-disciplined formations can be the bane of mounted knights in the Late Period.

Spearmen

The game features a number of spear-armed infantry units, ranging from the humble Spearmen to high-quality units such as the Order Foot Soldiers. Spearmen excel mainly at defense. The man in front can be supported by up to two men immediately behind, but for this to work the unit must be in good formation. Setting a spear-armed unit to Hold Formation is the best way to keep it well-formed and further magnifies its defensive properties.

Spear units are particularly good at resisting cavalry attacks. Even a few ranks of basic Spearmen can repel a charge by Feudal Knights if they can meet the mounted units head-on. Although spear units are likely to be defeated *eventually* by sword-armed infantry of similar cost, their tenacious defense means they can resist for a long time. Use spear-armed troops as a wall to shelter your more vulnerable units—archers, in particular—and to hold powerful enemy units in place while you win the battle elsewhere.

Spear units are much more vulnerable if struck in the flank or rear. This is the best way for cavalry to defeat spearmen. Even if only a few horsemen contact the flank, avoiding the wall of spears means they can kill many men on the first impact, which may be enough to break the spear unit. To avoid this, be sure your spearmen's flanks are well-protected.

Designer Notes

On Spearmen and Pikemen

Spearmen and pikemen can gain Attack, Defense, and Charge bonuses from their supporting ranks. Spear-armed units can claim up to 2 supporting ranks behind the first rank, while pike units can claim up to 4 supporting ranks behind their first rank. Whether or not spear and pike units get supporting rank bonuses depends very much on the situation, and on how tight and well-organized their formations are.

Here's how the rank bonuses work:

- For each supporting rank, 1 is added to the Defense factor.
- For each supporting rank, 1 is added to the Charge factor.
- For each 2 supporting ranks, 1 is added to the Attack factor.

Thus, a spear unit that normally has an Attack of -1 and a Defense of 1 could have an Attack of 0 and a Defense of 3, if it is in good formation and at least three ranks deep.

Also note that you can see when support factors are being applied because the men in the supporting ranks will engage in their fight animation, even though they're not directly in contact with the enemy.

The Developers

Almughavars

For a full description of this javelin- and spear-armed unit, look for Almughavars under "Javelin and Naptha Throwers."

Feudal Sergeants

Stat	Value	Stat	Value
Charge	5	Weapon	SPEAR
Attack	0 (+1 BONUS VS. CAVALRY)	Shield	LARGE
Defense	1 (+4 BONUS VS. CAVALRY)	March Speed	6
Morale	2	Run Speed	10
Armor (Value)	NONE (3)	Charge Speed	11

Feudal society is a hierarchy, and each rung of the ladder is expected to serve the one above it. Feudal Sergeants are a class below knights (but above landless peasants) and are often professional soldiers. Many lords will send these spearmen into battle as reliable medium infantry.

Chivalric Sergeants

Stat	Value	Stat	Value
Charge	5	Weapon	SPEAR
Attack	-1 (+1 BONUS VS. CAVALRY)	Shield	LARGE
Defense	5 (+4 BONUS VS. CAVALRY)	March Speed	6
Morale	0	Run Speed	10
Armor (Value)	MAIL (5)	Charge Speed	11

These heavy spearmen include professional soldiers and those hoping to be noticed and raised to the nobility. Their equipment may be a little old-fashioned or secondhand, but it is always well cared for, and their individual skill at arms is very good indeed. However, they can be undisciplined.

Gothic Sergeants

Stat	Value	Stat	Value
Charge	5	Weapon	SPEAR
Attack	0 (+1 BONUS VS. CAVALRY)	Shield	LARGE
Defense	6 (+4 BONUS VS. CAVALRY)	March Speed	4
Morale	2	Run Speed	8
Armor (Value)	THREE-QUARTER PLATE (6)	Charge Speed	9

Despite their old-fashioned plate armor, Gothic Sergeants are a mainstay of any army. Their spears allow them to stand in any battle line. They are well-motivated due to an emerging professionalism, and they operate without the impetuous desire for personal glory and fanatical bravery that can make noblemen troublesome.

Italian Light Infantry

Charge	5	Weapon	SPEAR
Attack	0 (+1 BONUS VS. CAVALRY)	Shield	LARGE
Defense	5 (+4 BONUS VS. CAVALRY)	March Speed	6
Morale	2	Run Speed	10
Armor (Value)	MAIL (5)	Charge Speed	11

The Italians have spent many years fighting enemies such as Norman, French, and Imperial armies, and each other. As a result, their medium infantry are better than average, and they're equipped with quilted armor, spears, and shields. They may lack the edge of hardened professionals, but they are reliable.

Muwahid Foot Soldiers

Charge	7	Weapon	SPEAR
Attack	1 (+1 BONUS VS. CAVALRY)	Shield	LARGE
Defense	1 (+4 BONUS VS. CAVALRY)	March Speed	6
Morale	4	Run Speed	12
Armor (Value)	NONE (3)	Charge Speed	13

These spearmen in the service of the Almohads are lightly equipped to stand in a line of battle. They are hardy desert men and carry only large shields for protection, but they are also swift and confident (possibly overconfident). In particular, note the effectiveness of their charge. Like all spearmen, they gain an advantage when fighting against cavalry.

Nubian Spearmen

Charge	4	Weapon	SPEAR
Attack	0 (+1 BONUS VS. CAVALRY)	Shield	SMALL ROUND
Defense	0 (+4 BONUS VS. CAVALRY)	March Speed	6
Morale	2	Run Speed	10
Armor (Value)	NONE (2)	Charge Speed	11

"Nubian Spearmen" is a slightly misleading title. These men come from all over Africa, having made their way north and ended up in the Sultan's military service. They carry the same kind of equipment as other spearmen, but they are often a little more disciplined and able.

Order Foot Soldiers

Charge	5	Weapon	SPEAR
Attack	0 (+1 BONUS VS. CAVALRY)	Shield	LARGE
Defense	5 (+4 BONUS VS. CAVALRY)	March Speed	6
Morale	2	Run Speed	10
Armor (Value)	MAIL (5)	Charge Speed	11

Not everyone has the social rank to become a Knight in a fighting order. Instead, these lesser men are taken on to fight in support of the knights. Often, they do very well because they are motivated by the prospect of salvation and are well-armored and equipped with spears.

Saracen Infantry

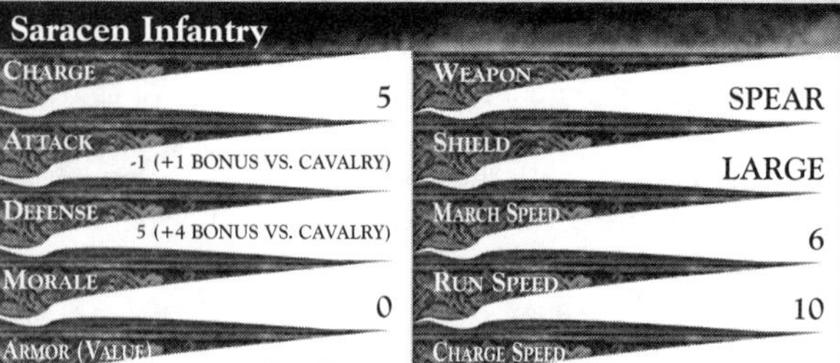

Stat	Value	Stat	Value
Charge	5	Weapon	SPEAR
Attack	-1 (+1 BONUS VS. CAVALRY)	Shield	LARGE
Defense	5 (+4 BONUS VS. CAVALRY)	March Speed	6
Morale	0	Run Speed	10
Armor (Value)	MAIL (5)	Charge Speed	11

Like many Saracens, these medium spearmen are well-disciplined when compared to Frankish or Crusader opponents. Saracen spears give them an advantage when fighting cavalry, and they are lightly armored so that they can move swiftly beneath the desert sun. They can also hold their own against comparable infantry.

Spearmen

Stat	Value	Stat	Value
Charge	5	Weapon	SPEAR
Attack	-1 (+1 BONUS VS. CAVALRY)	Shield	LARGE
Defense	1 (+4 BONUS VS. CAVALRY)	March Speed	6
Morale	0	Run Speed	10
Armor (Value)	NONE (3)	Charge Speed	11

Spearmen are useful in almost any army, particularly against cavalry—and unlike other troop types, the first two ranks can fight due to the length of their spears. They aren't likely to stand for long against professional men-at-arms, but they can give cavalry a nasty shock as long as they hold formation.

Swordsmen

In terms of combat factor per florin, sword-armed infantry are probably the best value in the game. They will defeat most other infantry of similar price. Swordsmen may be pressed back initially by a charge of pikemen or quality spearmen. However, if they have the morale to survive the initial onslaught, the nimbler swordsmen will gain the upper hand as the melee causes the pikemen's formation to break down. Swordsmen can be deployed a little wider than pike-armed units, too, so some men will be able to fall on their enemy's flanks. Use Engage At Will mode to get the best effect.

The big drawback to infantry units armed only with swords is that they resist cavalry attacks poorly. Swordsmen have little hope of defeating knights, and even light cavalry can cause them serious harm. If deployed in a thin line, swordsmen run the risk of being swept away almost immediately. When forced to face strong cavalry, the best tactic is to deploy them in a very deep formation (5 or more ranks). They may not win ultimately, but at least they won't be swept away by the initial cavalry charge.

Byzantine Infantry

Stat	Value	Stat	Value
Charge	3	Weapon	SWORD
Attack	2	Shield	LARGE
Defense	4	March Speed	6
Morale	0	Run Speed	10
Armor (Value)	MAIL (5)	Charge Speed	11

The Byzantine Empire's military tradition dates back to Roman times, and its armies have always included professional soldiers. These men-at-arms have mail armor, large shields, and swords, and they can be relied on to fight skillfully against most enemies. They are among the best heavy infantry in Eastern Europe.

Feudal Men-At-Arms

Stat	Value	Stat	Value
Charge	3	Weapon	SWORD
Attack	3	Shield	LARGE
Defense	4	March Speed	6
Morale	2	Run Speed	10
Armor (Value)	MAIL (5)	Charge Speed	11

Those seeking social position are often hardened warriors—war can bring wealth and social status. Because they are not rich yet, feudal men-at-arms wear second-hand mail looted from the dead, or mail that is just old-fashioned. They carry broadswords and large shields, making them equally good at attack and defense.

Chivalric Men-At-Arms

Stat	Value	Stat	Value
Charge	3	Weapon	SWORD
Attack	4	Shield	LARGE
Defense	4	March Speed	6
Morale	4	Run Speed	10
Armor (Value)	HALF PLATE (5)	Charge Speed	11

Not all the very heavy infantry are noble. Most are professionals or gentry who make do with old or second-hand armor. These swordsmen are good at both attack and defense, and they often form the backbone of a battle line. Heavily armored as they are, they can be slow moving.

Feudal Foot Knights

Stat	Value	Stat	Value
Charge	3	Weapon	SWORD
Attack	5	Shield	LARGE
Defense	4	March Speed	6
Morale	8	Run Speed	10
Armor (Value)	MAIL (5)	Charge Speed	11

These units are also the Feudal Knights when dismounted. They're a military elite who rule by the sword and hold land in return for their service. In combat, they favor horseback and lances that give them an advantage when charging opponents, but they may want to dismount and fight on foot against pikemen or halberdiers.

Gothic Foot Knights

Stat	Value	Stat	Value
Charge	4	Weapon	SWORD
Attack	5 (ARMOR PIERCING)	Shield	NONE
Defense	6	March Speed	4
Morale	8	Run Speed	8
Armor (Value)	FULL PLATE (6)	Charge Speed	9

These units are also the Gothic Knights when dismounted. Although it may look cumbersome, gothic armor is a cunning system of smooth surfaces, all devised to deflect attacks away from the wearer. Armed with a powerful two-handed sword when dismounted, these knights are capable of piercing a foe's armor and easily smashing their way into most defensive formations. Their desire for personal glory can make them impetuous, however.

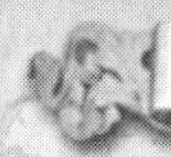
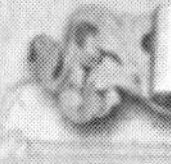

Hospitaller Foot Knights

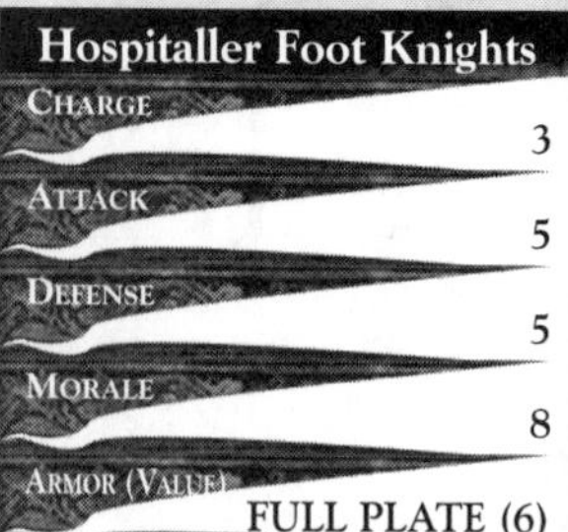

Stat	Value	Stat	Value
Charge	3	Weapon	SWORD
Attack	5	Shield	LARGE
Defense	5	March Speed	4
Morale	8	Run Speed	8
Armor (Value)	FULL PLATE (6)	Charge Speed	9

These units are also the Knights Hospitaller when dismounted. The Knights Hospitaller have adapted to changing fashions in warfare. Rather than traditional fighting from horseback, they can now take the field as armored infantry elite, well able to cut their way into enemy formations. Tactical flexibility, combined with their traditional discipline and courage, still makes them formidable.

Axemen

Axe-armed units share some of the characteristics of swordsmen, but they gain a bonus when fighting troops that wear heavy armor because their weapons have more penetrative force. Axemen are vulnerable to cavalry, too. However, since the most powerful cavalry have heavy armor, the axeman's bonus redresses the balance a little—if he can resist the cavalry's initial charge, that is.

Axes come in one-handed and two-handed varieties. Two-handed axes are more powerful, but their wielders can't use a shield in combat, leaving them more vulnerable. The game treats maces in the same way as one-handed axes. They are designed for use against armored foes, although they do their damage more by concussion than penetration.

Abyssinian Guards

Stat	Value	Stat	Value
Charge	4	Weapon	AXE
Attack	4 (ARMOR PIERCING)	Shield	NONE
Defense	0	March Speed	6
Morale	6	Run Speed	10
Armor (Value)	NONE (1)	Charge Speed	11

Abyssinians have been guarding Egyptian rulers for centuries. They are used on the battlefield as disciplined axemen, able to carve a path through enemies. Their lack of armor is a weakness, but their superb discipline is some compensation. They are best used to attack peasants, militia, and spearmen.

Ghazi Infantry

Stat	Value	Stat	Value
Charge	6	Weapon	AXE
Attack	5 (ARMOR PIERCING)	Shield	SMALL
Defense	-3	March Speed	6
Morale	8	Run Speed	12
Armor (Value)	NONE (2)	Charge Speed	13

The Ghazi are fanatical warriors who think nothing of facing tremendous odds. Wild and brave, they can be difficult to restrain. In an attack, Ghazis can smash into an enemy force, and their slashing, one-handed axes do terrible damage. On defense, they can rashly counterattack and therefore weaken a strong position.

Ottoman Infantry

For a full description of this bow and axe-armed unit, look for Ottoman Infantry under "Archers."

Varangian Guard

Stat	Value	Stat	Value
Charge	4	Weapon	AXE
Attack	4 (ARMOR PIERCING)	Shield	LARGE
Defense	5	March Speed	6
Morale	6	Run Speed	10
Armor (Value)	HALF PLATE (5)	Charge Speed	11

The Varangian Guard are part of the Imperial Household, a force of mercenary bodyguards. They have a history of being tough, loyal, and resourceful men from the north. Over the centuries, their ranks have included Vikings (and a Viking king!), Saxons, and Englishmen. Now, they are sometimes a ceremonial unit.

Vikings

Stat	Value	Stat	Value
Charge	3	Weapon	AXE
Attack	3 (ARMOR PIERCING)	Shield	LARGE
Defense	2	March Speed	6
Morale	4	Run Speed	10
Armor (Value)	LIGHT (4)	Charge Speed	11

Almost eclipsed by newer feudal fighting men, the Vikings are approaching the twilight of their glorious history. They are extremely tough, handpicked warriors whose tactical strength lies in the "shield wall," a formation that presents a solid front to the enemy. Vikings are only truly vulnerable if they break formation.

Woodsmen

Stat	Value	Stat	Value
Charge	8	Weapon	AXE
Attack	1 (ARMOR PIERCING)	Shield	SMALL
Defense	-1	March Speed	6
Morale	-2	Run Speed	10
Armor (Value)	LIGHT (2)	Charge Speed	11

Hardy woodsmen, the superiors of peasant levies, populate the vast forests of Eastern Europe. With their axes they can pierce armor and do terrible damage, even to "better" troops, and their light armor gives them some protection. They are still peasants, of course, and can run away like any other peasantry!

Pikemen

Pike-armed units share many of the characteristics of spearmen, but add some extra advantages. Due to the length of their weapons, up to 4 men can support the man fighting in the front rank, making them most effective 5 ranks deep. Deploying them 6 men deep means that full fighting effect can be maintained even after a few losses. However, this makes the units a little narrow, so it's best to protect their flanks by keeping several pike units close together.

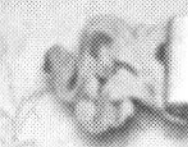

> Be sure to read "On Spearmen and Pikemen" earlier in this chapter!

Pikemen can be used defensively, similar to spearmen. Their longer weapons can repel even the strongest knights in the game. However, their deeper formation gives them real offensive potential too, particularly if several units are grouped together for flank protection. With their excellent morale and extra combat factors, Swiss Pikemen are one of the best offensive infantry units in the game.

Pikemen do have one disadvantage in comparison to spearmen. Their weapon requires two hands to grasp, so they cannot hold a shield. This makes them very vulnerable to missile fire. However, the awesome Swiss Armored Pikemen, with their half-plate armor, do not suffer this drawback.

Pikemen

Stat	Value	Stat	Value
Charge	4	Weapon	PIKE
Attack	1 (+2 BONUS VS. CAVALRY)	Shield	NONE
Defense	-1 (+6 BONUS VS. CAVALRY)	March Speed	6
Morale	2	Run Speed	10
Armor (Value)	NONE (1)	Charge Speed	11

Pikes are very long spears, so pikemen need proper training before they can act as a unit. Unlike other troops, the first 4 ranks of pikemen can fight against an enemy, presenting a wall of gleaming spear points to anyone foolish enough to charge them.

Swiss Pikemen

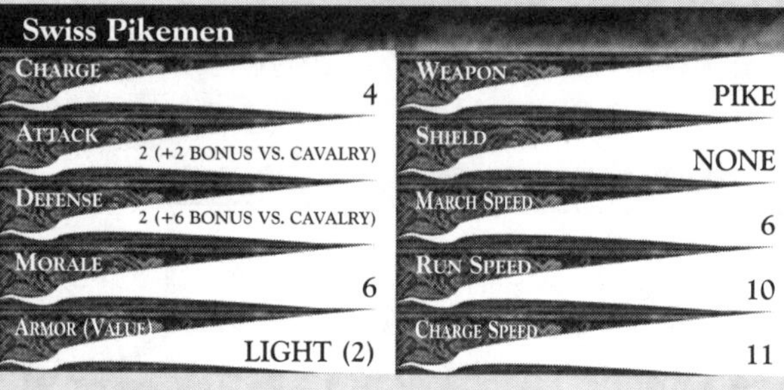

Stat	Value	Stat	Value
Charge	4	Weapon	PIKE
Attack	2 (+2 BONUS VS. CAVALRY)	Shield	NONE
Defense	2 (+6 BONUS VS. CAVALRY)	March Speed	6
Morale	6	Run Speed	10
Armor (Value)	LIGHT (2)	Charge Speed	11

Using a pike—which may be up to 4 meters long—takes training, and Swiss Pikemen are the best in Europe. They are superb against cavalry. No horse will charge against a wall of pike points, with 4 ranks of pikemen all capable of fighting at once.

Swiss Pikemen (Armored)

Stat	Value	Stat	Value
Charge	4	Weapon	PIKE
Attack	2 (+2 BONUS VS. CAVALRY)	Shield	SMALL
Defense	5 (+6 BONUS VS. CAVALRY)	March Speed	6
Morale	6	Run Speed	10
Armor (Value)	HALF PLATE (4)	Charge Speed	11

Swiss Armored Pikemen are very effective against cavalry. The first 4 ranks of any pike unit can fight, and horses will not charge into a wall of pike points. Swiss Armored Pikemen are highly regarded, thanks to their professionalism, but their solid formations can make them an easy target for missile fire.

Polearm Units

The various types of bills and halberds are known collectively as polearms. They have a long haft and a spear point for resisting cavalry charges, a hook for pulling a rider off his horse, and a large blade for cutting through heavy armor. Given this combination, units armed with polearms are quite formidable in the game. They're especially effective when fighting cavalry, against whom they get an attack bonus. Combine this with an extra bonus against armored troops, and you get a unit that can do real damage even to the toughest knights.

Polearm units fight well against foot units too, and they have no real weaknesses apart from their cost. However, they don't have quite the resistance to a charge that spearmen or pikemen do, because they don't get support from rear ranks. Examples include the fully armored Halberdiers (which are slow-moving but formidable in a fight), the lightweight Swiss Halberdiers, and the Janissary Heavy Infantry (who combine a halberd with decent armor and good speed).

Ch.4

Billmen

Stat	Value	Stat	Value
Charge	2	Weapon	BILLHOOK AXE
Attack	2 (+3 BONUS VS. CAVALRY, ARMOR PIERCING)	Shield	NONE
Defense	4 (+1 BONUS VS. CAVALRY)	March Speed	6
Morale	2	Run Speed	10
Armor (Value)	NONE (3)	Charge Speed	11

The billhook was originally a farming tool, an axe-and-hook with a long handle. After it evolved into a weapon, it could hack, stab, or drag a man to his death. English Billmen are well-trained in fighting against armored and mounted soldiers, pulling knights or men-at-arms to their deaths!

Chivalric Foot Knights

Stat	Value	Stat	Value
Charge	2	Weapon	POLEAXE
Attack	4 (+3 BONUS VS. CAVALRY, ARMOR PIERCING)	Shield	NONE
Defense	6 (+1 BONUS VS. CAVALRY)	March Speed	4
Morale	8	Run Speed	8
Armor (Value)	THREE-QUARTER PLATE (5)	Charge Speed	9

Chivalric Knights are a high point in the arms race between armor and killing weaponry. They wear superb plate armor and normally fight with lances on horseback. But when they dismount to fight on foot, they carry poleaxes—weapons intended to punch through any armor! They are an elite force trained from infancy in the art of war, and like any elite, they can be impetuous.

Halberdiers

Stat	Value	Stat	Value
Charge	2	Weapon	HALBERD
Attack	2 (+3 BONUS VS. CAVALRY, ARMOR PIERCING)	Shield	NONE
Defense	6 (+1 BONUS VS. CAVALRY)	March Speed	4
Morale	2	Run Speed	8
Armor (Value)	THREE-QUARTER PLATE (5)	Charge Speed	9

The halberd is a terrible weapon. Typically, it consists of a battle-axe and a pike mounted on a handle about six feet long. In the hands of a skilled man, a blow from one can fell a horse or cleave a man's head. It is a good weapon for assault troops, who have to break enemy formations and into fortifications. But its best function is defense. A 5- or 6-deep formation of Halberdiers can form a nearly impenetrable defensive barrier.

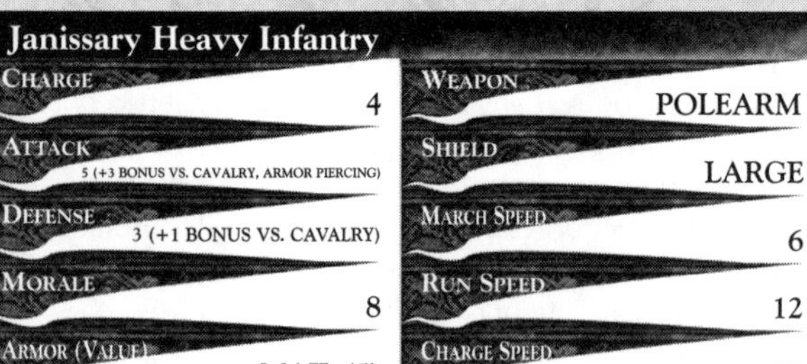

Janissary Heavy Infantry			
Charge	4	Weapon	POLEARM
Attack	5 (+3 BONUS VS. CAVALRY, ARMOR PIERCING)	Shield	LARGE
Defense	3 (+1 BONUS VS. CAVALRY)	March Speed	6
Morale	8	Run Speed	12
Armor (Value)	MAIL (5)	Charge Speed	13

Janissaries are the capable and disciplined elite of Turkish armies with a fearsome reputation. These heavy shock troops are deployed to batter a way through enemy armies so that others can pour through the gap. They are well-armored and armed with polearms that give them an advantage in close combat.

Militia Sergeants

For a full description of this poleaxe-armed unit, look under "Peasants and Militia."

Swiss Halberdiers			
Charge	2	Weapon	HALBERD
Attack	3 (+3 BONUS VS. CAVALRY, ARMOR PIERCING)	Shield	NONE
Defense	3 (+1 BONUS VS. CAVALRY)	March Speed	6
Morale	6	Run Speed	10
Armor (Value)	LIGHT (2)	Charge Speed	11

Swiss Halberdiers are extremely well-trained and disciplined—a product of the Swiss obsession with defending themselves. Although only lightly armored, they wield their halberds very effectively against most enemies. Unlike spears, which are good only for holding cavalry at bay, halberds also inflict heavy casualties against even heavily armored infantry opponents.

Urban Militia

For a full description of this poleaxe-armed unit, look under "Peasants and Militia."

Barbarians and Fanatics

All the units in this category are totally offense-oriented. They have an excellent charge, good attack factors, little or no armor, lousy defense, and a major lack of discipline. You may as well attack with these guys, because if you don't they'll charge of their own accord.

Designer Notes

On Barbarians and Fanatics

Some of these wild troops have very brittle morale and will run away if things start to go badly. So it's best to "use 'em before you lose 'em." Others, such as the Fanatics, Nizaris, and Ghazi Infantry, have excellent morale and will fight almost to the death… Of course, given their lack of defense, this tends not to take too long.

The Developers

Although it's no use trying to execute fancy maneuvers with these troops, you *can* try to hold them back until the critical moment. Given that barbarian and fanatic units can be so powerful when charging—and so poor if forced to defend or trapped in a long fight—timing is crucial. Under no circumstance should you leave them around to be shot at, or allow the enemy to charge them without counter-charging.

Some of the Arab fanatic units are also armed with bows, making for an interesting combination.

Fanatics

Charge	6	Weapon	CLUB
Attack	3	Shield	NONE
Defense	-4	March Speed	6
Morale	8	Run Speed	12
Armor (Value)	NONE (1)	Charge Speed	13

Simple, uneducated people are often willing to follow a charismatic leader who promises them Paradise. Existence for many of them is a hell of backbreaking work and grinding poverty. Fighting and dying with unquestioning, righteous faith is a chance for everlasting life in Heaven! And so, religious fanatics are inspired.

Futuwwas

Charge	3	Weapon	BOW, CURVED SWORD
Attack	4	Shield	SMALL
Defense	0	March Speed	6
Morale	0	Run Speed	10
Armor (Value)	NONE (3)	Charge Speed	11

Armored by faith and brave to the point of death, Futuwwa warriors are fanatical in battle, particularly against unbelievers. They are armed with bows and swords, making them very useful all-around soldiers. But rashness can be their undoing, and they may suffer heavy casualties during one of their typically brave attacks.

Gallowglasses

Charge	8	Weapon	SWORD
Attack	5 (Armor Piercing)	Shield	NONE
Defense	0	March Speed	6
Morale	0	Run Speed	10
Armor (Value)	LIGHT (2)	Charge Speed	11

In some ways Ireland is a relic of earlier times—Gallowglasses are Celtic warriors. Armed with two-handed swords, they are loyal to a clan chieftain, swift and fierce in battle, and have an almost berserker-like rage. They also are reputed to take the heads of slain enemies as trophies.

Ghazi Infantry

For a full description of this fanatic unit, look under "Axemen."

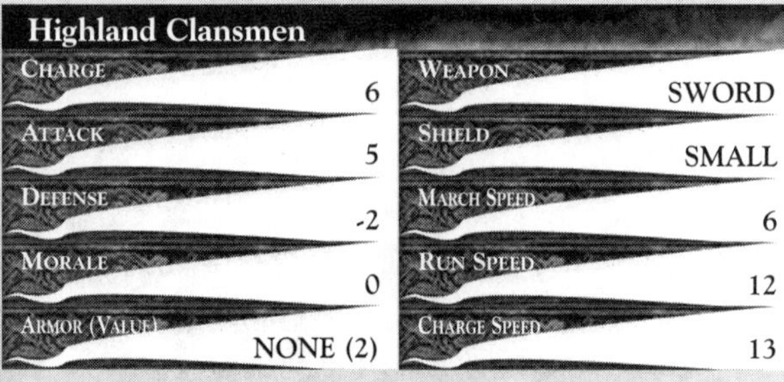

Highland Clansmen			
Charge	6	Weapon	SWORD
Attack	5	Shield	SMALL
Defense	-2	March Speed	6
Morale	0	Run Speed	12
Armor (Value)	NONE (2)	Charge Speed	13

Clansmen are the last tribal warriors in Western Europe, raised by a chieftain from his extended family. Although they're exceptionally brave by nature, they can also be stiff-necked and impetuous. Coming from lands where life is hard, these light infantry are usually poorly armed and can rarely afford much armor.

Kerns

For a full description of this barbarian unit, look under "Javelin and Naptha Throwers."

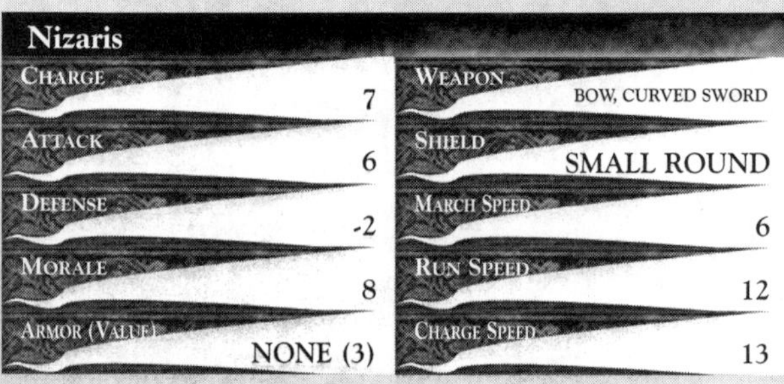

Nizaris			
Charge	7	Weapon	BOW, CURVED SWORD
Attack	6	Shield	SMALL ROUND
Defense	-2	March Speed	6
Morale	8	Run Speed	12
Armor (Value)	NONE (3)	Charge Speed	13

The Nizaris are members of a sect who have been inspired by faith to make war. They are armed with swords and bows, making them a flexible force for any Islamic general. Their fanaticism can sometimes make them impetuous in an attack because they ignore the odds against them.

Vikings

For a full description of this barbarian unit, look under "Axemen."

Peasants and Militia

The humble peasant is the cheapest and most easily available unit in the game. Particularly in the early stages, you may be forced to recruit peasants into your armies. They're poor all-around troops, and you should never rely upon them too much, but they do have their uses.

In general, it's best to keep them out of combat except in desperate circumstances, because their almost inevitable rout will undermine the morale of the rest of your army. However, they do have a reasonable charge, so they can tip the balance of a close melee by charging into the enemy's flank or rear, and the occasional downhill foray may sometimes produce results.

You can also use peasants to chase off enemy archers, or simply to stand and absorb arrow fire. Placing them close behind your front-line troops will bolster the morale of those in front, but don't expect the peasants to stay around to save the day if things go poorly. Never place a peasant unit off on its own, because it'll likely run as soon as the enemy comes in sight.

Designer Notes

Big Bad Peasant

A woodsman is a peasant with a large axe and a very bad attitude. Like all axe-armed units, woodsmen get a bonus against armored units, and also have a powerful charge. They won't defeat decent infantry units, but they may take down a good few before they flee.

The Developers

Almohad Urban Militia

Stat	Value	Stat	Value
Charge	3	Weapon	SWORD
Attack	3	Shield	LARGE
Defense	4	March Speed	6
Morale	2	Run Speed	10
Armor (Value)	HALF PLATE (5)	Charge Speed	11

As Islamic Spain comes under pressure, its cities look to their own defense and create urban militias. These men have plenty of opportunities for battle and are much more competent and aggressive than the usual run of militiamen. Well-armed and trained, they are qualitatively almost a standing army rather than a last-ditch defense.

Militia Sergeants

Stat	Value	Stat	Value
Charge	2	Weapon	POLEAXE
Attack	1 (+3 BONUS VS. CAVALRY, ARMOR PIERCING)	Shield	NONE
Defense	4 (+1 BONUS VS. CAVALRY)	March Speed	6
Morale	0	Run Speed	10
Armor (Value)	MAIL (3)	Charge Speed	11

Militia formations are drawn from the apprentices of growing towns. Armed with fearsome poleaxes, they can do significant damage to enemies, but their training is not always of the highest. They can do well against lesser troops, but they will quail before more professional soldiery.

Muslim Peasants

Stat	Value	Stat	Value
Charge	2	Weapon	SHORT SPEAR OR PITCHFORK
Attack	-2	Shield	NONE
Defense	-4	March Speed	6
Morale	-2	Run Speed	10
Armor (Value)	NONE (1)	Charge Speed	11

Life for peasants is never easy. They are the lowest social class, tied to the land or living in hovels in the growing cities. When war breaks out, peasants are sometimes forced into the army and then expected to fight. Peasants may see little reason to remain loyal when treated this way.

Peasants

CHARGE	4	WEAPON	SHORT SPEAR OR PITCHFORK
ATTACK	-2	SHIELD	NONE
DEFENSE	-4	MARCH SPEED	6
MORALE	-2	RUN SPEED	10
ARMOR (VALUE)	NONE (1)	CHARGE SPEED	11

Life is never easy for peasants, the bottom rung of a very long social ladder. When war comes, the levy takes them away from home and their crops. They are given few weapons, and they're just expected to fight and die for their betters. Peasants are therefore cheap but unreliable units.

Urban Militia

CHARGE	2	WEAPON	POLEAXE
ATTACK	1 (+3 BONUS VS. CAVALRY, ARMOR PIERCING)	SHIELD	NONE
DEFENSE	0 (+1 BONUS VS. CAVALRY)	MARCH SPEED	6
MORALE	0	RUN SPEED	10
ARMOR (VALUE)	NONE (1)	CHARGE SPEED	11

As cities and trade grow, so does the need for local defense. Some towns and cities can provide a locally raised force, recruited from among apprentices and journeymen. Although they only have limited training, their polearms give them an advantage against armored troops, and they are more disciplined than peasantry.

Woodsmen

For a full description of this peasant unit, look under "Axemen."

MISSILE UNITS

Missile fire is a double killer. It not only inflicts casualties, but also reduces enemy morale, sometimes significantly. Bows are particularly useful for dashing the enemy's spirit. They can fire arrows over friendly heads to rain death on distant foes. Plus, their reload time is short, letting them put down a lot of fire in a short time. Indeed, there's nothing like a thick shower of arrows to encourage an enemy formation to crack and run.

When their ammunition is used up, archers can be committed to melee combat. In fact, some of the archer units in the game are also skilled swordsmen and can hold their own in combat. However, other archers have difficulty fighting anything stronger than a peasant. If at all possible, try to spare these units from combat, or maneuver them around to the flanks and rear of an already-engaged enemy.

Missile/Melee Combo Units

All missile units carry melee weapons as well, but only a few types can actually fight hand-to-hand with any effectiveness. Missile units who fight reasonably well in melee action include the following:

Almughavars
Bulgarian Brigands
Futuwwas
Golden Horde Warriors
Hashishin
Janissary Infantry
Nizaris

For more on these units, see the "Archers" and "Javelin and Naptha Throwers" sections.

Archers

The bow is the most common type of missile weapon in the game. Bow-armed units range from pure archer units, such as Desert Archers, to high-quality units such as Turkish Janissaries, who can shoot *and* give a good account of themselves in hand-to-hand combat. The main characteristics of the bow are good range, good rate of fire, and a high trajectory that allows it to fire over other troops.

Although the archer's ammunition supply is fair, it can be used up quickly because of his high rate of fire. In the Early Period, archers are very deadly, but as you encounter better-armored targets in the High and Late Periods, they're less effective.

Remember: Damp bowstrings lose power and accuracy, so it's best to avoid attacking in wet weather if you have lots of archers.

When to Fire into the Melee

Firing into a massed melee runs the risk of shooting some of your own men. But this tactic is often worthwhile, especially if your units are more heavily armored than the enemy, or if the enemy troops are in a denser formation.

Designer Notes

Where to Deploy Archers?

Should you deploy bow-armed units in front of your melee units or behind them? Putting archers in front gives them a clear line of sight and allows them to open fire at the longest range. However, as the enemy closes, archers will have to retreat to safety behind other troops. This causes them to lose valuable short-range shooting time, and it might disorder the troops behind them as they pass through.

On the other hand, if you place archers *behind* your main battle line, they won't be able to see their target (unless shooting down a steep hill) and thus will fire less accurately. However, they can rain death on the enemy right up until the battle lines clash.

The Developers

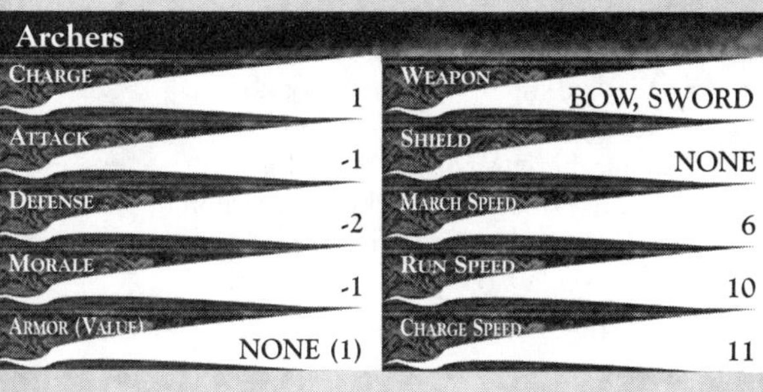

Archers

Stat	Value	Stat	Value
Charge	1	Weapon	BOW, SWORD
Attack	-1	Shield	NONE
Defense	-2	March Speed	6
Morale	-1	Run Speed	10
Armor (Value)	NONE (1)	Charge Speed	11

Archery is a survival skill. It helps put food on the table, assuming that the archer isn't hanged as a poacher! Using the same skill in battle can bring down an armored man, although the Archers' short bows are not quite as efficient as true war bows.

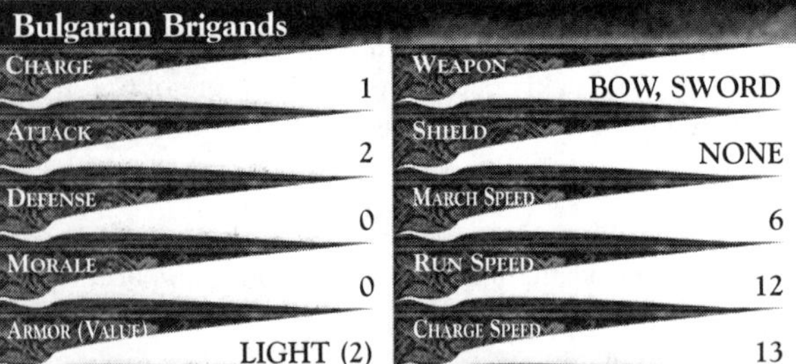

Bulgarian Brigands			
Charge	1	Weapon	BOW, SWORD
Attack	2	Shield	NONE
Defense	0	March Speed	6
Morale	0	Run Speed	12
Armor (Value)	LIGHT (2)	Charge Speed	13

The independent peoples in the Balkans have always been difficult for outsiders to rule. The Bulgar Brigands are organized enough and tough enough to be mercenaries. They are tactically flexible fighters, well able to use both bows and swords. But brigands may lack moral fiber in a crisis.

Desert Archers			
Charge	1	Weapon	BOW, SWORD
Attack	-1	Shield	SMALL
Defense	-1	March Speed	6
Morale	0	Run Speed	12
Armor (Value)	NONE (2)	Charge Speed	13

All desert peoples need superior skills and hardiness to survive, let alone prosper. Desert Archers are generally superlative, and their compound bows are excellent weapons. It is their role to pepper enemy troops with arrows and stay out of reach, for they do not fight well in melee.

FUTUWWAS

For a full description of this archer unit, look under "Barbarians and Fanatics."

Genoese Sailors			
Charge	1	Weapon	BOW, SWORD
Attack	0	Shield	NONE
Defense	-2	March Speed	6
Morale	2	Run Speed	12
Armor (Value)	NONE (1)	Charge Speed	13

Acting as more than just hastily levied infantry, Genoese Sailors make very effective units of light archers when away from their ships. They are fast moving and lightly armored, but they're not equipped to fight hand-to-hand except as a last resort.

Golden Horde Warriors

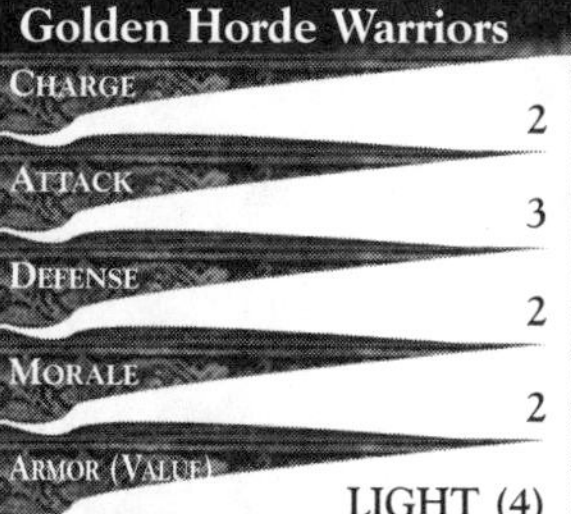

Charge	2	Weapon	BOW, SWORD
Attack	3	Shield	LARGE
Defense	2	March Speed	6
Morale	2	Run Speed	10
Armor (Value)	LIGHT (4)	Charge Speed	11

Away from their precious horses, the Golden Horde are formidable and highly disciplined warriors, expert in the use of their powerful compound bows and swords. They are not suitable for assaults against heavy infantry, being better at breaking formations with arrow fire and then moving in to crush already-beaten men!

Hashishin

Charge	2	Weapon	BOW, CURVED SWORD
Attack	6	Shield	NONE
Defense	3	March Speed	6
Morale	12	Run Speed	12
Armor (Value)	LIGHT (2)	Charge Speed	13

The Hashasin are a sect originally from Persia, and they are masters of stealth, deception, and murder. On a battlefield, they can hide in almost any terrain and are ideal for ambushing enemy generals. When committed to action, they can strike at their victims with both sword and bow. Check the Morale value. This unit's morale is very hard to break.

Janissary Archers

Charge	1	Weapon	BOW, CURVED SWORD
Attack	1	Shield	NONE
Defense	0	March Speed	6
Morale	4	Run Speed	10
Armor (Value)	LIGHT (2)	Charge Speed	11

"Yeni Cheri" (the "New Soldiers") are a new Turkish system of national and royal (not feudal) armies. Disciplined, drilled, and professional, Janissary Archers are intended to break up and weaken enemy formations so that other soldiers of the Janissary corps can move in for the kill.

Janissary Infantry

Charge	1	Weapon	BOW, SWORD
Attack	4	Shield	NONE
Defense	2	March Speed	6
Morale	4	Run Speed	10
Armor (Value)	MAIL (3)	Charge Speed	11

The Janissaries are raised from provincial children, taken into the Sultan's service, and trained to do nothing but fight and obey. Janissaries do not fight for personal honor. They fight to win. These soldiers are armed with bows *and* swords, making them a tactically flexible and powerful unit.

NIZARIS

For a full description of this bow-armed fanatic unit, look under "Barbarians and Fanatics."

Ottoman Infantry

Stat	Value	Stat	Value
Charge	2	Weapon	BOW, AXE
Attack	1 (ARMOR PIERCING)	Shield	SMALL ROUND
Defense	1	March Speed	6
Morale	0	Run Speed	10
Armor (Value)	LIGHT (3)	Charge Speed	11

Well-armed and armored, Ottoman Infantry are tough enough to be in the vanguard of any Turkish army. They are well-equipped with bows and axes (which give them an advantage against armored enemies), and they're well-trained and disciplined. Usually, they can be relied on to defeat most infantry.

Trebizond Archers

Stat	Value	Stat	Value
Charge	1	Weapon	BOW, SWORD
Attack	3	Shield	SMALL
Defense	-1	March Speed	6
Morale	2	Run Speed	10
Armor (Value)	NONE (2)	Charge Speed	11

Compound bows give these soldiers an advantage thanks to their range, accuracy, and penetrative power. Trebizond Archers are well-trained and disciplined, and they can act as a light infantry in a pinch. Although they can fight in a melee, it would be a foolish commander who used them to attack unbroken enemies.

Turcoman Foot Soldiers

Stat	Value	Stat	Value
Charge	1	Weapon	BOW, SWORD
Attack	-1	Shield	SMALL
Defense	3	March Speed	6
Morale	-1	Run Speed	12
Armor (Value)	MAIL (4)	Charge Speed	13

The Turcomans, from Turkmenistan and Northeastern Persia, are adept at desert warfare. They are primarily archers, but they can fight as light infantry if they need to do so. They are best used to weaken an enemy for others to attack. Their melee combat abilities are best reserved for self-defense.

LONGBOW, CROSSBOW, AND ARBALESTER

Longbow units share all the attributes of other archers, with the extra benefits of longer range and better penetration against armored targets. Longbowmen are also armed with a handy axe, giving them bonuses in hand-to-hand combat against armored enemies. They can be very effective against the flanks of knight units. Their only drawback is their expense.

Crossbows have a much lower rate of fire than normal bows, and their flatter trajectory means they can only fire over troops in front of them if they are downhill or at long range. However, crossbows are more accurate than normal bows and have *much* better armor penetration. Thus, during a battle, crossbow units will most likely inflict more casualties than archer units. However, they'll take much longer to expend their ammunition. Crossbows are best for slow tactical battles, or for castle assaults.

Designer Notes

How to Use Pavise Crossbowmen

The regular Crossbowmen in the game are well-armored, but the Pavise Crossbowmen have even better protection due to the large wooden shield (called a pavise) they carry with them. This makes them a bit slow and thus not well-suited to offensive operations. However, they can be an excellent defensive unit to soak up missile fire.

Pavise Crossbowmen are also very useful in castle assault situations, because their pavise lets them make a close approach to the structure without taking too many casualties from the castle defenses.

The Developers

Arbalests are similar to crossbows, but they have greater range and even greater armor penetration. Also, because of their steel strings, they are not affected by damp weather. Both crossbow and arbalest units are best deployed in formations only 2 ranks deep (3 if in loose formation) because men further back find it very hard to shoot over the heads of those in front.

Arbalesters

Stat	Value	Stat	Value
Charge	1	Weapon	CROSSBOW
Attack	-1	Shield	NONE
Defense	2	March Speed	6
Morale	0	Run Speed	10
Armor (Value)	MAIL (3)	Charge Speed	11

The arbalest is a heavy crossbow that can fire a bolt that will penetrate most armored targets. It has a very slow rate of fire and needs a small windlass to pull back the string. Properly protected by other troops, Arbalesters can be deadly.

Crossbowmen

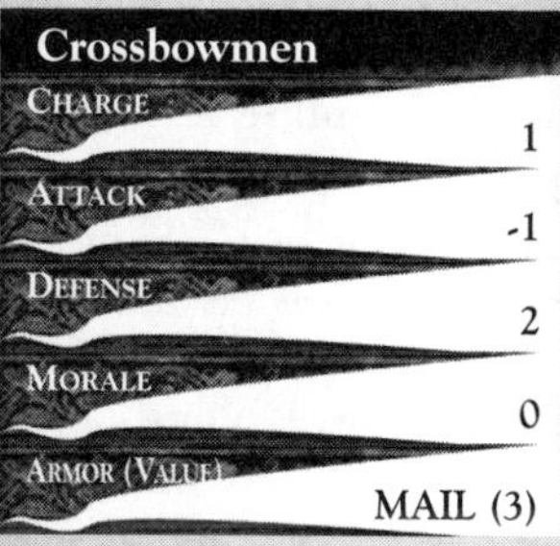

Stat	Value	Stat	Value
Charge	1	Weapon	CROSSBOW, SWORD
Attack	-1	Shield	NONE
Defense	2	March Speed	6
Morale	0	Run Speed	10
Armor (Value)	MAIL (3)	Charge Speed	11

Anyone can use a crossbow. A few weeks of practice will make anyone a master of it. (Archers, on the other hand, have to be trained for years.) Once trained as a Crossbowman, even the humblest peasant can kill the mightiest king. This weapon is often seen as "unfair"—by the mighty, of course.

Longbowmen

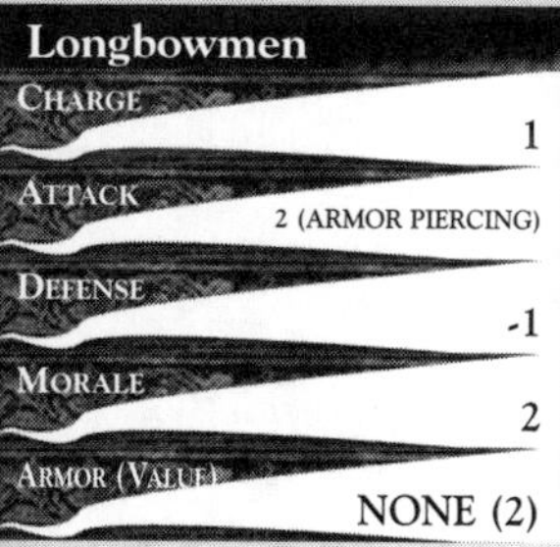

Stat	Value	Stat	Value
Charge	1	Weapon	LONGBOW, AXE
Attack	2 (ARMOR PIERCING)	Shield	SMALL
Defense	-1	March Speed	6
Morale	2	Run Speed	10
Armor (Value)	NONE (2)	Charge Speed	11

English and Welsh Longbowmen are the finest archers in Europe, able to direct a storm of arrows against targets up to 300 meters away. Even knights are vulnerable, thanks to the longbows' armor-piercing bodkin arrowheads. Longbowmen are often best when the enemy is forced to attack and then shot down!

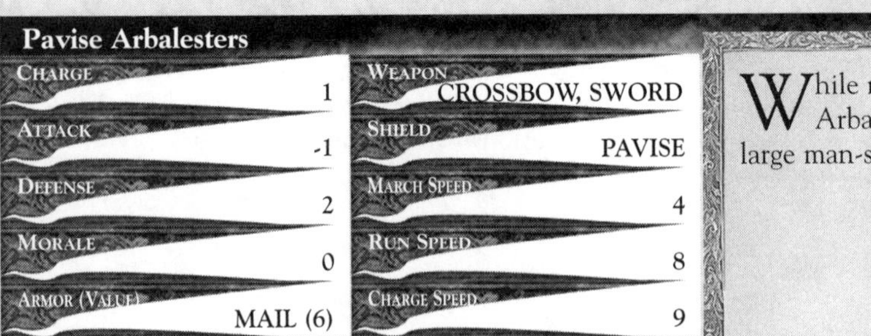

Pavise Arbalesters

Stat	Value	Stat	Value
Charge	1	Weapon	CROSSBOW, SWORD
Attack	-1	Shield	PAVISE
Defense	2	March Speed	4
Morale	0	Run Speed	8
Armor (Value)	MAIL (6)	Charge Speed	9

While reloading, a Pavise Arbalester hides behind his large man-sized shield.

Ch.4

Pavise Crossbowmen

Stat	Value	Stat	Value
Charge	1	Weapon	CROSSBOW, AXE
Attack	-1	Shield	PAVISE
Defense	2	March Speed	4
Morale	0	Run Speed	8
Armor (Value)	NONE (6)	Charge Speed	9

Anyone can master a crossbow in a few weeks—but it is not a perfect weapon. It has a slow rate of fire, and during reloading a crossbowman is vulnerable unless he has a pavise, or large shield, to shelter behind. The Italians are famous for their crossbowmen.

Arquebusier and Handgunner

Although armed with only primitive guns, these soldiers were the first to depend on massed gunfire. Their main drawbacks are their long reload time and an inability to fire in wet weather. They have reasonable range, but since their weapons are very inaccurate, they may not cause much damage at longer ranges.

You can deploy Arquebusiers in 1 or 2 ranks to deliver massed volleys. Or, if you deploy them in 3 or more ranks, only the first rank will shoot. After firing, it will move to the rear to reload, allowing the second rank to come forward to shoot. This revolving formation helps offset the long reload times and gives more continuous fire.

Designer Notes

The "Fear Effect" of Gunfire

Gunfire can be a real morale-buster. In an age with little technology, the combination of the noise, the smoke, and the sight of their comrades dropping dead for no apparent reason will often cause units to break and run in terror. Another point to note is that even the heaviest armor offers only slight protection from gunfire.

The Developers

Handgunners use the earliest form of handguns, often just a short tube on a stick. These weapons are very crude, inaccurate, short-ranged, and take a long time to reload. However, the noise and smoke they produce elicit profound terror in their targets, and their bullets can penetrate even the heaviest armor.

Because of the need to get in close to discharge their pieces, Handgunners are heavily armored and can give a good account with the sword. Like the Arquebusier, the Handgunner can use a rotating mode of fire if desired. The front rank fires and then withdraws to the rear so the next rank can shoot. But his preferred mode of operation is to close on a foe, deliver a couple of close-range volleys, and then finish him off with the sword.

Mamluk Handgunners don't have the armor of their European counterparts, so they prefer to avoid close combat.

Ch.4

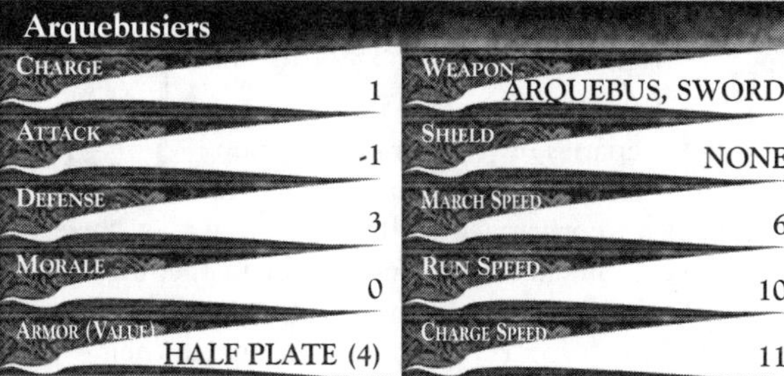

Arquebusiers

Charge	1	Weapon	ARQUEBUS, SWORD
Attack	-1	Shield	NONE
Defense	3	March Speed	6
Morale	0	Run Speed	10
Armor (Value)	HALF PLATE (4)	Charge Speed	11

The arquebus or matchlock is a relatively sophisticated firearm. It is easy to use, can be aimed with some accuracy, and rarely explodes and kills the user! Arquebusiers can fire volleys, damaging the enemy's morale as well as his frail flesh, but they cannot fire at all in wet weather.

Handgunners

Charge	1	Weapon	HANDGUN, SWORD
Attack	4	Shield	NONE
Defense	3	March Speed	6
Morale	4	Run Speed	10
Armor (Value)	HALF PLATE (4)	Charge Speed	11

Handguns are not accurate—or safe!—and are useless in damp weather. But it is relatively easy to train troops to use them. Even though Handgunners are slow, short-range missile troops, they are useful because of the frightening noise and smoke they produce!

Mamluk Handgunners

Charge	1	Weapon	HANDGUN, DAGGER
Attack	0	Shield	NONE
Defense	-2	March Speed	6
Morale	2	Run Speed	10
Armor (Value)	NONE (1)	Charge Speed	11

Islamic science has allowed the Mamluks to produce better gunpowder than other peoples, and their handguns are also skillfully made. Mamluk handgunners have greater discipline than their Christian counterparts, although they must still deal with the handgun's slow rate of fire and low accuracy.

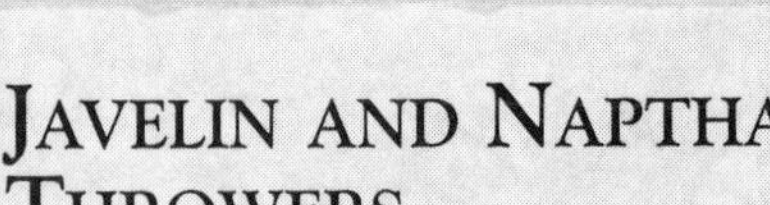

Javelin and Naptha Throwers

Medieval: Total War includes several javelin-tossing units. At first sight, javelins would appear to be poor weapons because of their short range and limited ammunition. However, a powerfully thrown javelin can pierce even heavy armor, and a soldier can throw his bundle of javelins in quick succession. Well-placed javelin units can devastate their targets in short order.

Due to their short range, it is difficult to use javelins in Skirmish mode against advancing enemies. Your javelin units will withdraw before the enemy gets close enough to attack. Javelin tossers are best employed against the flanks of enemy units.

With their crude grenades of incendiary liquid, Naptha Throwers can be dangerous to friend and foe alike. They can cause great carnage to nearby enemy units, and their bombs will cause great fear. However, these unpredictable weapons can often go astray and injure friends too. A Naptha Thrower cannot carry a shield, but he wears chain-mail and a helmet and carries a dagger.

Almughavars

Charge	6	Weapon	JAVELINS, SPEAR
Attack	4 (+1 BONUS VS. CAVALRY)	Shield	NONE
Defense	1 (+4 BONUS VS. CAVALRY)	March Speed	6
Morale	8	Run Speed	12
Armor (Value)	LIGHT (2)	Charge Speed	13

These lightly armored Catalan mercenaries ply their trade all around the Mediterranean. Almughavars are shock troops armed with javelins that give them a fearsome missile attack, opening gaps in the enemy line for a subsequent charge with their spears. Few others can match their professional determination and ferocity.

Kerns

Charge	3	Weapon	JAVELINS, SHORT SWORD
Attack	2	Shield	NONE
Defense	-3	March Speed	6
Morale	0	Run Speed	12
Armor (Value)	NONE (1)	Charge Speed	13

The Irish keep to the Celtic way of warfare. Constant skirmishing between Irish warlords and English invaders gives even the peasants a warlike attitude. They fight as kerns—light, harassing javelin-men—rather than as untrained farm laborers, and they bring their particularly bloody-minded savagery to the battlefield.

Murabitin Infantry

Charge	2	Weapon	JAVELINS, SWORD
Attack	1	Shield	LARGE
Defense	0	March Speed	6
Morale	4	Run Speed	12
Armor (Value)	NONE (3)	Charge Speed	13

The tough Murabitin are recruited from the desolate Almohad provinces along the North African coast. Armed with javelins, they are good for harassing enemy formations and can cause a surprising number of casualties. Their swords are only sufficient for limited self-defense, so they are best used as skirmishers.

Naptha Throwers

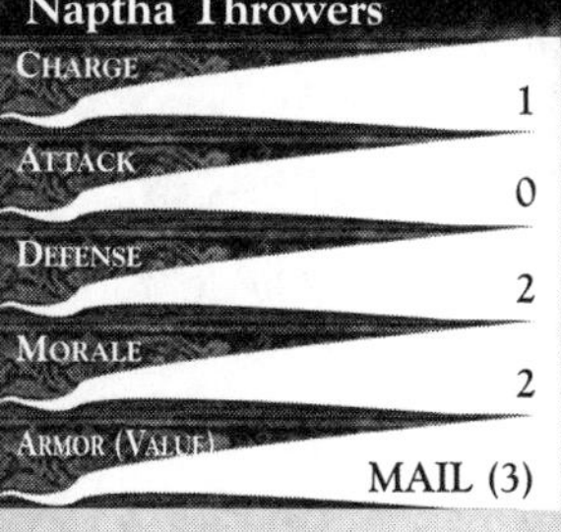

Stat	Value	Stat	Value
Charge	1	Weapon	POT, DAGGER
Attack	0	Shield	NONE
Defense	2	March Speed	6
Morale	2	Run Speed	10
Armor (Value)	MAIL (3)	Charge Speed	11

Naptha is a fiery mixture of chemicals that is very difficult to put out. It's placed in ceramic pots, which are then thrown so that they burst open on contact. Naptha is dangerous, and it is possible for the thrower to set fire to himself rather than a target!

Spanish Jinete

For a detailed description of this mounted javelin-tossing unit, look under "Mounted Missile Units."

Mounted Missile Units

Many *Medieval: Total War* cavalry units are armed with bows. Remember that mounted archers fire less accurately than foot archers. So the best tactic is to use the horse archer's speed to move into an advantageous position on the enemy's flank or rear.

We should also reiterate two other important points mentioned in Chapter 3, "Battle Map Tactics." First, you can move mounted missile units to close range against infantry targets, because their speed will keep them out of danger. Second, *never* engage in shooting matches with infantry bow units. Your mounted unit will almost always lose, since it fires less accurately and offers a much bigger target.

Most of the previous comments apply to mounted crossbowmen too. Their speed lets them maneuver for good shots on armored targets that other missile units may find hard to damage. If confronted by infantry bowmen with no protective screen of spearmen or other troops, the mounted crossbowmen's best tactic is often to charge home, swords out, rather than stand and shoot it out. Against supported infantry archers, the best tactic is to simply fall back out of range and look for an unprotected flank.

Berber Camels

For a detailed description of this camel-mounted archer unit, look under "Camel Units."

Boyars

For a detailed description of this heavy cavalry archer unit, look under "Heavy Cavalry (Missile-Armed)."

Byzantine Cavalry

For a detailed description of this heavy cavalry archer unit, look under "Heavy Cavalry (Missile-Armed)."

Golden Horde Horse Archers

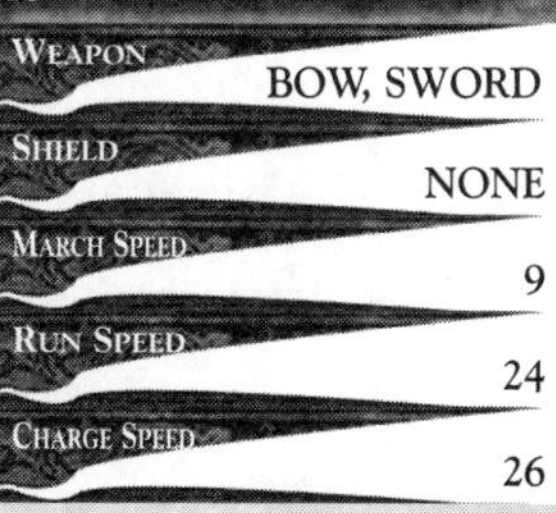

Stat	Value	Stat	Value
Charge	2	Weapon	BOW, SWORD
Attack	3	Shield	NONE
Defense	1	March Speed	9
Morale	4	Run Speed	24
Armor (Value)	LIGHT (3)	Charge Speed	26

Golden Horde Horse Archers should be used primarily to harass and ambush enemies. They are ideally suited to the battlefield hit-and-run tactics favored by the Mongols. Their superior speed gives them the ability to mass swiftly, attack, withdraw, and then repeat as often as needed—and all without fighting in a melee!

Horse Archers

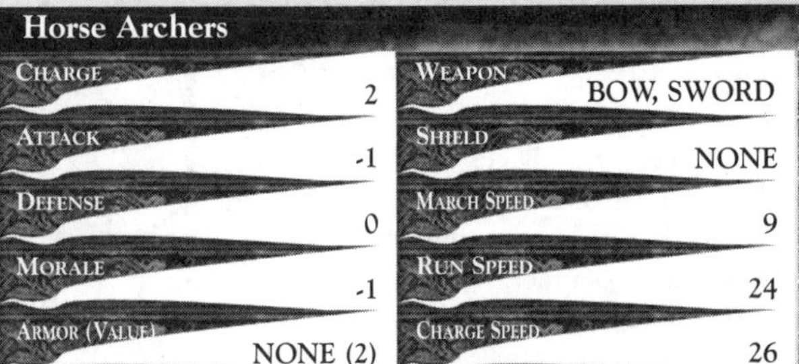

Stat	Value	Stat	Value
Charge	2	Weapon	BOW, SWORD
Attack	-1	Shield	NONE
Defense	0	March Speed	9
Morale	-1	Run Speed	24
Armor (Value)	NONE (2)	Charge Speed	26

Many eastern European peoples use horse archers, and their fighting style requires them to be masterful horsemen *and* bowmen. They pepper enemies with arrows while staying tantalizingly out of reach because they are vulnerable in hand-to-hand fighting—something a wise commander remembers!

Mamluk Horse Archers

Stat	Value	Stat	Value
Charge	2	Weapon	BOW, SWORD
Attack	3	Shield	SMALL
Defense	2	March Speed	9
Morale	4	Run Speed	20
Armor (Value)	LIGHT (4)	Charge Speed	22

The Mamluks are a slave warrior elite. Almost without exception, their troops are highly disciplined, motivated, and organized. Their Horse Archers are both good shots and skilled horsemen, able to destroy slower opponents. They can fight hand-to-hand in their own defense, but they should not be committed to such fights recklessly.

Mounted Crossbowmen

Stat	Value	Stat	Value
Charge	2	Weapon	CROSSBOW, SWORD
Attack	0	Shield	NONE
Defense	2	March Speed	9
Morale	2	Run Speed	24
Armor (Value)	LIGHT MAIL (3)	Charge Speed	26

Armed with slightly smaller crossbows than their infantry equivalents, Mounted Crossbowmen are one response by western armies to eastern mounted archers. But while crossbows have killing power, they also have a slow rate of fire, so these crossbowmen must use their cavalry mobility to stay out of trouble.

Sipahi of the Porte

For a detailed description of this heavy cavalry archer unit, look under "Heavy Cavalry (Missile-Armed)."

Spanish Jinetes

Stat	Value	Stat	Value
Charge	2	Weapon	JAVELINS, SWORD
Attack	2	Shield	SMALL
Defense	3	March Speed	9
Morale	2	Run Speed	24
Armor (Value)	LIGHT MAIL (4)	Charge Speed	26

Formerly Moorish soldiery, Jinetes are lightly armored cavalry, both fast and maneuverable. They often manage to surprise enemies, because instead of using lances, they hurl javelins before closing to fight hand-to-hand with swords. This double ability makes them handy warriors and a fine addition to any Spanish army.

Turcoman Horsemen

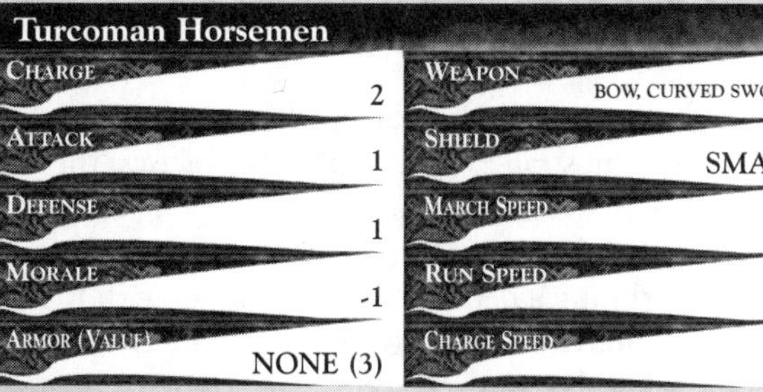

Stat	Value	Stat	Value
Charge	2	Weapon	BOW, CURVED SWORD
Attack	1	Shield	SMALL
Defense	1	March Speed	9
Morale	-1	Run Speed	24
Armor (Value)	NONE (3)	Charge Speed	26

These fast and light cavalry, lightly armored and equipped with bows and swords, are ideally suited to desert warfare. They can harass and weaken units with missile fire, and then press home attacks. Against Frankish Crusaders, they have little trouble in staying out of range while wearing down the enemy.

Turcopole

Stat	Value	Stat	Value
Charge	2	Weapon	BOW, SWORD
Attack	-1	Shield	SMALL
Defense	2	March Speed	9
Morale	0	Run Speed	24
Armor (Value)	LIGHT (4)	Charge Speed	26

After fighting Saracen cavalry, the Crusaders realized that knights were not suited to war in the Holy Land. To counter the nimble Saracens, the Westerners recruited local mercenaries. These Turcopoles are lightly armored and carry both bows and swords, making them a flexible unit type in combat.

Chapter 5: The Full Campaign

The Full Campaign lets you guide your faction through 400 years of Medieval European history.

At the design team's suggestion, we combined the strategies for all three medieval time periods (Early, High, and Late) into one discussion for each faction. When you select the Early Period and choose a faction, you end up playing that faction through the years of the High and Late Periods as well. Therefore, having separate sections for the two later periods would merely present redundant material.

Welcome to the Single Player Full Campaign, where you put it all together—Campaign Map strategy and Battle Map tactics, the best of both worlds. If you've played any of the Full Campaign scenarios yet, you know how open-ended the gameplay is. And the truth is, any step-by-step walkthrough outlining a detailed series of moves with highly specific battle plans would inevitably diverge (perhaps widely) from your own experience of playing the campaign.

However, the creators of *Medieval: Total War* did design each faction's campaign with an optimal overall success strategy in mind. We've gathered together their suggestions in this chapter. Yet another example of this book's obsession with information from the highest sources! Again, these suggestions cannot guarantee victory. You still have to win your tactical battles, and the game's AI will react in different ways depending on your course of action. But these suggestions will point you in directions that offer the best chances of success.

THE ALMOHADS

Valencia and Portugal are not aligned with any faction at the start of the Early Period. The army in Valencia is commanded by El Cid (a high-ranking general), so it will be a valuable addition to your forces. Bribe the armies in these provinces right away, because the Spanish and Aragonese will try to do this within a few years.

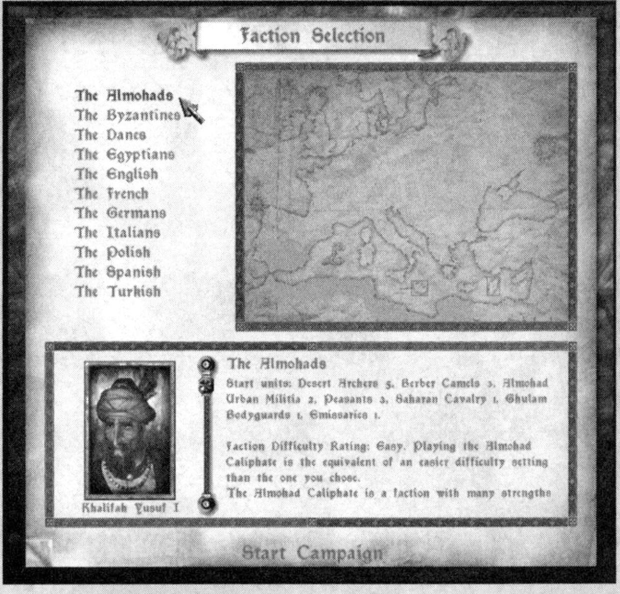

Now you have three neighbouring factions—the Egyptians, the Spanish, and the Aragonese. If possible, ally with the Egyptians and then leave only a small army in Cyrenacia. A small force in a bordering province will indicate trust and reduce the chances of your neighbour breaking the alliance… maybe. The force should be balanced, however, so build a Fort, Town Watch, and Horse Farmer to give you some Urban Militia and Saharan Cavalry. Then send some Nubian Spearmen and Desert Archers down from Morocco. Add a few Peasants and a low-ranking heir, and the province should be safe.

In any case, the Egyptians are most likely distracted by the Turks, Byzantines, and various crusading factions. So you should be able to concentrate on the Iberian peninsula. Historically, the Spanish steadily drove the Muslims from the region and allied with the Aragonese to create what is now Spain, so it is important not to trust them.

Group large armies in Cordoba, and send some Alims or Imams into all the non-Muslim provinces. Remember, the difference in faith between a faction and its subjects is often the cause of rebellions. It is also worth noting that leaving holy men and Spies in provinces you have lost to Christian factions will stir up trouble for the new rulers, but you run a high risk of having them assassinated. By the same token, training Assassins is also important in order to cope with the influx of Bishops. The Spanish and Aragonese will be trying to convert Muslims to Christianity too!

Attack Leon first, and then sweep eastward through Castille, Navarre, and Aragon. By the end of the Early period, the Almohads need to be in control of all provinces south of the Pyrenhees.

If you're starting in the High Period, Valencia will already be under Almohad control and you will already have major strongholds in Algeria and Granada, so higher-caliber troops will be available. It won't be possible to rely much on lighter infantry, such as Almohad Urban Militia, because the Age of Chivalry has begun. Christians will be fielding units of very heavy cavalry and knights against you.

Trade is now essential to raise the necessary funds for heavier units. Building ships and ports around the Iberian peninsula—and allying with those Christian factions around the Mediterranean who do not pose an immediate threat—should net you all the florins you need. Beware, though, because Christian factions are still Christian factions, and they will crusade against you if the Pope decrees. After all, you *are* wiping out the Catholic Spaniards.

Starting in the Late Period requires the Almohads to take back most of their former territory from the Spanish. Historically, by this time the "Reconquista" was almost at an end. By 1491, the Moors (as the Almohads were more commonly known) had abandoned even their stronghold at Granada and been pushed back into North Africa. But when the Late Period begins, there is still a chance to divert the course of history.

It may be possible to expand eastward into Egyptian territory, but it is unlikely that the Egyptians will be passive neighbors and allies, as in other periods. The warlike Mamluks are now in control, and the Egyptians—assuming the Ottoman Turks will be chiefly concerned with wiping out the Byzantine Empire—may turn their attentions to Almohad territory. So you must defend on two fronts, which is never an easy task. But Egyptian spices can be a source of high income for your eventual push into Europe.

THE BYZANTINES

A good start in the Early Period is vital for the Byzantines. You open with several islands in the eastern Mediterranean—Crete, Rhodes, and Cyprus. These will be safe from attack in the early going, so use them to produce boats and Spies. Concentrate on defending your mainland regions. Surprisingly easy pickings are available in the Balkans (Serbia, Bulgaria, Moldavia, and Wallachia) and on the southern steppes (Kiev, Khazar, etc.), providing these provinces can be reached first and the Turks can be kept in line.

Build plenty of Byzantine Infantry and Trebizond Archers. These are strong units that are good for defense. Do not build any Varangian Guard until later. These elite troops take too long to build and are best for strengthening large armies. Once your borders are defended and you are safe from invasion, you can increase your income. Constantinople can generate large amounts of trade income. Send out the fleets you have built in Crete and Cyprus, and start forming your trade network.

In the long term, the big problem is that the Empire and Constantinople are on the route that *every* Crusade from the west will take toward the Holy Land. Expect to be looted, attacked, or generally done down by at least one mob of religiously inspired psychotics during the game!

In the High Period, Constantinople is the Byzantine Empire. Hold off the Turks—ally with them, even—and concentrate all efforts on making Constantinople the capital of the Byzantine Empire once more. Again, it's one of the richest provinces on the map when connected to a trade network. Conquest is good, but bribery is better, because the buildings in the province won by bribes will be undamaged. Once this is done, the rest of the game should consist of picking enemies carefully and crushing them without mercy. Byzantine units are starting to become old-fashioned, and eventually they will be outclassed by other factions' troops, so mercenaries will be required to keep up.

Assassins, Emissaries, Spies, and mercenaries are the keys to the Byzantine Empire's success in the Late Period. Buy mercenaries to obtain up-to-date troops, send Assassins to kill enemy generals, use Spies to foment disloyalty and revolts, and use Emissaries to buy up rebellious provinces. There's an urgent need to stifle the Turks before they can get going. The Turkish military is a "late developer," while the Byzantine native forces are now old-fashioned. (The Kataphraktoi are fearsome, but not war-winners on their own.) The Byzantine position at this time is difficult, but it's far from hopeless!

THE DANES

The Danes begin the game in the High Period with just one province, so early expansion into Scandinavia and Norway (secured by naval superiority) is essential. Historically, the Kalmar Union successfully controlled trade routes between Norway, Sweden, and Denmark, and across the Baltic Sea. First you must secure these two provinces to your north, and then build ports and trading posts/merchants there.

A strong navy is necessary to keep control of trade, as are alliances with the Russians, English, Polish, and Germans. Be careful, though, because eventually you will need to conquer territory belonging to at least one of these factions to keep your economy afloat. And before then, your neighbors may decide that they too would benefit by having Danish provinces absorbed into their regimes.

Attacking England first may be the most desirable option for the Danes. The island is well placed to stage an invasion of the Northwest European mainland. Germany and the Holy Roman Empire are also worth considering, because the Germans' unpopularity with the Pope can allow the Danes to take vital North and Baltic Sea provinces and maybe push further south without fear of excommunication. But beware, because Papal politics are notoriously fickle. Factions fall in and out of favor regularly, so timing is vital.

The Russians, as Orthodox Christians, may offer a safer option for expansion (in terms of the religious repercussions, of course), but their lands are vast and so are their armies. If you decide to take on the Russians, build Inns as soon as you can to take advantage of the superior troop types who can be hired as mercenaries. Take advantage of all opportunities to increase any agricultural and mining income that is available, too.

The Polish hold some useful territory around the Baltic region, but any attack on them should be measured. They are pious people, and unless you can wipe them out within a few years, you will attract Papal displeasure.

THE EGYPTIANS

Syria is an immediate threat. As long as the Turks hold it, they can threaten Arabia, Tripoli, Palestine, and Antioch. Attack as soon as you feel strong enough, because this will give you some breathing room and reduce your border with foes from a four-province front to a two-province front. Strengthen your armies and then finish off the Turks, driving north through Edessa and Armenia in Rum. Do *not* ally with the Byzantines to do this! They will also be attacking the Turks and will assist you by invading when you do. Make sure you attack with more men than the Byzantines. If you do this, the Byzantines won't turn on you during the battle. Plus, they'll leave the province to you afterward.

Now take some time to strengthen your armies again. In your newly acquired regions of Rum and Armenia, train Armenian Heavy Cavalry, a most useful unit. Increase your farmland and trade income, and form a trade network using Sinai as your shipbuilding center. Maintain a garrison of one strong army in Egypt. This will discourage the Almohads from attacking you. They will concentrate on central Europe and will try only to match the strength of your Egyptian defense force. As an extra safety net, send an Emissary to forge an alliance with them.

When you are ready for war with Byzantium, send Spies to Constantinople, Greece, and Bulgaria. Generate revolts to distract them. Send plenty of Alims as well, to increase the Muslim populace in preparation for your assault.

Ch. 5

Begin by taking Lesser Armenia, using your armies in Antioch and Edessa. Then take Georgia, but make sure you leave enough men behind in Armenia to defend it. Keep building units and sending them up through Syria and into Armenia. Use these armies in Armenia to invade Trebizond, which is key to your invasion of the rest of Byzantium. A channel will be formed; your armies in Lesser Armenia and Rum can march immediately into Anatolia and then Nicaea without stopping. But leave behind one strong unit and some Spies in each conquered province to prevent rebellions by the predominantly Orthodox populations. Let your Alims slowly convert the people to your faith.

Join your army in Nicaea with your army in Trebizond. When Constantinople finally falls, the Byzantine empire will be broken beyond recovery. Finish off their remaining regions at your leisure, and expect some assistance from the Hungarians.

THE ENGLISH

The fellows at The Creative Assembly were divided on the proper strategy for their home country, offering us two very different approaches. This underscores the beauty of *Medieval: Total War*. The gameplay is so open-ended that it lends itself to multiple strategies. We'll present both competing English strategies and let you decide which one suits your tastes. Or try them both!

The "Home Islands First" Approach

The first order of business is to crush the Welsh and Scots. Start using these areas to produce their specialist troop types quickly. It's possible to take rebel-held Navarre (and its valuable weapon-bonus iron deposits) quickly through bribery. Ireland can wait, because any army sent there is out of action for four years while a port is being built. Establishing a fleet in the English Channel should also be a priority. Otherwise, an assault into Flanders and an early war with the French will be needed to link England and your English holdings in France. In the longer term, build the infrastructure needed to create Longbowmen and Billmen as quickly as possible, because these are among the most useful troops in the game.

In the High Period, try to secure the home islands as a matter of course, and make sure that your fleets control the English Channel. Otherwise, it's difficult (impossible?) to get troops from Wessex to the English territories in France. Try to take Wales early, and build, build, build in that province. A Bowyers' Guild is the aim (pardon the pun) in Wales, because this trains Longbowmen—some of the best killers in the game—and Welsh Longbowmen get +1 Valor. The same holds true for Mercia, but here the goal is to create a Spearmakers' Guild for Billmen with +1 Valor. Be nice to the French (marry into the family!), but only until the moment of attack.

In the Late Period, secure Scotland, because the Scots have a nasty tendency to invade Northumbria. The English can't afford to lose any provinces, because they don't have many! Recruit Longbowmen into your armies as fast as possible, and attack the French early and often (ransoms can meet some of the costs of war), particularly the French king. (Kill your prisoners if you capture him in battle.) The Pope may enter the political fray and threaten excommunication. But without fleets, the only way for Catholic enemies to invade England itself is through Wessex. As long as the English maintain a strong navy, excommunication is not a huge problem. When the last French heir is killed, France will dissolve and the door to European domination will be open.

The "France First" Approach

The rebel regions of Wales and Scotland give you plenty of room for expansion. But do *not* attack them just yet. Your immediate threat is the French. Their lands have been split by your presence in Normandy, Anjou, and Aquitaine, and they will invade at the first opportunity, seeking to forge their empire into one land. If you are fighting with the Welsh and Scottish rebels at the same time, you're forced to split your resources and you may not be able to adequately defend yourself.

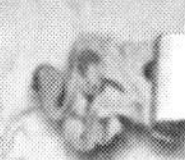

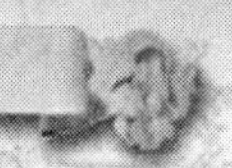

Build large armies in Wessex and Aquitaine. Send some of your men from Aquitaine up into Anjou and Normandy. Then build Inns and develop farmland in these two regions. Keep an eye out for mercenaries attracted by your Inns; you will need them to successfully defend against the French. Each time you are attacked, counterattack quickly.

Invade the other French regions one at a time, consolidating and rebuilding after each conquest. By all means, begin by taking Flanders! This will join your lands together and let you pass troops back and forth between them. From there, take Brittany, place a Peasant garrison in the province, and then send the Brittany invasion army back to Normandy. Pick up the defending army there and invade Ile de France.

Your war with the French may take some time. While it rages, remember to send some Spearmen units and Cavalry to Mercia and Northumbria. If you forget about these two homeland provinces, rebel armies may mount a surprise attack and take them from you. Sending an Emissary to bribe the rebels is a good way of dealing with them.

Keep a strong presence in Aquitaine. Once the Aragonese have finished conquering the Iberian peninsular, they will turn their attention to Central Europe—and you. Bribe the rebel army in Navarre. This will distract Aragon because there will be two of your provinces to attack instead of one. An alliance with the Aragonese can hold them at bay for a little longer, and when they break it, the King of Aragon will find his Influence reduced and his generals less loyal. When that happens, you can make your move south.

An invasion of the Iberian peninsula will prove difficult and costly, however. Take Toulose from the French and then form a line of armies across the Pyrenees to prevent invasion by Aragonese forces. Then sit tight for awhile. By waging war with two Catholic factions, you will upset the Pope. Take some time to build up your armies and increase your income. This will give the pontiff plenty of time to calm down and become friendly again. (Or you could just carry on your war, and eliminate the Pope with an assassin's blade if he excommunicates you.)

THE FRENCH

The French start on a knife's edge. As the Early Period begins, they find themselves divided by the English and in a very vulnerable position. When you're playing the French faction, the key to survival is to make sure you do *not* lose Ile de France.

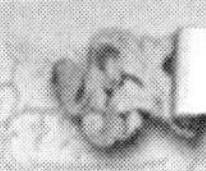

First, build some Inns and make good use of mercenaries to bolster your army. Build as many troops as you can in Ile de France, and send some to Flanders and Champagne. Train Peasants and recruit mercenaries in Toulose and Brittany. These troops are your only hope of holding those regions in the first 15 years.

The English will waste no time in attacking you. In fact, they will risk everything for victory. This exposes them to attack from the Aragonese, a suitable ally for you. Hang on for as long as you can. The English will weaken, and you can counterattack at the right moments to drive them from the continent.

Keep your eye on stray attacks from Germany. Their Emperor will be fighting the Italians, Danes, and Poles, but he'll still find time to take a pop at you. Defend yourself, but don't follow up with invasion to the east. Concentrate on defeating the English and making your borders secure.

Develop as much farmland as possible, and use Flanders as your trade center. Despite these measures, you will find that you'll soon develop cash flow problems. When this happens, invade England. Make sure your attack is swift, and end any sieges as soon as you can. The Pope won't like you attacking another Christian kingdom, so you must take as much land as you can before he asks you to cease your attack.

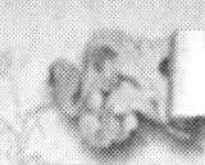
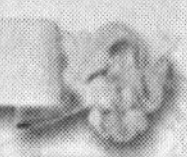
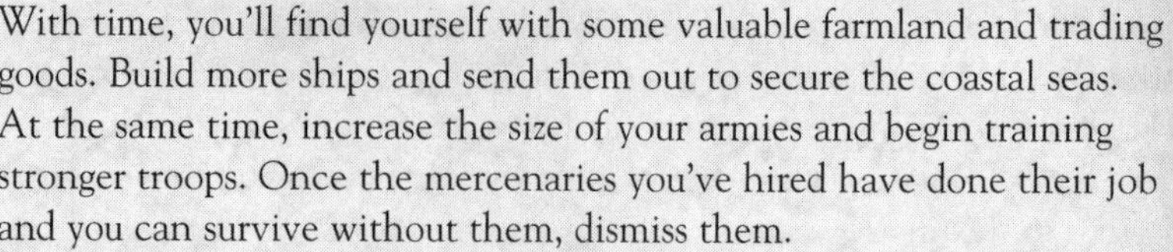

With time, you'll find yourself with some valuable farmland and trading goods. Build more ships and send them out to secure the coastal seas. At the same time, increase the size of your armies and begin training stronger troops. Once the mercenaries you've hired have done their job and you can survive without them, dismiss them.

From here, you should have secured a stable, well-defended corner of the map. This forms an excellent platform to launch attacks. Now you can start planning your attack on the Iberian peninsula.

THE GERMANS

Playing as the Germans is possibly the most difficult position in the Full Campaign scenarios. The game starts with the Holy Roman Empire in control of a large number of provinces in the center and north of the mainland. A number of emerging factions are trying to establish themselves in the same area, and they won't take kindly to being considered Imperial subjects. Expect to be attacked by the Italians, French, and Polish. Also expect to find it difficult to forge lasting alliances, especially with Catholic factions.

In reality, the Empire saw themselves as the successors to Rome and therefore viewed Italy and Southern Europe as theirs by right. Germanic emperors constantly fell in and out of favor with the Pope. Catholic factions tend to hang on the pontiff's every word (in order to stay in favor themselves!), so it's essential to make an alliance with the Papal faction and keep it solid in order to pacify the pious nations surrounding the German provinces. Due to geography, the Italians and Sicilians will probably encroach into Papal lands before the start of the High Period. So the opportunity is there for the German faction to offer alliance to the Pope, fight the common enemy, and thus gain favor.

Historically, the German Hansa controlled North Sea trade, so establishing ports, fleets, and trading posts/merchants in Friesland and Saxony is essential. You may consider expanding northward into Denmark to secure the trade routes in the region, and eastward into Pomerania, Silesia, Prussia, and Poland. Poland has relatively few provinces, so you might be able to wipe out the Poles before the Pope has even noticed.

By the Late Period, the Empire will have lost a sizeable chunk of their lands to France. Expanding east may be the only way to raise the funds needed to seize back Franconia, Lorraine, and Burgundy from the French. At all times, the short-term nature of alliances and the frequency of attacks against Germany will require a high concentration of forces along your borders. (Of course, this in itself will agitate your neighbours!) Build Border Forts to stop the movement of Spies, and put up Inns to hire the mercenaries you need to respond quickly to any threat.

Finally, always maintain a good level of loyalty among your generals by promoting them and marrying them to your Princesses. If generals have questionable loyalty, use Emissaries to strip them of titles, Spies to investigate them and bring charges of treason, and Inquisitors to keep up a healthy level of fear.

THE ITALIANS

To your north sits the Holy Roman Empire of Germany. It is huge but surrounded by enemies on all sides, so it has plenty of options for expansion. Make sure the Emperor does not choose you as a target! Build large armies in Venice, Milan, and Genoa.

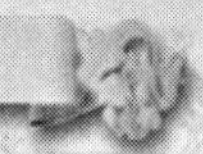

Build workshops in Venice for your armies, and then improve your farmland. Do the same in Milan. Use Spies to destabilize the regions around you and prevent other factions from attacking. Train plenty of foot troops and use your heirs to command the armies. Then turn Venice into your shipbuilding center, sailing out galley after galley to form a chain of ships to the western Mediterranean, via Malta. Trade will be a very important component of Italian success!

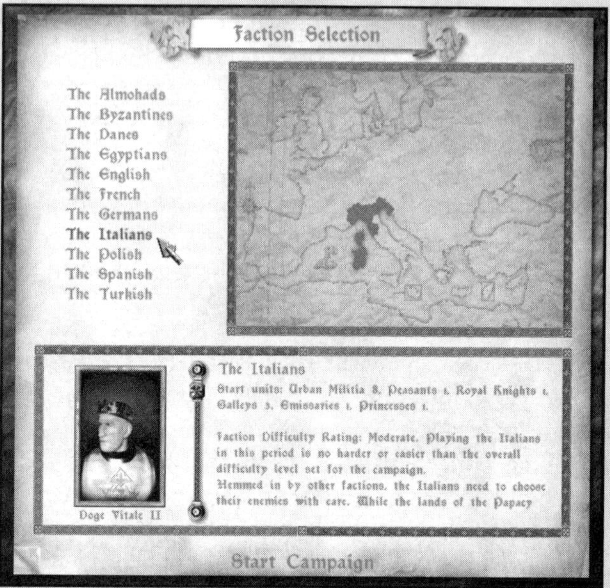

The first Cavalry you can train are the Mounted Sergeants, and it takes time to build the required buildings. For a long time, you can train only infantry in your provinces. To gain a mounted force, build an Inn in Genoa and recruit mercenary knights, preferably those of the Holy Orders.

Keep building your armies and improving your trade, and then send Crusades along your trade routes to the Holy Land. Once Palestine and Sinai are captured, build Inns and various workshops so that you have plenty of well-equipped troops to defend with.

Expansion to the north will be difficult. If the Germans attack you, or if they become weakened, seize the opportunity to gain some land. Otherwise, look south. Try to take some Almohad regions in Africa. Declare Crusades to the Iberian peninsula. They will pass through several Catholic factions along the way, so they should become strong by the time they reach the target.

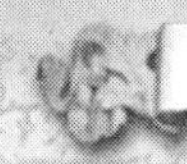

THE POLISH

Playing as the Polish is a game of constantly holding the enemy back from the gates. Throughout the three historical periods featured, the Poles manage to hold the same territory, despite being sandwiched between the fiercely expansionist Holy Roman Empire and the hungry Russians. Eventually, both of these factions, as well as the Hungarians, will want a piece of Polish territory. So it is vital to make alliances with *at least* two of these factions, and to bring the rebel provinces to the north and east under Polish control.

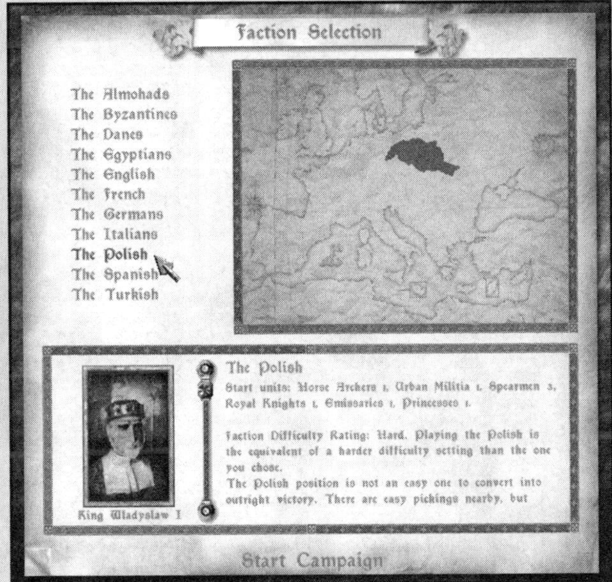

This may not be as straightforward as it sounds. At the beginning of the Early Period, Poland has only recently accepted Christianity, and the surrounding regions will be Pagan. Thus, building a Church and getting Bishops into the rebel provinces will greatly reduce the chances of rebellions in provinces you have bribed/conquered. We also recommend that you build Inns in all provinces as soon as possible, so mercenaries can be used to quell any uprisings that might occur.

Once the rebel provinces of Pomerania and Prussia are secure, it is important to build Ports and Trading Posts there to take advantage of sea trade with Russia, Denmark, and Germany. With trade in full bloom, it should be easy to build facilities to train the higher-quality troops needed to expand.

At the beginning of the High Period, the Russians are still organizing themselves into a faction. With the correct timing, a wily Polish leader can successfully expand east and crush the Russians before they become a threat.

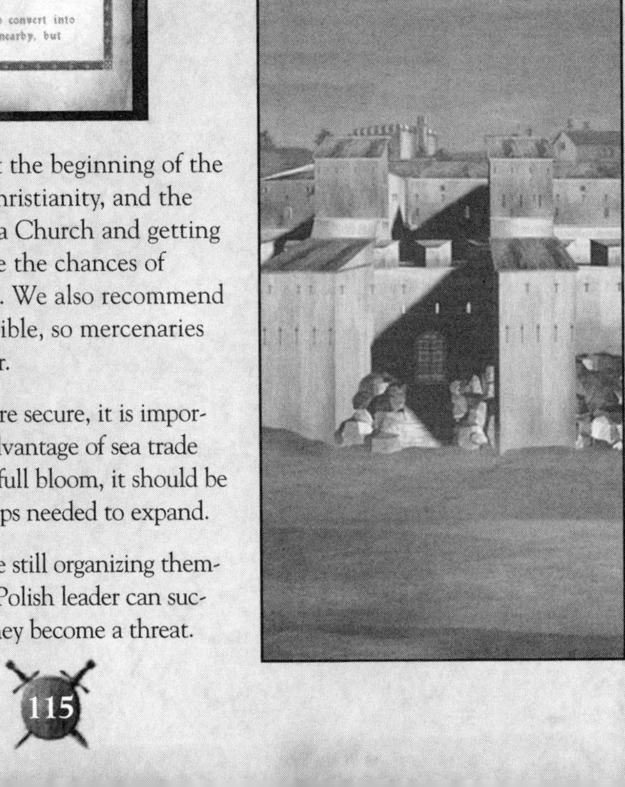

THE RUSSIANS

At the start of the High Period, the Russians are only just moving from being a mere conglomeration of steppe warrior tribes into a recognizable country. Only the provinces of Muscovy and Novgorod in the north and Pereyaslavl and Kiev in the south are established, so your first move must be to unite the various rebel provinces under your banner. You can bribe some, but others require an invasion. Of these provinces, Lithuania and Livonia have castles and a range of troop types that can resist your assault, so make sure your army has a good mix of cavalry, infantry, and missile troops. Be careful not to spread your forces too thinly across the conquered provinces, because rebellions are very likely at this early stage.

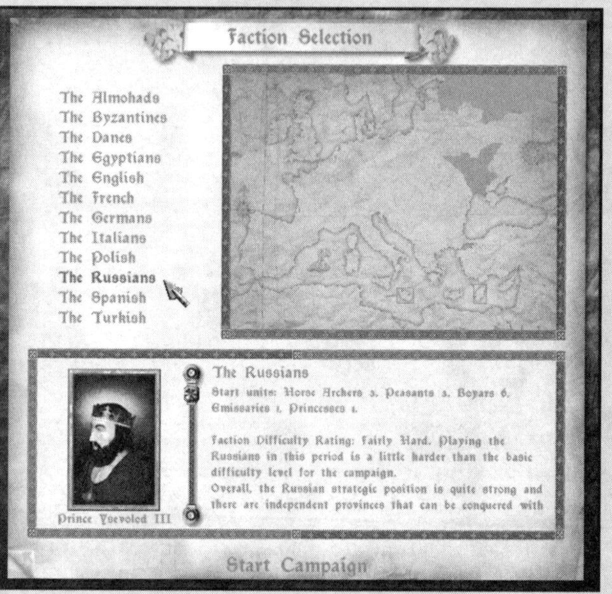

Some of the steppe regions are low on resources and potential income, so it is advisable to form some alliances and begin trading as soon as possible before your money runs out. Byzantium and Hungary could be important allies, and the Black Sea region, bordered by Kiev, has massive trade potential. The same is true of the Baltic Sea region, so an alliance with the Danes and the development of ship-building capability are essential.

After securing these lands, you can look at further growth. The Polish are a natural choice—they hold only a few provinces and will ally with you almost straight away to avoid becoming targets of Russian expansion for as long as possible.

Once your Russian army is at full strength, crushing the Polish should be a question of just two or three years of campaigning. There is no call for religious retaliation from the Papacy, of course, because Russia is Orthodox Christian. The other great Orthodox power, the Byzantine empire, has no interest in your affairs at this time and will most likely support you as the only other Orthodox faction. Plus, the Byzantines will have problems of their own before the middle of the 13th century as the Turks move westward.

Pushing further westward into the Holy Roman Empire is an option as well. Just remember that fortifying eastern Russian territories—particularly Kiev, Ryazan, Volga-Bulgaria, and Pereyaslavl—before 1240 is absolutely essential. In that year, the Mongol Golden Horde will arrive at the steppes, and you will need considerable defenses and siege weaponry to defend against their unholy onslaught.

THE SPANISH

The Spanish have simple goals: To drive the Almohads out of Spain as quickly as possible, and to pursue them into North Africa if necessary. All other considerations are secondary. An early alliance with the Aragonese can be important, and the army in Valencia is well worth bribing because it is led by the legendary general El Cid. If the Spanish don't secure El Cid's services, someone else will! The Spanish have the potential to train some dangerous troops, if only because of the iron ore in many Iberian provinces. These soldiers, and Crusades, can lead to many Spanish conquests.

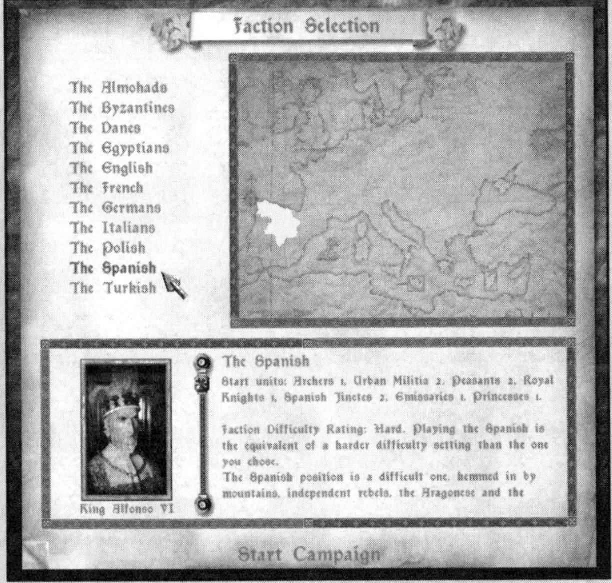

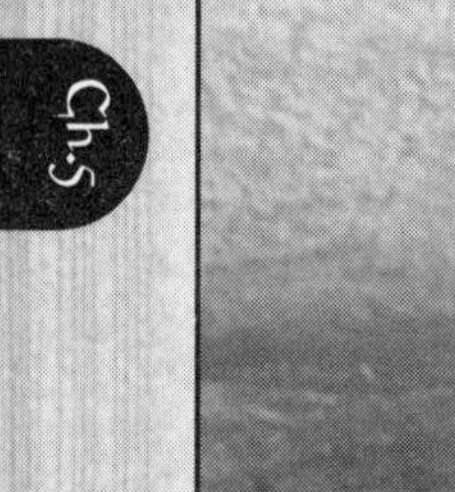

In the High Period, the Almohads are the first target, as always. Crusades launched against Almohad possessions can be surprisingly effective, and they give the Spanish access to Knights of Santiago units. These are powerful heavy cavalry, something the Spanish lack at this time. For the moment, an alliance with the Aragonese is useful. But sooner or later it will have to be broken, as will any deal with the English or French to the north. Getting a province on the other side of the natural defensive line of the Pyrenees is a necessary step to European (as opposed to North African) greatness.

By the Late Period, the first item on the Spanish agenda is still the destruction of the Almohads, but now Catholic opponents must be confronted as well. To achieve victory over Catholic enemies, the Spanish are blessed with Inquisitors. These "religious character assassins" should be used to weaken enemies by selectively removing as many generals as possible before any attack starts. Burning a general or two isn't an act of war, after all, no matter how much it damages a foe! So, kill off the Almohads, and then deal with the Aragonese. After that, the Mediterranean or southern France can be Spanish.

THE TURKISH

The Turks have a simple first choice—attack either the Byzantines or the Egyptians. Access to the steppes is limited by the need to conquer (Byzantine) Georgia, and there are no nearby rebel provinces for instant and easy conquest. Whichever enemy is chosen, keep the peace with the other bordering faction! A two-front war will be difficult to survive, let alone win.

That said, the Egyptians to the south own some very rich land, with gems and spices that can create a large amount of trade income. On the other hand, every province taken from the Byzantine Empire to the west is a double bonus, because most have special troops you can train. Seizing these provinces also means you've weakened the Byzantine armies by depriving them of specialist troops. But be aware that the Byzantines have many high-ranking generals and strong armies. A war with them will be long, costly, and difficult.

The key region to take if you are to defeat Byzantium is Trebizond. But before you can take it, you must capture Lesser Armenia and Georgia. If you are allied with the Egyptians, they will help with Lesser Armenia, but you will have to take Georgia on your own. Take too long and the Byzantines will move their forces north into Khazar. This makes it difficult to take Trebizond, and it means the Byzantines have a strong counterattack when their northern army turns around to attack you.

Capture Trebizond, sweep through Anatolia and Nicea, and then move on to Constantinople. You may find the Hungarians will attack the Byzantines as well. This joint offensive will drive them from the mainland and leave them confined to the islands of Crete, Cyprus, and Rhodes. Once this is done, push on north into the Novgorod lands. Their regions surrounding the Black Sea have many tradable goods. Increase your trade network. Enhanced by the addition of the great port at Constantinople, it will fund your march through Europe.

Now get ready for the coming storm. The Mongols! The Mongols! As the High Period begins, the Turks are likely to be in the front line against the "numberless hordes" from the steppe, and any strategy you choose needs to take this into account. The Byzantine Empire makes a very tempting target, however. It is at its most vulnerable before it has chance to retake Constantinople, so the temptation to crush the Empire may be worth indulging to the full! Grab as many rebellious provinces as possible, as *early* as possible. Destroy the Byzantines, and then turn south and plan to weather the great Mongol migration. The Turks, if they can prosper, have some excellent exclusive military units and can do very well at this time.

In terms of military potential, the Late Period may be the best of the Turkish starting positions. Turkish exclusive units are late arrivals in the game, and there are nearby rebel provinces that can be quickly overrun. There are also several wealthy provinces nearby to finance it all (Palestine, for example). Decide quickly whether your main early effort will be to conquer the Byzantines or to take the Middle East. The Byzantine Empire can only get relatively weaker over time, unless it has enough time to gather a war chest to pay for mercenaries. Georgia also needs to be secured at some point to delay invasion from the north.

Chapter 6: Historical Campaigns

Henry V at Agincourt. Jeanne d'Arc at Orleans. Richard the Lionhearted versus Saladin at Arsuff in 1191. What could be cooler than recreating such historic confrontations and matching wits with some of the greatest military minds in history? *Medieval: Total War* gives you that unprecedented opportunity in its series of Historical Campaigns.

These campaigns differ from the Full Campaign because there is no turn-based component. Each Historical Campaign reenacts a famous sequence of battles. Once you win the first battle, you jump immediately to the second without a strategy map interlude. The action is fast, furious, and best of all, historically accurate.

Once again, this chapter relies almost entirely on the guidance of the design team at The Creative Assembly. For the Hundred Years' War, the creators of this campaign series have given you a detailed, step—by-step tactical walkthrough of every battle from both sides, French and English.

For the Golden Horde, Barbarossa, Richard, and Saladin campaigns, the designers cut right to the chase. Here, the experts give you a set of Quick Tips that form a kind of "pocket guide" for each campaign, laying out the simple strategic directives you need to win each battle in the campaign series.

THE HUNDRED YEARS' WAR: A TACTICAL WALKTHROUGH

The Hundred Years' War was fought by England and France from 1337 to 1457, although warfare was by no means continuous during this period. English kings felt that they had good claims to much of France, and even to the French throne. Most of the fighting took place on French soil, but there were occasional attacks on English coastal towns by French raiders. When there was fighting, it was bloody and often merciless. The French nobility regarded war as their vocation, and they were horrified to be confronted and beaten by "lesser"—but more professional—English soldiers.

The walkthroughs for both sides of this conflict, English and French, are detailed and specific about the battlefield tactics. Play through these campaigns under the design team's guidance. Think of it as a kind of advanced tutorial for tactical combat.

Fighting as the English

The three battles in this campaign show the differences in war-making between the English and the French. By 1420 the English, under their finest warrior-king, Henry V, had very nearly achieved their goals. But even victories at Crécy, Poitiers, and Agincourt would not be quite enough.

As an historical aside, the English owe their traditional two-fingered gesture of contempt to the Hundred Years' War. The French threatened to cut off the first two fingers of any longbowman they captured, thus crippling the man as a warrior. Waving two fingers at the French thus became a way of defying them and daring them to come and make good their threats of mutilation!

Crecy 1346

Crécy was the opening battle of Edward the Black Prince's assault on Normandy, one of the early campaigns of the Hundred Years' War. The French had been careful to avoid battle with the tactically superior English, but at Crécy they had the advantage of numbers and, apparently, better morale. Edward chose a defensive position for his army and waited for the French attack.

After exchanges between the English longbowmen and the French crossbows, the French knights lost patience and charged forward—they even managed to trample their own crossbowmen! With this lack of discipline, the French were cut down in droves and French knighthood lost its bravest and best.

Battle Objectives

- Edward, the Black Prince, must survive the battle.
- Ensure that your army does not run from the battlefield.
- King Phillip of France cannot be allowed victory. Defeat his army.

Walkthrough

A quick survey of the battlefield at the start reveals two units that have become isolated, far off past the windmill on the English right flank. One unit consists of 20 Feudal Knights, the personal unit of your commander Edward the Black Prince. The other is a unit of 30 Spearmen. The moment the battle begins, Edward will be pursued by 120 French Feudal Knights, 60 Feudal Men-at-Arms, and a unit of Crossbowmen to boot!

You have to make sure that Edward survives the battle, so the first thing to do is to click on his unit icon (the one with a star) on the bottom-right corner of the screen to select it, and then double-click on the hill near the rest of your army. This gets Edward's unit galloping away from danger. Next, double-click on the unit icon for your 30 isolated Spearmen, near the middle of the unit lineup at the bottom of the screen. The camera view quickly pans to that unit.

You see Edward and his knights running away, with the enemy cavalry in pursuit. Click and drag your Spearmen in a 3-deep formation, right across the front of the charging enemy knights. The Spearmen deploy to intercept the units that are chasing Edward. These brave men will make the ultimate sacrifice to allow Edward to escape.

Rush your commander, Prince Edward, away from his pursuers, and then block their pursuit with the nearby Spearmen.

Now it's time to organize your units back at the top of the hill to make sure they're ready for King Phillip's charge. Use your Spearmen in the front. Drag them out into 3-deep lines across the hillside to provide a barrier against the enemy charge. You can also use your other foot units in this manner, but your Spearmen will be the most effective against Phillip's cavalry. We recommend you spread your Men-at-Arms behind the Spearmen for quick support. Then place your deadly Longbowmen along the top of the hill behind these men, and order them to pepper the charging enemy with arrows.

While you're doing this, don't forget those enemy units who were attacking Edward. By now they've destroyed the Spearmen you sent to fend them off, and they'll be endangering your right flank. If they manage to flank you, they could cause a lot of damage. Move Edward's knight unit further up the hill to make sure that he's safe. Then set up a defense in front of him, similar to the one used against the main French force—Spearmen in front, Feudal Men-at-Arms behind.

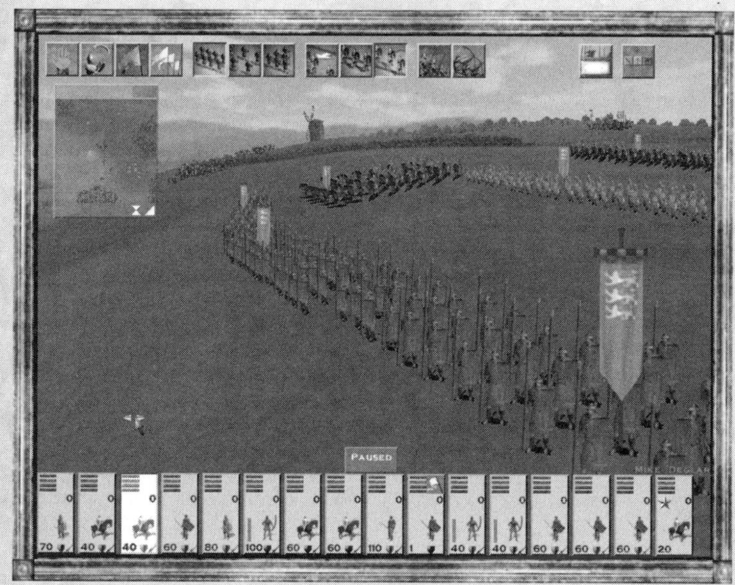

Remember to put your Spearmen in the front rank whenever your army takes up a defensive posture.

You should now be in a very strong position to defend against the French assault. You have the high ground, and you have several units of mounted Feudal Knights to rush into any gaps or breakthroughs. Once the attack is halted and the French have retreated, send the knights galloping to attack the enemy. Remember that a charge into the flank or rear provides that extra level of shock to infantry units.

Poitiers 1356

Ten years after his victory at Crécy, Edward the Black Prince was still campaigning in France. In 1356, an army under King Jean Le Bon of France caught up with an English raiding force near Bordeaux. Once again, the English proved themselves to be masters of selecting ground for a fight that suited them, not the French. The English longbows wreaked terrible damage, and the French *battles* (or divisions) did not attack together.

Surprised by an English counterattack, the French broke and fled, but their king was captured. Legend has it that after the battle, the chivalrous Edward served dinner to his chief captive, King Jean, before sending him back to the Tower of London to await ransom.

Battle Objectives

- The Black Prince's survival is paramount. Protect him at all costs.
- Though outnumbered, your forces must stand firm. Rally any that flee!
- Victory can only be achieved by defeating the army of King Jean. The key to this battle is survival until the reinforcements arrive. You are heavily outnumbered, so keep your general alive until help is at hand.

Walkthrough

Your army starts out arrayed across several farm fields on low ground. First, select all of your troops by pressing Ctrl+A, and move them to the top of the hill behind them (with a double-click, so they run). You definitely want to have a good defensive position for this fight.

The key to success at Poitiers is to hustle your army up the hill behind them and set up a defensive line facing downhill.

Once your troops start jogging up the hill, you can look at what the French are doing and try to set up your defenses accordingly. You need to create a strong defense line. As in the previous battle, array your Spearmen across the front with your Feudal Men-at-Arms and Peasants providing backup. Position your archers behind them to fire at the enemy. If you establish a strong defensive line, the enemy will hesitate before attacking—therefore allowing time for your considerable reinforcements to arrive.

The French now begin their rush up the hill. Make sure you know where your general is! Keep him safe and away from threat. Also make sure that your Longbowmen are back far enough that they do not rout too early. The French may try to outflank you around the left side of the hill. Simply shift troops from right to left, avoiding gaps in the line and backing up your front-line soldiers.

Now just hold on until the reinforcements arrive. When they do, you should have superior numbers. Immediately charge directly downhill into the French, who will be tired from trying to fight uphill. Watch them flee…

Agincourt 1415

Agincourt is perhaps the most famous English victory in the Hundred Years' War. Following a siege at Harfleur, Henry V led his small, tired army on a march towards Calais and safety. He was trapped by a larger French army—some say five times as many men—and most of the English expected to die.

The French nobility proved to be their own worst enemies. They charged forward in search of glory and easy victory, and met only death as they were shot down by English longbowmen. With Agincourt, Henry V began a campaign that almost put him on the French throne, but his triumphs were squandered by his successors.

Battle Objectives

- Protect King Henry. The battle is lost if he is killed.
- Make sure your army isn't routed or slaughtered.
- Break the French army. Kill them or force them to rout.

Walkthrough

In this battle, you must provide a platform that gives your Longbowmen time to weaken the enemy.

Place your Spearmen in a line in front, and then array your Feudal Men-At-Arms behind them in a parallel line. At either end of your lines of Spearmen, deploy your Billmen back at an angle towards the English side so the formation is semihexagonal. Line up your archers behind your infantry and wait for the enemy to come.

Immediately deploy your Spearmen and Billmen in a half-hexagon to protect your flanks.

As soon as the French march into range, fire your arrows at the enemy cavalry units. Do not waste time going for the foot soldiers. The cavalry are more of a threat. In the meantime, place your own Feudal Knights behind your Archers to make the line stronger and the enemy less likely to attack. Careful! The enemy may attempt to flank you, so be ready to counter this threat with your Feudal Knights and more Archers.

Once you have beaten back the initial French assault, counterattack with your Billmen and Spearmen. In order to get the French to rout, use your cavalry, but make sure you do not get your general killed!

Fighting as the French

With the death of Henry V of England in 1422, the French were spared the humiliation of an English king on their throne. King Charles of France, although irredeemably mad, did his country one last service just by outliving Henry, and the French crown never passed to an English monarch.

The English, for their part, were too busy with political infighting for control of young King Henry VI to wage another effective campaign. But the tide of war had yet to turn in favor of the French. That is, until the appearance of a charismatic young woman named Jeanne d'Arc, who was to lead the French armies to new victories and drive out the hated English.

This was to be the endgame of the Hundred Years' War, and the time that defined France as a unified nation. The three battles presented here reflect this period of French resurgence.

Orleans 1429

Once Jeanne d'Arc had convinced King Charles of France and his religious advisors that she wasn't mad or a heretic, it became clear that not only was she an inspirational leader, but she also had the practical military skills of a general many years her senior. With Orléans surrounded by an English army, the French needed a victory to lift the protracted siege, and with Jeanne as their living banner, they had a good chance of success.

Battle Objectives

- If your army falls to the English, this battle is lost.
- Destroy all 4 of the English ballistae to claim victory.

Walkthrough

This battle is about *speed of attack*. To break the siege, you must destroy all four of the enemy ballistae before the English reinforcements arrive.

First, select all of your troops using Ctrl+A and double-click to get them out of the castle. As your army pours out of the gates, you can click on them and reassign them as you see fit. The best-guarded English ballista is on the left side of the castle, so order your cavalry troops over there. However, do *not* attack straight away. Your horsemen need more support.

Get to the two ballistae in front of the castle as soon as you can, or your access will be cut off by late-arriving English reinforcements.

Meanwhile, select the next unit out of the gate to take on the English cavalry attacking from the right. It's important to attack them *immediately* so that they don't block your gate and make it difficult for you to get more troops out. If you keep the cavalry busy with one unit, this frees up another unit to attack the ballista. This same tactic—one unit ties up the English cavalry, another hits the ballista—should be used on the other siege machines.

Do not get too distracted by the ballistae at the castle's sides, however. You need to rush the two ballistae sitting straight ahead quickly, because this is where the English reinforcements will arrive. If you wait too long, the oncoming troops cut off your path and you can't reach the siege weapons.

Your ultimate target is the Keep inside the castle walls.

Once you have destroyed both of the forward ballistae, send your troops to attack the ballista on the left. The key here is to draw the enemy troops down below the ballista and then swing a unit of cavalry up behind them to destroy the machine.

Loire Valley 1429

Even with Orléans saved from its English attackers, there were more problems for the French. The Loire Valley was still crawling with English troops. The English had replaced their old strategy of raiding and despoiling the countryside with a new strategy of occupation and siege. Unless this valley could be cleared of English soldiers, the victory at Orléans would be a hollow one. If the English could be driven out, the French would have a new freedom of action. Jeanne led her troops into the attack.

Battle Objectives

- Stand fast and strong in the face of the enemy! If you die or run, this day is theirs.
- Get at least 100 men within the castle walls to claim victory.

Walkthrough

First, click on each of your five Demi-Cannons and aim at the walls. (They're arrayed around the fort, so the easiest way to find them is to double-click on their unit icons and let the camera pan to them.) The object here is to create as many different entry points into the castle as you can. This lets you attack from all angles, which then divides the enemy response.

As soon as you open the bombardment, check the mini-map. You'll notice 5 small units of English defenders emerging from the trees onto the field behind your Demi-Cannons. These troops did not make it inside the castle before you laid siege to it. You need to eliminate them so that they do not aid those who are in the castle. Hunt them down! You have them greatly outnumbered, but watch out for the Longbowmen.

Once the outer walls have been breached, aim your Demi-Cannons at the inner walls of the Keep. Getting your men inside that is your ultimate target. During the bombardment, keep your troops a safe distance away to avoid getting caught in crossfire from the Arrow Towers.

Once you've breached the Keep walls, make your assault on the castle. Use a combination of tactics here to penetrate the Keep. First, try to draw the enemy out of the castle using your Halbardiers and other spear troops. Then use your faster cavalry units to charge in and take the Keep.

Patay 1429

As the French continued to attack in the Loire Valley, the English garrison of Beaugency suspected that they had been abandoned. They left the town and moved off, without expecting the French to be so close or to pursue them. Even so, they took the usual precautions for a march through hostile territory. The French pursued closely but carefully, determined that this time an English army would not get the chance to choose defensive ground of their own liking, and that their own forces would not enter the fight in a piecemeal fashion to be shot down by longbowmen. The whole French force succeeded in catching the English before they could set a defensive position, and battle was joined.

Battle Objectives

- Protect Jeanne d'Arc's life. If she falls, who knows what the English will do to her?
- If your armies fall, the English have won. You cannot let this happen.
- You must repel the English intruders. Rout them or kill them, but defeat them you must.

Walkthrough

This is the final battle of the campaign. Your French army has been marching hard in their attempt to take the English by surprise, so your men are strung out vertically and not in the best starting position. Thus, it is important that you organize your troops properly at the start of the battle. Remember: You can pause the action while you do this.

The English will withdraw and take up positions on the hill rising up just behind them. Bring your Spearmen to the front and line them up 3-deep to create a defense against the enemy cavalry. Meanwhile, take two units of your Chivalric Knights (not your general's unit!) and deploy them to the right and left of the English position so that they can flank it if they choose to attack.

Then move your men toward the enemy. Try to tempt the English to attack you by sending your Chivalric Knights in for a charge at their frontline units. As the English cavalry rides down the hill to counterattack, order your Knights to retreat behind your Spearmen. Gallop off at an angle to prepare for a flank attack. Use your Crossbowmen and Chivalric Men-at-Arms to provide support.

Draw the impetuous English knights down the hill onto level ground.

Hold your cavalry back until your Spearmen are in the thick of the battle, and let your Crossbowmen exact a toll from the English knights for a few moments. Then charge your own Knights back into the fray, hitting the English hard in the flank. Watch the tide turn fiercely!

THE GOLDEN HORDE CAMPAIGN

"The horde of the Tartars is numberless. When one is killed, another ten spring from the hell whence he came. Each of them has the head of a dog, and carries with him sufficient weapons for three or four warriors."

So wrote Benedict the Pole, and he had every reason to be fearful, even if he had confused Tartars and Mongols. The Golden Horde were more terrible than anything he could have wished to see: cruel, uncompromising, and the most efficient military force since the Caesars. They erased cities, slaughtered thousands, and enslaved any survivors. That they turned aside from reaching farther into Europe is one of the quirks of history, and is due to one death.

Their Khan, Ogadai, drank himself to death, and a replacement had to be selected from among the Golden Family by the Horde. If Ogadai had not died, who knows where the Horde would have stopped. They could easily have camped in the ruins of Paris, Rome, or Cadiz. The battles in this campaign show how efficient their military machine could be with the right leadership.

Kalka River 1223

In 1221, having conquered a large portion of Asia, Genghis Khan turned his attention to Eastern Europe. He ordered Jebei Noyon and Subadai Bahadur to lead a reconnaissance into Russia, a move that would bring dire consequences for medieval Europe.

The Mongols had a major decisive victory at the Kalka River in 1223 against a fragile alliance of Russian princes, where they used their infamous "feigned retreat" for the first time on European soil. Drawing the disorganized army across the river, the Mongols surrounded the Russians on the opposite bank and then pursued them as they fled from the battlefield.

After the battle, the Mongols marched eastward to rejoin Genghis Khan. They were not to return to Europe until 1237, ten years after the Great Khan's death, when his son Ogadai ordered the Golden Horde to return and continue the conquest.

Battle Objectives

- Do not let your men's resolve fail them or allow them to fall in great numbers.
- Crush the Russian army under your boot, or send them weeping back to the soft arms of their women.

Quick Tips

Feign retreat across the three bridges, drawing the enemy across by using your Horse Archers as bait before sending in your powerful heavy cavalry and foot warriors. Important: Keep the bridges covered by arrow fire as much as possible.

Try the infamous Mongol "feigned retreat" by pulling your Horse Archers back over the bridges and then pinning the Russians down with arrows as they try to cross.

Kiev 1240

When the Golden Horde returned to Europe in 1236, they began by crushing the Kipchaks and Bulgars of the Steppes, before reaching Russia in late 1237. After decisive victories in Riazan, Vladimir, and Moscow during the following year, they stopped short of Novgorod and waited throughout 1239, resting in the Don basin before recommencing their onslaught at Kiev in 1240. The inhabitants of Kiev showed their defiance by executing the Mongol emissaries sent to demand their surrender.

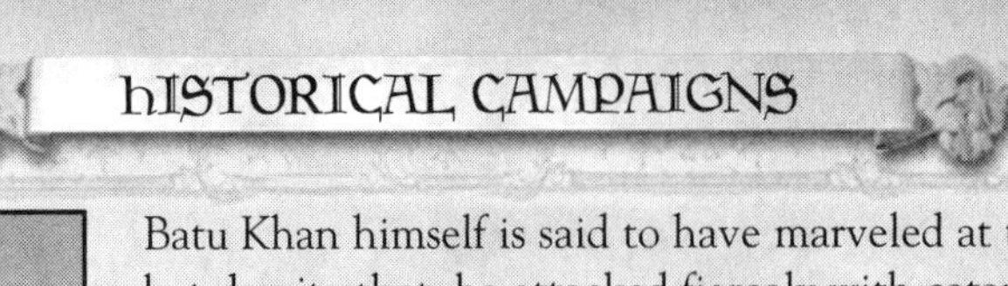

Batu Khan himself is said to have marveled at the great city's beauty, but despite that, he attacked fiercely with catapults, arrows, and naptha. When Kiev fell in December 1240, there was much slaughter. People were impaled and some had wood splinters driven under their fingernails, while priests were roasted alive and nuns were ravished upon the church altars.

Battle Objectives

- Protect the catapults. If even one is destroyed, you will know defeat this day.
- If the Horde is routed or killed, the enemy will claim victory. Do not allow this to happen.
- Take the Russian general's head.
- Get at least 100 of the Horde inside the castle walls.

Quick Tips

Protect your Catapults with your Naptha Throwers and infantry while you pound the walls of the castle with the artillery. While this is going on, use heavy cavalry to rout the Russian knights. Once the castle walls are breached, order your heavy cavalry and foot warriors to assault the troops inside. Remember: You must crush the Royal Knights and kill their general.

LIEGNITZ 1241

After destroying Kiev in December 1240, the Golden Horde turned its attention to Hungary, which offered a solid base for future attacks on Western Europe. The court of King Bela IV had also provided sanctuary for Russian princes fleeing the fall of Kiev. Whereas the main thrust of the attack was the Hungarian plains, the Mongols also invaded Poland to fully outflank the enemy.

After the Horde had captured Cracow and Sandomir, the Silesian King Henry the Pious met them at Liegnitz in the spring of 1241 with a combined force, including Teutonic Knights, led by their Grand Master. The Mongols managed to confuse and divide the Polish and German army before surrounding and beheading Henry.

Battle Objectives

- Kill both the Polish King *and* the Teutonic Grand Master. If either one flees the battlefield, his cowardice actually wins the day for your enemies.
- Kill or rout at least half of the combined opposing forces.
- Ensure that the Horde stands firm and does not suffer overwhelming death.

Quick Tips

Use Horse Archers and heavy cavalry to wear down the German troops (Teutonic Knights and Teutonic Sergeants) up front, while your Warriors wait in the woods. When the Polish move forward down the road, fall on them in ambush from the trees. Retain a unit of heavy cavalry to block the rear of the field, and capture the Polish and German leaders if they attempt to escape. If either leader manages to escape, you will lose.

Mohi 1241

When Batu Khan and Subadai Bahadur reached Hungary in the spring of 1241, they faced a large force of Hungarians supported by the Knights Templar. Feigning retreat for 9 miles after reaching the city of Pest, the Mongols drew their enemies to the banks of a river near the village of Mohi, where they set up camp on high ground overlooking the bridge. Concealing their own camp, the Mongols watched as the Hungarians pitched their tents on the opposite bank, unaware that only a thin stretch of water separated them from the Golden Horde!

As Batu led an attack on the bridge and the Templars guarding it, Subadai forded the river upstream, outflanked and routed the Hungarians. What followed was terrible carnage as the Mongols hunted down the fleeing troops all the way to Pest, which they razed to the ground. The Horde then marched on towards Vienna, only turning back when the death of Ogadai Khan required them to return to the East to choose his successor.

Battle Objectives

- Kill or rout the Hungarian army.
- Defeat the Templar forces—rout them or kill them.
- Prevent the Horde from routing or dying in too great a number.

Quick Tips

Engage the Templars by attacking their camp with heavy cavalry, infantry, and the catapult. Meanwhile, send the remaining cavalry and Horse Archers to the second river crossing and outflank the Hungarian forces until a rout occurs.

THE BARBAROSSA CAMPAIGN

Frederick Barbarossa was the King of Germany and Holy Roman Emperor for nearly 40 years. Like all Emperors, he dreamed of bringing the Empire back to its former greatness, which meant bringing both Italy and the Papacy back into the Imperial fold. These two strategic aims would take Barbarossa into Italy at the head of his armies, and would lead to his excommunication by Pope Alexander III in 1160. In return, Frederick simply chose to regard another churchman as the "real Pope" and ignored Alexander!

Barbarossa also launched many attacks into Northern Italy, but eventually he was forced to realize that he couldn't retake the Italian parts of the Holy Roman Empire by force. Some of those battles make up the campaign here. In 1177, he and Pope Alexander came to an agreement and his excommunication was cancelled. Frederick Babarossa drowned while leading his crusading army across the River Saleph (in what is now Turkey), but during the later Middle Ages he was believed to be sleeping beneath the Imperial castle of Kyffhauser, waiting to rescue his people from dire peril!

MILAN BORDER FORT 1158

This engagement is typical of many battles fought during Frederick Barbarossa's advance into northern Italy. The cities of Italy were rich, by European standards, and could afford better defenses than just city walls. They could also finance the construction of outlying forts and fortified villages, which would either delay an attacker with yet another siege or allow the defenders to sally forth and harass an attacker's supply lines.

To forestall such attacks, a prudent commander—and Barbarossa was—would make sure the outlying defenses were destroyed before moving on to his main objective. In this case, the small town had to be taken and held.

Battle Objectives

- If Barbarossa dies or flees, this day will be lost.
- Defeat is your only reward if you fail to capture the fort before 21 minutes pass.
- You need to get at least 10 men inside the fort and hold it for 1 minute.

Quick Tips

Quickly knock down the enemy walls. You must achieve at least two breaches, keeping your troops out of reach of the enemy towers. Then overcome the defense and attack the second gate with your infantry.

Carcano 1160

Carcano was the site of an epic battle between the Holy Roman Emperor Frederick and the joint forces of Milan and its near neighbors. According to some accounts of the battle, Barbarossa was forced to withdraw behind the walls of Baradello when his forces were attacked in the flank by cavalry from Milan. The Milanese victors subsequently destroyed the castle of Carcano. You must do better than Barbarossa and win the battle.

Battle Objectives

- Barbarossa must remain on the battlefield and must not fall.
- If over 60 percent of your troops rout or die, the battle is lost.
- You must defeat both Milanese armies to win.

Quick Tips

Move the cavalry positioned on your left flank to the right, where they can stand ground together. (Press the Hold Position button.) Attack the Papal general to make his forces rout. When his army is on the run, swing your right flank by 90 degrees and face the onslaught of the charging Italian army.

If you can't keep within the maximum limit for casualties, try to pull your whole force back and gather them on a hill. This should give you sufficient advantage to press home the final attack.

The Milan Road 1161

Frederick Barbarossa's campaign in Italy was to reestablish the authority—indeed, the very concept—of the Holy Roman Empire. The Italians, having been independent for so long, were reluctant to yield to any external authority, especially one that wasn't even Italian!

Therefore, Barbarossa's campaign strategy in Italy was everything that could be expected from a medieval warlord. It was thorough, brutal, and effective. Barbarossa correctly guessed that the inhabitants of Milan would be more amenable to his demands if they were starving when he besieged them, so he cut off their supplies.

Battle Objectives

- Ensure that Barbarossa remains alive and on the field until the end.
- You have only 8 minutes to achieve victory.
- Take at least 10 men into the marked town and hold it for 3 minutes.

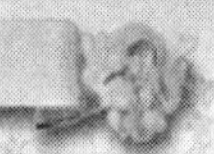

Quick Tips

Charge with one cavalry unit straight through the gaps in the enemy line to the small village ahead of you. Keep the other forces busy with the rest of your army, and you should have sufficient time to occupy the marked zone.

Get at least 10 men into the marked zone for 3 minutes.

San Romano 1161

Under siege by the Imperial Army led by Frederick Barbarossa, the citizens of Milan became desperate enough to try any stratagem that would break the siege. With help unlikely to reach them from beyond the besieging army, their best option was to sally forth and attack. A wise commander such as Barbarossa could still be caught off balance by such a sally, but would soon organize a temporary defense to counter it. If the Milanese could reach and destroy the Imperial baggage train, the besiegers would have to lift the siege. If they could destroy some of Barbarossa's siege engines and artillery as well, this too would benefit them.

Battle Objectives

- Do not let the enemy claim victory by defeating your army.
- Barbarossa must oversee his troops. Keep him alive and on the field.
- Hold out against the invaders for 20 minutes and they will abandon their assault.

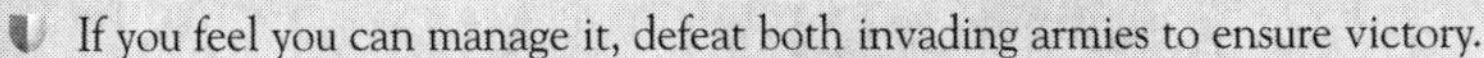

- If you feel you can manage it, defeat both invading armies to ensure victory.
- Do not abandon your baggage train! Maintain a guard of at least 40 men inside your picket. The Milanese will capture your train if they get just 1 man inside the picket.

Quick Tips

Position your army on top of the hill where the supply train is stationed, and prepare to defend both flanks. The Milanese will approach your forces in a piecemeal fashion, so you can send down troops to take out the most dangerous units. When a mass rout sets in, send in your cavalry forces to keep them on the run.

Legnano 1176

Over a period of 16 years, Frederick Barbarossa continued to campaign in Italy. At Legnano, he ran into an enemy that was ready and waiting and, on that day, better organized and led. Barbarossa's army was defeated at Legnano by a combined force including troops from Lombardy, Milan, and the Papal armies. His enemies even managed to kill his standard-bearer and force Barbarossa to escape after abandoning his horse. This defeat compelled him to abandon his dreams of Imperial glory and make his peace with Pope Alexander III, finally being forgiven and accepted back into the church in 1177. You have a chance to reverse this disastrous result for the Holy Roman Emperor.

Battle Objectives

- Increase your chance of victory by keeping your troops alive and steady.
- Keep Barbarossa alive and on the field until victory is achieved.
- End the battle quickly by killing the Papal general.
- Victory can also be yours if you can defeat the Milanese force.

Quick Tips

Try to hit the enemy general immediately in order to weaken the morale of his forces. Target the strongest units with your missile troops, and try to outflank the enemy forces with your strongest cavalry reserve.

THE RICHARD CAMPAIGN

Richard the Lionhearted, or "Coeur de Lion," is one of the great warrior kings of English history. He spent only six months in England during his ten years on the throne—and even that was just to squeeze more money out of the country! The rest of the time he was doing what he enjoyed and did best: soldiering.

Richard's fame as a warrior was well-earned. He was personally brave, a formidable strategist, and a master castle builder, and was seen as the embodiment of chivalry. His skills eventually gave him command of the Third Crusade, and while he failed to take Jerusalem, it was not for want of trying. His battles were conducted with a good deal of military skill and political savvy, as he alternated attacks on the Saracens and negotiations with Saladin.

Richard came to an appropriate soldier's end after his crusading days. He died after being shot by a crossbowman while besieging a rebellious vassal in France. Despite his personal wish that the crossbowman not be harmed for carrying out his duty, once Richard was safely dead, his lieutenants captured and flayed his killer in revenge.

ARSUF 1191

The Frankish kingdoms in the Holy Land had met with mixed fortunes before the arrival of reinforcements, in the shape of the Third Crusade. Before Richard Coeur de Lion and Philip II Augustus of France arrived, the Crusaders had been too weak to be much of a threat to Saladin. But with help from these European monarchs, they managed to break into Acre and take it from the Saracens.

In September 1191, after a year of frustration and unhappiness with their lack of further progress, the Crusaders moved south from Acre, making for the town of Jaffa. Outside the small settlement of Arsuf, they met a Saracen army in the open. Richard's tactical sense proved to be the decisive factor, and his victory at Arsuf restored the morale of the Third Crusade. It proved that the Saracens were not invincible, even with the example of Saladin to inspire them.

Battle Objectives

- Keep King Richard alive.
- Make sure enough of your troops stand fast and survive Saladin's onslaught.
- Rout or kill Saladin's army in its entirety.

Quick Tips

Run your entire force to the opposite side of the map and position your units on top of the hill. Put your missile units in the front ranks and pepper the enemy. As soon as they climb the hill, countercharge downhill with your infantry. Keep your cavalry in reserve—use them only when you need to plug the gaps. Pull your countercharging infantry units back to your line, because they can't keep pace with the routing enemy and will tire out quickly. After you've withstood the second and third Saracen charges, try to keep them on the run with the cavalry you've held back. If you spot the enemy general close to your units, attack him immediately. If you hit him hard enough, you will likely achieve a mass rout of the enemy.

Jaffa 1191

The capture of Jaffa marked a high point for the warriors of the Third Crusade under their leader, Richard Coeur de Lion. After their victory at Arsuf in September 1191, the Crusaders took the city but got no closer to their final goal of capturing Jerusalem. Richard's army encamped outside the city because of the stench of the dead within the walls. In medieval times, it was well known that foul smells caused disease.

As you begin this battle, a large Saracen force has appeared, cutting off any chance of withdrawal. With the city walls at their backs, Richard's army has no easy avenue of retreat. The Crusaders' position is far from hopeless, however. Defeating Saladin's army requires nerve and a little daring. The trick is to stand fast and use Archers to weaken the Saracens as they approach, and then launch a counter-charge at the right moment. Learning to judge the "right moment" is part of matching King Richard's strategic skill!

Battle Objectives

- Keep King Richard alive.
- Make sure enough of your troops stand fast to survive Saladin's onslaught.
- Rout or kill Saladin's army in its entirety.

Quick Tips

The Saracens have a *massive* cavalry force, so your only chance to win this one is to stay put. Don't pursue the units that rout first. You can't keep pace with them. Use your Spearmen to shield your missile units. Hold back your knights as reserves, and throw them into the fray when the battle is at its most critical point (some judgement required here).

If either flank is not engaged (usually the right flank), withdraw some of the units from there to bolster your defense elsewhere. When the enemy is sufficiently thinned out and breaks rank, chase the routing units. The now-returning rallied enemy units should suffer collapsed Morale and join in the rout.

SALADIN

Saladin, or Salah al-Din Yusuf ibn Ayyub, was the founder of the Ayyubid dynasty in Egypt and the eventual conqueror of the Crusaders' kingdom of Jerusalem. He brought the city back into Muslim control in 1187, and then defended it against the attacks of, among others, Richard the Lionhearted during the Third Crusade. Before this, however, he fought many successful battles against the Frankish Crusaders, always being sensible enough to let the Crusaders' own weaknesses work against them before he moved in for the kill.

MARJ'AYYUN 1179

Saladin was not a commander to wait for the enemy, or to allow earlier problems to deflect him. On hearing that he had invaded towards Sidon, King Baldwin IV of Jerusalem ordered a counter-march to intercept the Saracen forces. Eventually, they reached a hilltop overlooking the Saracen encampment. However, rather than waiting for their infantry to recover from the wearying march, the Frankish Crusaders immediately advanced.

Always impetuous—and in this case, absolutely convinced that they were to have an easy victory by destroying the Saracens in camp—the nobles, knights, and cavalry were soon disorganized and separated from the rest of the army. The supporting infantry was left straggling after, exhausted by the heat.

As the battle begins, although there has been a delay as Saracen skirmishers hold off the Crusaders for a while, the Crusader infantry forces are still not in proper positions to immediately affect the battle. The heavy knights are too far forward and isolated from proper support, and they're getting tired in their unsuitably heavy armor.

Battle Objectives

- Saladin must survive the battle to continue his campaign.
- Protect your army. Suffer too many deaths or routings and the battle is lost.
- King Baldwin's army must be driven off or slaughtered.

Quick Tips

Keep the enemy knights busy with the four units located at the edge of the map. This keeps them from joining the attack against the main body of your army. Engage the enemy as soon as possible. Use the high ground to your advantage, and try to turn King Baldwin's flank with your fast cavalry units by attacking from the rear.

The Horns of Hattin

Thanks to early Muslim successes, the Crusaders were forced to set aside their internal disputes and campaign together. Saladin didn't wait for them to come to him, though. He attacked along the main road to Tiberias and Sennabra, threatening both towns and the castle. An appeal for help against the Saracens was sent to King Guy of Jerusalem. Count Raymond of Tripoli advised waiting where there was water and pasture for the cavalry, even though his own wife was under siege at Tiberias.

King Guy, however, chose to listen to the Master of the Temple, the commander of the Knights Templar, whose plan involved an immediate attack. The Franks broke camp, left the road, and moved across the barren wasteland of the Plain of Toran. Whether through spies or traitors, Saladin was warned of the approaching Crusaders and moved his army to the hills at Hattin, ready to fall on the Crusaders as they came out of the waterless plain and before they had a chance to form a battle line. Thus, Saladin's forces were in a perfect place to harass the tired, thirsty Crusaders as they advanced piecemeal into the fray.

Battle Objectives

- Saladin must survive to continue the fight to drive away the Crusaders.
- Avoid overwhelming losses through death or routing.
- Kill the Frankish army or drive them from the battlefield.

Quick Tips

Attack the rearguard as quickly as you can and eliminate them. This should be fairly easy because they are pulling away from you and attempting to form a defensive formation with their comrades. Remember: You receive a combat bonus when attacking from the rear. Try to hit the enemy knights with your Archers to thin out their ranks.

Now you should face the main body of the Crusader army, which may still be in disarray due to the rout of their comrades. Send in your infantry to keep them busy, and try again to flank them with your cavalry. As soon as they start routing, keep the pressure on until the better-armored knights lose heart. They will eventually, due to the Morale loss caused by the routing of friendly units.

Acre

Under the leadership of King Guy of Jerusalem, the Crusaders besieged Acre, but they were both discomfited by the arrival of a relief force under Saladin and encouraged by the arrival of their own reinforcements. King Guy and his advisors decided to launch an attack on the Muslim encampment, rather than simply concentrating on their siege works. Guy ordered his army to make ready for a pitched battle, and initially everything seemed to go well. He had chosen a reasonably strong position for his army, with one flank protected by the sea, the other by the River Belus, and his archers and crossbowmen in the front.

But soon his men—and especially the more mobile cavalry—realized there was the prospect of loot from the nearby Muslim encampment. Once the Crusaders had dispersed to look for money and valuables, Saladin was able to rally his forces and counterattack. The great Muslim leader managed to capture and then execute the Master of the Temple, thus finishing off one of his most implacable enemies.

Battle Objectives

- Protect Sultan Saladin. If he falls, the Crusaders will claim victory.
- Maintain your army long enough to ensure the defeat of Guy's forces.
- The Crusaders must be defeated. Rout or destroy King Guy's army.

Quick Tips

It's almost impossible to hold your ground if you keep your starting position. Therefore, order your forces up to the top of the hill and await the onslaught of the enemy attack. Here you should have the advantage of height. Fight a defensive battle, keeping your forces facing downhill in good support positions.

Appendix 1: Technology Tree

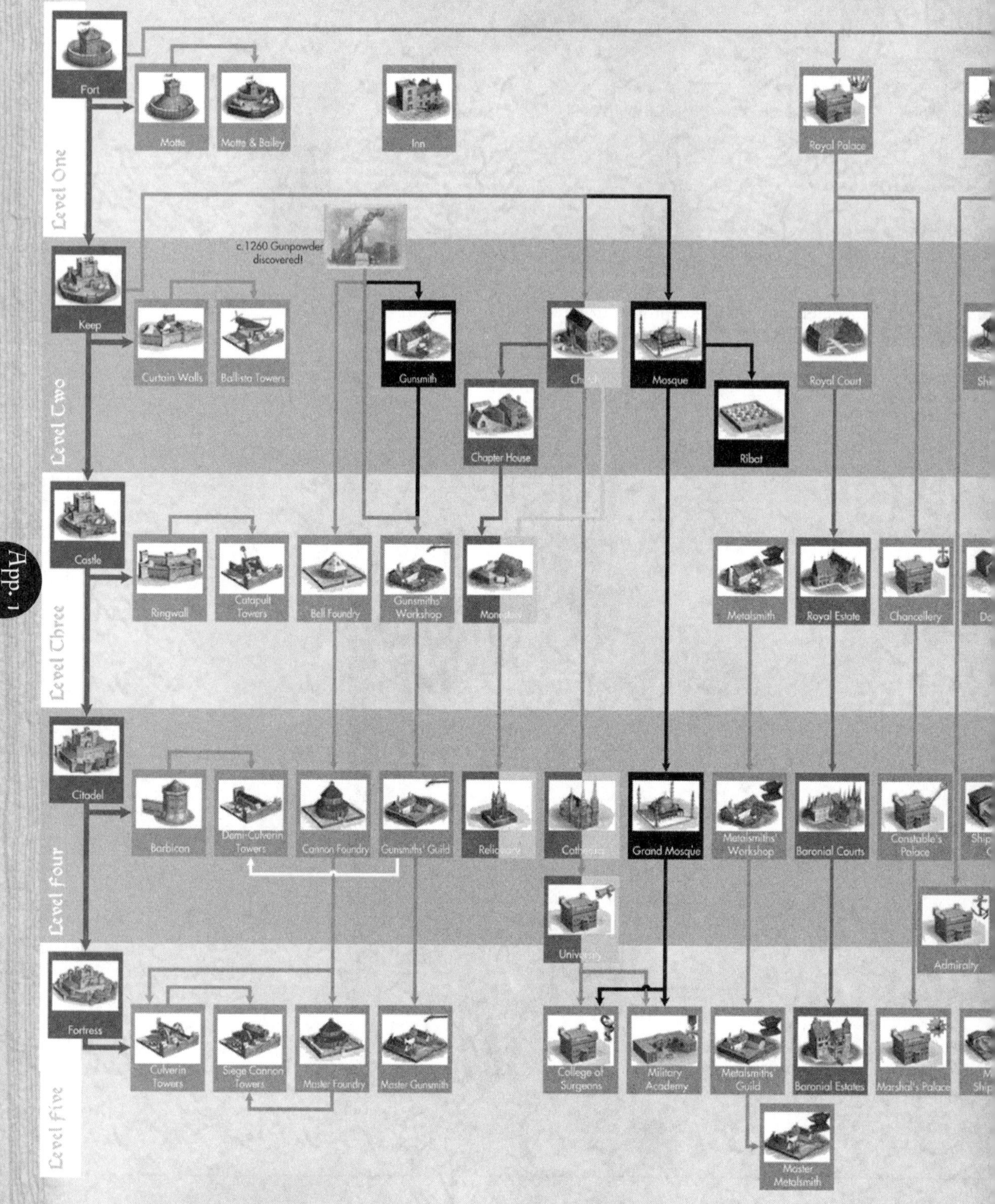

App. 1

Appendix 1: Technology Tree

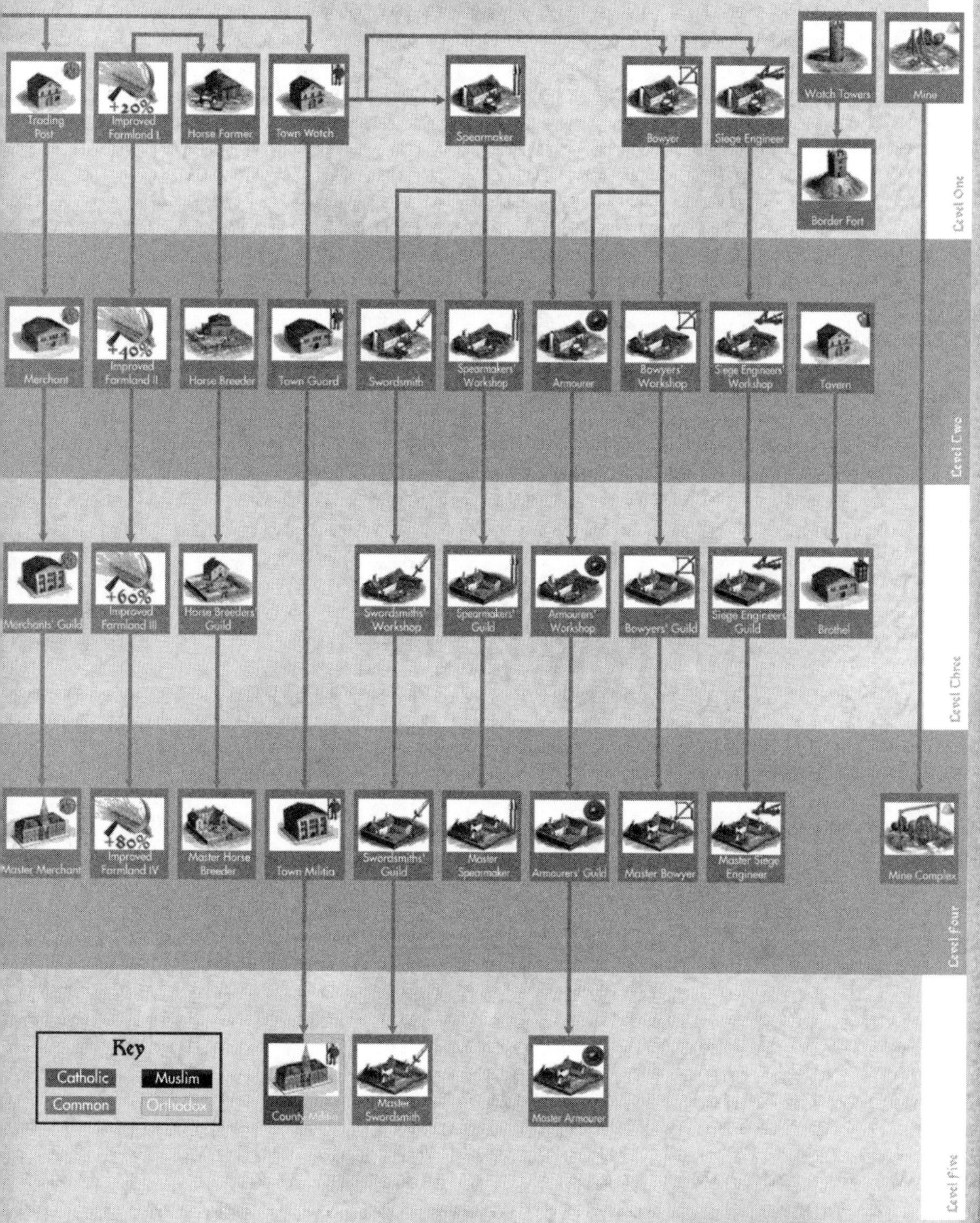

Strategic Agents etc.

Agent		Building	Building	Building
	Emissary  	 Royal Palace	 Royal Palace	 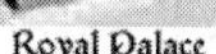 Royal Palace
	Assassin	Tavern	  Tavern	 Tavern
	Spy 	 Brothel	Brothel	 Brothel
Catholic Bishop	Orthodox Priest	 Church	  Church	
Catholic Cardinal 	Orthodox Bishop 	 Cathedral	 Cathedral	
	Crusade 	  Chapter House		
	Jihad 	 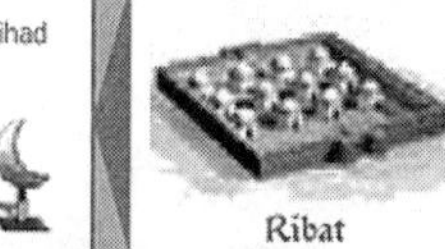 Ribat		
	Inquisitor 	  Monastery		
	Grand Inquisitor 	  Reliquary		
	Alim 	 Mosque		
	Imam	 Grand Mosque		

Light Cavalry

Horse Archers

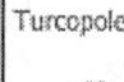

Horse Archers ← Horse Farmer ← Horse Farmer

Turcopoles ← Inn + Antioch, Edessa, Syria, Tripoli

Turcoman Horse ← Mounted Crossbows ← Horse Breeder ← Horse Breeder

Berber Camels ← Bowyers Workshop + Morocco, Algeria, Tunisia, Cyrenacia

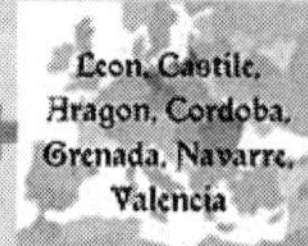

Boyars ← Horse Breeders Guild + Armourers Guild

Spanish Jinettes ← Horse Breeder + Leon, Castile, Aragon, Cordoba, Grenada, Navarre, Valencia

Mamluk Horse Archers ← Bowyers Guild + Horse Breeders Guild

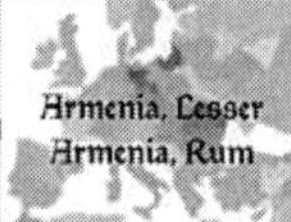

Byzantine Cavalry ← Horse Breeder + Bowyers Workshop + Swordsmiths Workshop

Heavy Cavalry

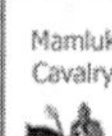

Armenian Heavy Cavalry ← Horse Breeder + Armenia, Lesser Armenia, Rum

Mamluk Cavalry ← Horse Breeder

Feudal Foot Knights ← Feudal Knights ← Royal Estate + Armourers Workshop + Horse Breeder

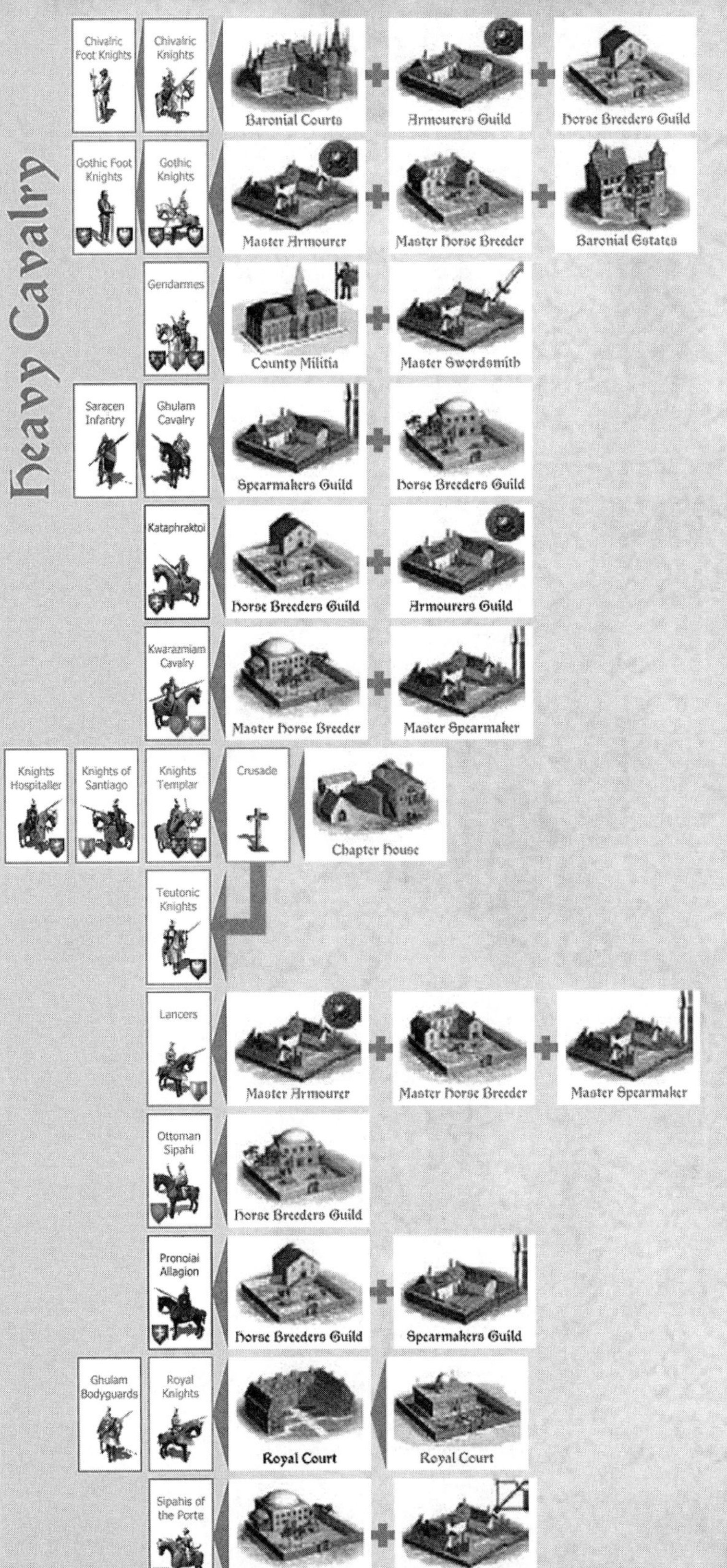
Heavy Cavalry
Chivalric Foot Knights
Chivalric Knights
Baronial Courts
Armourers Guild
Horse Breeders Guild
Gothic Foot Knights
Gothic Knights
Master Armourer
Master Horse Breeder
Baronial Estates
Gendarmes
County Militia
Master Swordsmith
Saracen Infantry
Ghulam Cavalry
Spearmakers Guild
Horse Breeders Guild
Kataphraktoi
Horse Breeders Guild
Armourers Guild
Kwarazmiam Cavalry
Master Horse Breeder
Master Spearmaker
Knights Hospitaller
Knights of Santiago
Knights Templar
Crusade
Chapter House
Teutonic Knights
Lancers
Master Armourer
Master Horse Breeder
Master Spearmaker
Ottoman Sipahi
Horse Breeders Guild
Pronoiai Allagion
Horse Breeders Guild
Spearmakers Guild
Ghulam Bodyguards
Royal Knights
Royal Court
Royal Court
Sipahis of the Porte
Master Horse Breeder
Master Bowyer

Heavy Infantry

Unit	Requirement	Additional requirement
Billmen	Spearmakers Guild	
Varangian Guard	Spearmakers Guild	Royal Palace
Ghazi Infantry	Mosque	Swordsmith
Feudal Men-at-Arms	Swordsmith	
Janissary Heavy Infantry	Military Academy	Master Spearmaker
Halberdiers	Town Militia	
Swiss Halberdiers	Town Militia	Switzerland

Medium Infantry

Upgrade	Unit	Requirement	Additional requirement
	Gallowglasses	Swordsmith	Ireland
	Highland Clansmen	Fort	Scotland
Byzantine Infantry	Abyssinian Guard	Swordsmith	
	Vikings	Fort	
Hospitaller Foot Knights	Order Foot Soldiers	Crusade	Chapter House
	Ottoman Infantry	Bowyers Workshop	
	Chivalric Men-at-Arms	Swordsmiths Workshop	

Skirmishers

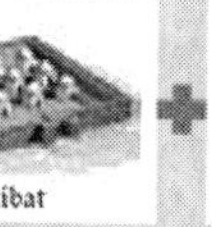

Peasants etc.

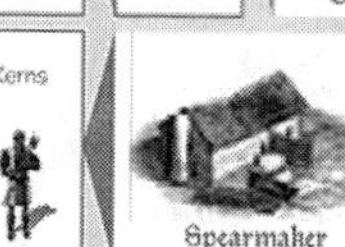

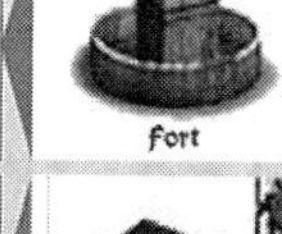

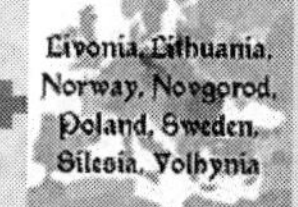

Missiles

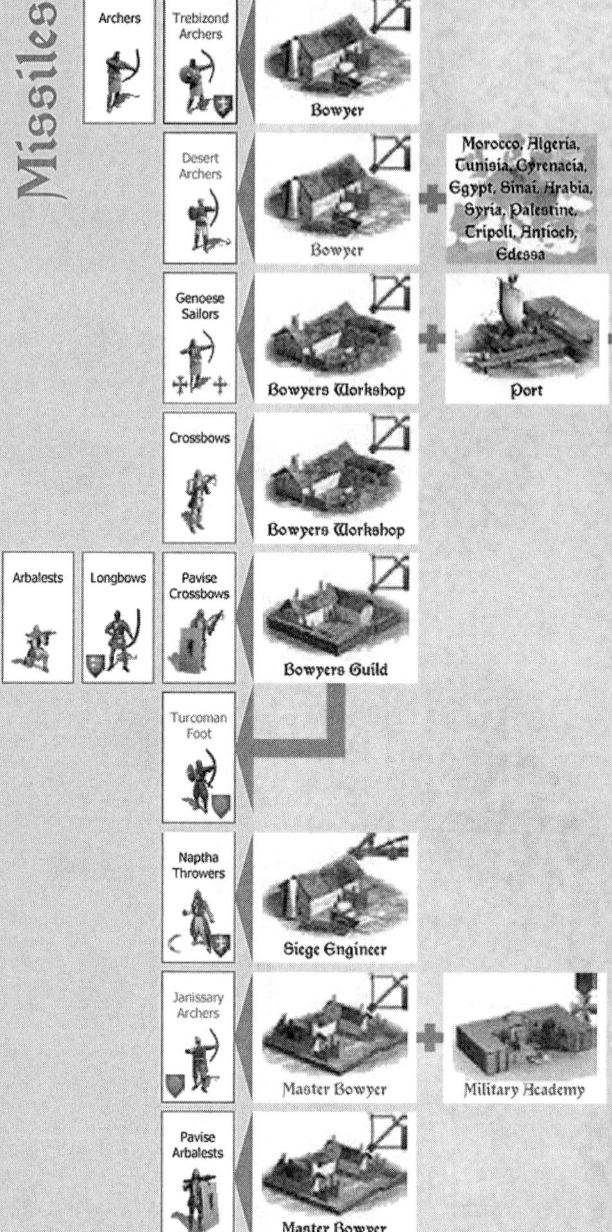

Archers
Trebizond Archers
Bowyer
Desert Archers
Bowyer
Morocco, Algeria, Tunisia, Cyrenacia, Egypt, Sinai, Arabia, Syria, Palestine, Tripoli, Antioch, Edessa
Genoese Sailors
Bowyers Workshop
Port
Genoa
Crossbows
Bowyers Workshop
Arbalests
Longbows
Pavise Crossbows
Bowyers Guild
Turcoman Foot
Naptha Throwers
Siege Engineer
Janissary Archers
Master Bowyer
Military Academy
Pavise Arbalests
Master Bowyer

Spearmen

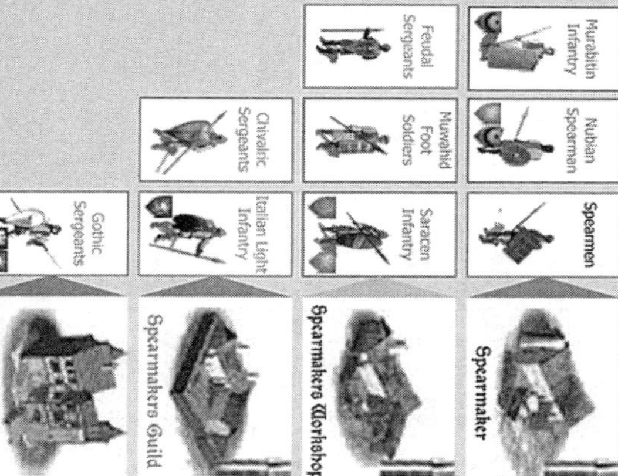

Handguns

- Arquebusiers: Gunsmiths Guild
- Handguns: Gunsmiths Workshop
- Mamluk Handguns: Gunsmith

Artillery Pieces

Artillery Piece	Alternative	Required Building
Ballista		Siege Engineer
Catapult		Siege Engineers Workshop
Trebuchet		Siege Engineers Guild
Mangonel		Master Siege Engineer
Bombard	Mortar	Bell Foundry
Demi-Culverin	Demi-Cannon	Cannon Foundry
Culverin	Siege Cannon	Master Foundry
Serpentine		Master Foundry + Gunsmiths Guild

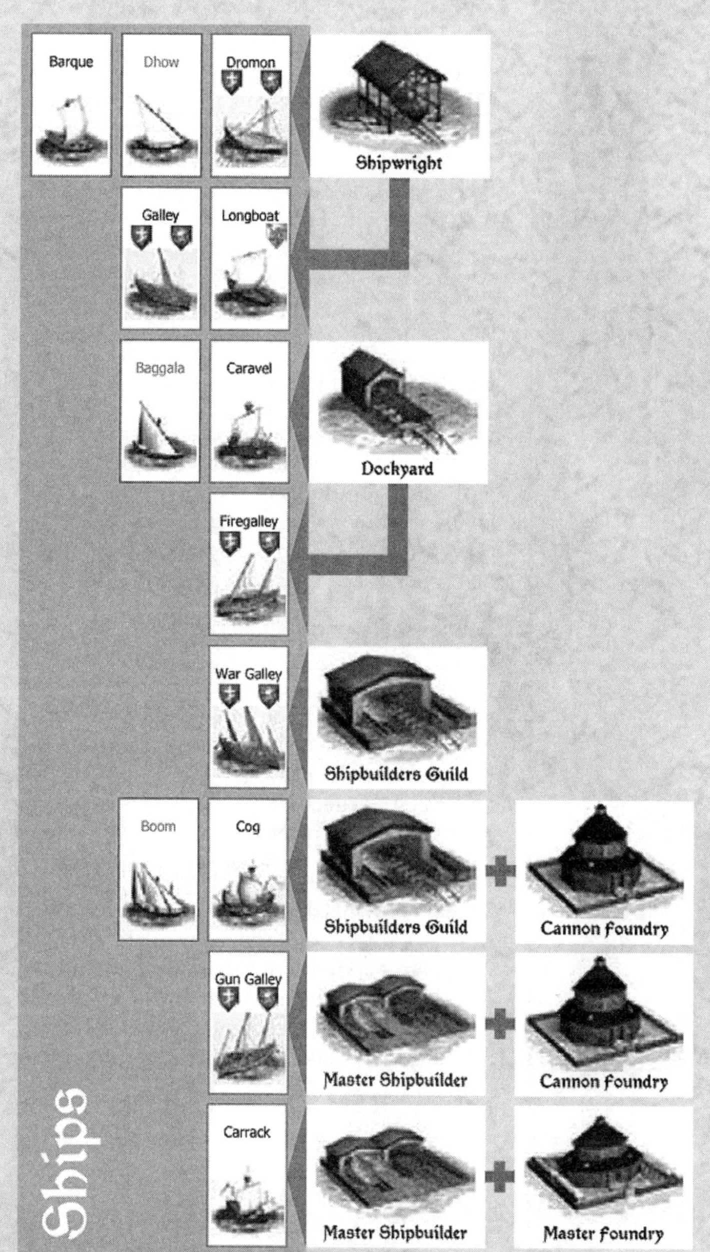

Ships
Barque
Dhow
Dromon
Shipwright
Galley
Longboat
Baggala
Caravel
Dockyard
Firegalley
War Galley
Shipbuilders Guild
Boom
Cog
Shipbuilders Guild
Cannon foundry
Gun Galley
Master Shipbuilder
Cannon foundry
Carrack
Master Shipbuilder
Master foundry

Appendix 3: Vices and Virtues

Faction leaders, governors, and generals acquire vices and virtues during a game. Some of these can have a very significant effect on your strategic situation on the Campaign Map, or your tactical considerations on the Battle Map. For example, a governor who is a Compulsive Gambler lowers both his province's agricultural output *and* trade income by 20 percent—a pretty hefty penalty for a vice. On the other hand, if your faction leader acquires the virtue of being a Magnificent Builder, this increases Happiness by +10 in all of your provinces, and it gives a +2 Loyalty boost to every general in your faction.

Here's a recap of how vices and virtues work in the game:

If an army commander has a vice or virtue that affects Morale or Command, the penalty or bonus applies to his entire army—that is, to each of the units in the army. If his vice/virtue affects only Valor, the penalty or bonus applies only to the general's own unit. These combat-oriented vices and virtues affect governors or your faction leader just as they would a normal general.

But governors and your faction leader can acquire certain vices and virtues that affect province-wide or kingdom-wide relations (Happiness, Dread, Acumen, Loyalty, Piety), building, agriculture, or trade. If the king of France is a Great Trader, for example, this adds +10 Happiness in *all* provinces controlled by the French faction, and it boosts *all* French trade income by +20 percent. If a French provincial governor is a Great Trader, however, the effects apply only to his province. So if the Duke of Burgundy gains the Great Trader virtue, the same bonuses of +10 Happiness and +20 percent trade income apply only to Burgundy.

When a provincial governor acquires a vice or virtue that has a province-wide effect, its bonus or penalty applies to his province, no matter where he is or who is currently sitting in his province—the king, other governors, it doesn't matter. The only person whose location *does* matter is the faction leader. The loyalty of both generals and regions depends on their distance to the faction leader. The further away he is, the more loyalty drops.

Following is a complete list of all vices and virtues available in the game:

NAME OF VICE/VIRTUE	EFFECTS
Able Lieutenant	With a lieutenant to carry out many of his duties extremely well, this man inspires confidence just through his choice of servants! +2 Acumen, +20 Happiness
Able Scholar	This man's abilities as a learned man have few equals, but his time to study the practical arts of war has been severely limited. +2 Acumen, -2 Valor
Absentee Landlord	He pays no attention whatsoever to his estates, leaving corrupt and incompetent lackeys to do his duty. It is causing widespread hunger and much discontent. -20 Happiness, -30% agricultural output.
Administratively Greedy	When he is involved in any activity, money usually changes hands and often ends up in his purse. -10% agricultural output, -10% trade income.
Adultery	Rumors have spread about his adulterous affair with another noble's wife. -2 piety.
Affable	This man's abilities to put everyone at ease in his presence inspire loyalty and hard work in all who know him. +3 Acumen, +30 Happiness
Alcoholic	He engages in epic bouts of drinking lasting days at a time, punctuated by deep depressions and sudden violence. -3 command, -2 acumen, +1 dread.
Always Drunk	He drinks constantly and is very often drunk. Needless to say, this affects his ability to command. -2 command, -1 acumen.
Ambitious	He seeks power and glory, and focuses much effort on political intrigue to achieve this. +1 dread, -1 loyalty.
Approachable Manner	This man's demeanor naturally puts underlings at their ease and aids him in managing state affairs. +1 Acumen, +10 Happiness
Argumentative	He argues fiercely, often shouting wildly. His anger is swift, simmers briefly, and then pours out in a torrent of violence. This can be useful on the battlefield. +1 dread, +2 valor.
Art Lover	He believes that Great Art is worthy of support and encouragement wherever it is found. He has the confidence to spend money well, on the work of the very best artists. -10% agricultural output, -10% trade income.
Artistic Leanings	While he recognizes that art is worthwhile, his tastes are not yet fully defined. He is confident when commissioning new works for his enjoyment. -5% agricultural output, -5% trade income.
Artistic Temperament	While he would never publicly admit to it, his tastes in art are refined and precise. This interest is an expensive obsession. -20% agricultural output, -20% trade income.

NAME OF VICE/VIRTUE	EFFECTS
Assassinator	His network of assassins has been penetrated and exposed. The families of his victims clamor for vengeance. He is not a popular man. +2 valor vs. spies, -5 loyalty, -40 happiness.
Assault Specialist	He is a specialist in organizing and leading castle assaults. +3 Command when assaulting castles.
Assured Loyalty	His acquittal on charges of treason have made this man keen to show his faithfulness to his faction. +1 loyalty.
Atheist	He has been exposed as a non-believer in a world ruled by the devout and faithful. It will be hard for him to survive. -8 piety.
Authoritarian	He is quick to use his power to enforce his commands, and brooks no disobedience. +1 Dread.
Autocrat	He is firmly in control, and takes measures to ensure his commands are obeyed without question or dissent. +2 Dread.
Avarice	His various dubious enterprises to make money at the expense of his subordinates have been exposed. +2 acumen, -40 Happiness.
Awful Risky Attacks	Attacking against the odds is always difficult, but he manages to make it a disaster almost every time. -3 Command in this situation.
Bad Assault Defender	He really isn't cut out to defend castles. He should let someone else do it. -3 Command when defending castles.
Bad Assaulter	He really isn't cut out to lead castle assaults. He should let someone else do it. -3 Command when assaulting castles.
Bad Attacker	When attacking, all reason seems to escape him. His tactics often confuse his enemies, regularly talking of them during their victory celebrations. -3 to Command when attacking.
Bad Defender	He is incapable of sitting and waiting for the enemy to come to him. Attack is not always the best form of defense. -3 Command when defending.
Bad Last Stand	He makes hideous errors when defending against a superior force. -3 Command in this situation.
Bad Risky Attacks	He is particularly bad at attacking stronger foes. -2 Command in this situation.
Bad Siege Defender	He is very bad at organizing effective resistance to sieges. -3 years to siege duration.
Bad Sieger	He is not cut out for sitting around sieging castles. +3 years to siege length.

NAME OF VICE/VIRTUE	EFFECTS
Bad Steward	He neglects his duty to manage his estates well, causing poverty and discontent. -10 Happiness, -10% agricultural output.
Believer	He is a true believer. +1 piety.
Blackmailer	He has been caught blackmailing a senior official, and fined a large sum. He is most unhappy about this and seeks revenge. -3 loyalty.
Blood Lover	It has become known that he kills prisoners for his own pleasure, denying his men their share of any ransom money. +3 Dread, -3 Morale, -2 Piety.
Born Again	He has repented his sins and claims to be washed in the blood of the Lamb of God. He has taken a vow of personal poverty and donated his wealth to the Church. The Inquisition will find him hard to fault now. -6 dread, +6 piety
Brave Beyond Belief	Fear is a unknown to this man. On the battlefield, he has no thought of danger or death and his example leads others to perform great deeds! +3 Valor, +3 Morale
Brigand and Thief	His position is a hollow sham to protect the widespread thievery he controls and encourages. Little is safe from his thievery, and his subjects know it. -10% agricultural output, -10% trade income, and -20 Happiness.
Builder (Province)	His extensive program of building has brought prosperity to the people in his province. +10 Happiness.
Builder (Kingdom)	His extensive program of building has brought prosperity to the people. +10 Happiness in all provinces.
Butcher	He is famous for the massacre of thousands of prisoners in a single battle. Few can match the horror of this deed. +2 Dread.
Captivating Nature	This man's winning ways with the masses have caused many to see him as a natural leader, and to do their best to please him. +20 Happiness, +2 Morale
Captured	He did not enjoy the process of being captured and ransomed, and instills a fear of being captured in all his men. This makes them less likely to rout, but makes them harder to command. +3 morale, -1 command.
Careful with Money	This man finds it hard to say goodbye to any money, ever, even to the point of not rewarding those in his service. +2 Acumen, -20 Happiness
Charismatic Leader	This man's impact on a crowd is such that he inspires respect - even love - and great deeds just by his presence. +30 Happiness, +3 Morale
Charismatic	This man's personal aura inspires great efforts from, and the confidence of, everyone he commands. +10 Happiness, +1 Morale

NAME OF VICE/VIRTUE	EFFECTS
Charitable	He believes it is his duty to make some effort to help the poor. +10 Happiness.
Charming	This man's behavior not only puts people at their ease, but gets them to go just that little bit further in carrying out their duties. -2 Dread, +1 Acumen
Chinless Wonder	Perhaps one or two of this man's close ancestors were a little too close, resulting in an unconventional family tree. -1 Acumen, -1 Command
Chivalrous	Chivalry and honor are meat and drink to this man. He is incapable of taking advantage of an enemy in a fair fight. +2 Morale, -2 Dread
Clever Assistants	This man is aided in his day to day work by able servants, who carry out many of his duties very well. +1 Acumen, +10 Happiness
Clever with Words	This man's ready wit and repartee is indicative of a clever mind and clear thinking. +1 Acumen
Compulsive Gambler	Although he manages to keep it quiet, his gambling is completely out of hand. Any money to which he has access will be rashly gambled away. -20% agricultural output, -20% trade income.
Compulsively Charitable	He has a deep need to do good works. Often this need overrides financial reality, and causes problems. -10% agricultural output, -10% trade income, +10 happiness.
Connoisseur of Art	He has a finely developed taste in artwork, sculpture and architecture, and this helps encourage artists and artisans achieve truly great works. -20% agricultural output, -20% trade income.
Connoisseur	He enjoys life's little luxuries, and if these cost money, that's just too bad - regardless of whose money is actually being spent! -10% agricultural output, -10% trade income.
Corrupt	He has a certain flexibility, and often accepts small bribes to speed up the carrying out of his duties. -10% agricultural output, -10% trade income.
Coward	He is considered by all to be a coward in battle, and men who serve him on the battlefield are just waiting for him to turn and run. It makes it hard for him to keep his army on the field. -9 morale.
Cowardly	His deliberate avoidance of combat in the past has become a source of ridicule. No efforts on his part are likely to change this now. His men are reluctant to risk their lives when he will not. -6 morale, -2 valor.

NAME OF VICE/VIRTUE	EFFECTS
Crack-Brained	This man's habits of dancing in moonbeams, painting his servants blue and sucking horseshoes has lead some to suspect he may be unbalanced. -2 Morale, -20 Happiness
Dead Drunk	
Deep Religious Urges	His religious leanings are central to his character, and his faith leads him to support (financially and practically) religious authorities at all times. -15% agricultural output, -15% trade income.
Deep Thinker (Philosopher)	His is a more than passing acquaintance with the works of classical scholars, making him a properly educated, if sometimes impractical man. -10% agricultural output, -10% trade income.
Deep Thinker (Man of Reason)	This man's ability to think clearly about any problem gives him insight denied to ordinary men, but perhaps at the cost of unquestioning faith. -3 Piety, +3 Acumen
Degenerate Gambler	He will wager on anything. Winning is secondary to the thrill of betting, although there is always the chance that this time he will win... -20% agricultural output, -20% trade income.
Delegates Authority	This man has a rare gift to find good men and get them to work hard in his service, aiding him in much that he does. +2 Acumen, +2 Command
Despot	He treats his advisors and opponents alike with brutal force. All who oppose him and many who he just doesn't like are arrested, imprisoned or assassinated. He is not popular. +4 Dread, -40 Happiness.
Devout (Paranoid)	After a recent interview with the Inquisition he has taken to spending long hours in prayer, and is vociferous in his support for the Church. -2 dread, +2 piety
Devout (Pious)	He is a devout believer, and acts in accordance with his beliefs. +2 piety.
Dominant Trader	He has a desire to be the sole trading power in his domain. No competitors can be allowed to flourish. -30% trade income.
Doubtful Courage	There are serious doubts about his courage in the face of the enemy. Reports of him screaming like a girl as he departed the field are not too exaggerated. His men are not inspired. -6 morale.
Drinker	He enjoys drinking slightly more than is prudent. Most things can wait until he sobers up, but battles cannot... -1 command.
Drinking himself to Death	He is mostly bedridden, but occasionally his retainers strap him to a horse and lead him out. His retainers are fairly competent now at making decisions for him. -20 health.

NAME OF VICE/VIRTUE	EFFECTS
Dubious Accounting	It is widely known that he misappropriates a small portion of local taxes for his own use. -10% agricultural output, -10% trade income, -10 Happiness.
Eager to Retreat	He has a reputation for being very quick to decide retreat is the best strategy, perhaps because he is always put in difficult positions. -1 Loyalty, -2 Morale.
Educated	He has a good education, having a basic understanding of philosophy, theology, and the classics. +1 acumen.
Eloquent	He has a gift for being able to talk himself out of any difficulty, making it hard to fault his religious views, and making him a persuasive administrator. +1 piety, +1 acumen.
Embezzler	It is widely known that when governing he misappropriates a large portion of the funds under his control, to the detriment of the local economy. -20% agricultural output, -20% trade income, -20 Happiness.
Envy	He so passionately wants power and glory, he cannot stand to see others enjoying it. He has been caught engaging spies and assassins to plot against them. +2 dread, -3 loyalty.
Exclusive Trader	He has a desire to be the best, if not only with mercantile power where he holds authority. Others wishing to trade are discouraged by whatever means necessary. -20% trade income.
Expert Assault Defender	He is an expert at defending castles against assaults. +2 Command when in this situation.
Expert Assaulter	He is an expert in assaulting castles. +2 Command when assaulting castles.
Expert Attacker	He is an expert in the art of attacking defensive positions. +2 Command when attacking.
Expert Defender	He is an expert in defense, well known for his ability to exploit terrain, lay ambushes, and force attackers in to unwise decisions. +2 Command when defending.
Expert Last Stand	He is a specialist in defending when outnumbered more than 2 to 1. +2 to Command in this situation.
Expert Risky Attacks	He is expert at attacking when outnumbered. +2 to Command in this situation.
Expert Siege Defender	He is an expert at organizing men and supplies, penetrating enemy lines and maintaining a disciplined garrison. +3 years to siege duration.
Expert Sieger	He is an expert in the art of sieging castles into submission without resorting to battle. -2 years to siege duration.
Extreme Loyalty	Accusations of treason have left this man with the desire to prove himself more loyal than anyone else. +3 loyalty.

NAME OF VICE/VIRTUE	EFFECTS
Faithful Servants	This man has a talent spotting the right people and giving them granting authority and responsibility to carry out some of his duties. +1 Acumen, +1 Command
Family Above All	He shows loyalty to his family at all times. He gives them employment even when it is obvious that they are without talent and actually harmful. -20% agricultural output, -10% trade income.
Family Favorites	While pretending that he chooses servants and aides by merit, he favors relatives on every possible occasion. Their poor abilities are less important to him than kinship. -20% agricultural output, -10% trade income.
Famous Warrior	He is famous for his skill on the battlefield and few can hope to match him in single combat. +20 health, +3 valor.
Famously Brave	This man's courage naturally raises the fighting spirit of anyone who fights at his side. +1 Valor, +1 Morale
Fanatic	He follows religious doctrine to the letter, arresting and executing any he judges to be heretics. +40% zeal when governing, +1 dread.
Fast Talker	Court Jesters come to this man for lessons in how to turn a pithy phrase. His mind is as sharp as his conversation. +2 Acumen
Fervent	He applies religious doctrine to the way he lives his life and the way he governs. +1 piety, +10% zeal when governing.
Field Defense Specialist	He specializes in defending in the field. +3 Command when defending.
Fine Leader	He leads from the front, taking risks but gaining much respect and inspiring his men by example. +4 morale, +2 loyalty.
Foully Corrupt	He sees corruption as a necessary evil, and forces himself to accept bribes when carrying out duties he should be doing anyway. He does little without an extra payment from somebody. -15% agricultural output, -15% trade income.
Frequent Mercy	He is known for showing mercy to captured rebels. +20 Happiness, -1 Dread.
Friendly	This man's natural ability to put others at their ease inspires confidence in his leadership on many levels. +2 Acumen, +20 Happiness
Frugal	This man is careful when spending money, even to the point of not rewarding faithful service. +1 Acumen, -10 Happiness

NAME OF VICE/VIRTUE	EFFECTS
Gambler	He enjoys gambling, and will wager on the outcome of almost any chance event. For him, the money at stake is less important than the thrill. -10% agricultural output, -10% trade income.
Generous To A Fault	His generosity towards his fellow human beings has few bounds, and his natural nobility of spirit further encourages his charity. -10% agricultural output, -10% trade income, +20 happiness.
Gentle Knight	This man's adherence to the code of chivalry is the very stuff of legend, an inspiration to troubadours and storytellers! +3 Morale, -3 Dread
Gives Away Power	This man has the ability to give his followers powers, but lacks the wisdom to see that some powers should not be given away. +1 Acumen, +1 Command
Gluttony	He binges on luxury foods, spending vast fortunes on rare delicacies and huge feasts, while his peasants starve. They resent this greatly. He is so overweight he can hardly mount his horse. -4 valor, -10 Happiness.
God Fearing	He has attracted much interest from the Inquisition, despite spending most of his time praying and much of the rest engaged in good works. -4 dread, +4 piety
Good Assault Defender	He has a talent for defending castles against assaults. +1 Command when in this situation.
Good Runner	He is remembered for the way he ran from the battlefield on more than one occasion. Perhaps he had no choice, but whispers among his men say otherwise. -3 morale.
Great Builder (Province)	His extensive program of building has brought prosperity to the people, and also to himself. +10 Happiness, +1 Loyalty.
Great Builder (Kingdom)	His extensive program of building has brought prosperity to the people, and to the nobility. +10 Happiness in all provinces, +1 Loyalty to all generals.
Great Leader	He leads from the front with great courage, and all who follow him love him for it and are inspired to great deeds. +6 morale, +3 loyalty.
Great Steward (Kingdom)	His extensive program of developing farmlands has brought prosperity to the ordinary people and his constant attention to farming matters has greatly increased agricultural output across the realm. +10 Happiness in all provinces, +20% to all agricultural production.
Great Steward (Province)	His extensive program of developing local farmlands has brought prosperity to the ordinary people and his constant attention to farming matters has greatly increased local agricultural output. +10 Happiness, +20% to agricultural production.

NAME OF VICE/VIRTUE	EFFECTS
Great Trader (Province)	His policies have greatly encouraged local trade in the province, bringing prosperity to the townsfolk and increasing trade income. +10 Happiness, +20% to trade income.
Great Trader (Kingdom)	His policies have greatly encouraged trade in all provinces, bringing prosperity to the townsfolk and increasing trade income across the realm. +10 Happiness in all provinces, +20% to all trade income.
Great Warrior	He has a natural talent for personal combat, making him less likely to die in battle. +5 health.
Greed	His desire for wealth makes him an unpopular master, as he squeezes every last florin out of his lands. +1 acumen, -10 Happiness.
Guaranteed Loyalty	Perhaps it was a flirtation with treason that has made this man realize that his true worth lies in fidelity. +2 loyalty.
Hard Sums	This man's ability to add up and get the same result every time gives him an envied monetary ability. +1 Acumen
Hard to Kill	His constitution is strong and his vigilance relentless, making him a very difficult man to assassinate. +4 valor vs. assassins.
Head In The Clouds	His abiding and excessive interest in classical scholarship leads him to neglect his day-to-day duties. -20% agricultural output, -20% trade income.
Heavy Gambler	Gambling is an obsession for this man. He enjoys staking large sums of money - from whatever source - in games of chance. Winning is an occasional pleasure for him. -15% agricultural output, -15% trade income.
Hedonist	He devotes much of his time to good food and other pleasures of the flesh. He is a little overweight. -1 valor.
Heretic	It has become widely know that he is a heretic. -5 piety.
Hesitant	He has been known to call off attacks at the last minute, perhaps because ordered to. His men do not like this habit. -1 Loyalty, -2 Morale.
Hideous Scars	His hideous scars make him terrible to behold, and have given him a matching temperament. He also is almost crippled by several old wounds, making combat difficult. -5 health, +3 dread, -3 valor.
High Security	He spends much of his time devising ingenious new security measures to defend against assassins. He has made himself a master of self defense. +3 valor -3 acumen.

NAME OF VICE/VIRTUE	EFFECTS
Highly Educated	His excellent education makes him a good administrator and a fine leader, but he questions things just a little too much. +1 acumen, +1 command, -1 piety.
Highly Learned	Learning has given this man a taste for the intellectual, but at the cost of his physical prowess. +3 Acumen, -3 Valor
Highly Organized	This man has a talent for organization and getting the best from his servants and underlings. +2 Acumen, +20 Happiness
Honest	He is basically an honest man. +1 loyalty.
Honorable Warrior	This man's chivalrous conduct has been noted with approval by his friends and enemies. +1 Morale, -1 Dread
Humanist	This man's ability to think clearly makes him worldly-wise, but his knowledge also leads him to set up Reason in the place of Faith. -4 Piety, +4 Acumen
Impressive Scars	His habit of putting himself in harm's way has given him some gruesome scars, and one or two war wounds that trouble him from time to time. -5 health, +2 dread.
Inbred	Most men manage to have eight great-grandparents, but this man has been badly short-changed! -3 Acumen, -3 Command
Incest (1)	He has an incestuous relationship with his daughter and this has become public knowledge. The pious are outraged with this and have demanded that action be taken. -5 piety.
Incest (2)	He has an incestuous relationship with his sister and this has become public knowledge. The pious are outraged with this and have demanded that action be taken. -5 piety.
Indecisive	He often calls off attacks at the last minute, perhaps because of orders. His men hate this tendency. -2 Loyalty, -4 Morale.
'Informal' Merchant	He sees nothing wrong with indulging in trade that does not pay the necessary duties and taxes, always assuming that he is enriched in the process! -10% agricultural output, -20% trade income.
Informant Network	His network of informants stretches far and wide, often giving advanced warning of plots against him. +4 valor vs. spies, -1 loyalty.
Informants	He has built up a local group of informants giving him some warning of plots against him. +2 valor vs. spies.
Invulnerable	He regularly takes small doses of poison, building up considerable resistance, and his security measures are second to none. This makes him almost impossible to assassinate. +6 valor vs. assassins.

NAME OF VICE/VIRTUE	EFFECTS
Irredeemably Witty	This man's quips, epigrams and well-turned phrases show an ability to rapidly grasp the essentials of many subjects. +3 Acumen
Irritable	He is quick to anger, and slow to forget a grudge. +1 dread.
Killer Instinct	He has a talent for killing, making him quite effective on the battlefield, and discomfiting those who stand against him. +2 Valor, +1 Dread
Kleptocracy	When governing his whole administration is geared towards misappropriating as much cash as possible. It ruins the local economy. Everyone is aware of this. -30% agricultural output, -30% trade income, -30 Happiness.
Law Maker	He has a talent for making and enforcing laws, making his territory an unsafe place for bandits or thieves to operate. +2 Dread
Lawman	He has shown himself to be adept at dealing with bandits and other lawbreakers. +1 Dread
Lazy	He suffers from sloth, finding it difficult to attend to his duties. -1 command, -1 acumen.
Legendary Leader	He leads from the front magnificently, inspiring awe in his troops and pride in his people. +6 morale, +3 loyalty, +10 happiness.
Literate	While this man's love of books is exceptional, it has also left him with a distaste for more manly pursuits. +1 Acumen, -1 Valor
Lover of Books	This man's love of books has few equals, but his literary pursuits have left him with little time for warlike activity. +2 Acumen, -1 Valor
Loyal	His natural instinct is to be loyal. +1 loyalty.
Magnificent Builder (Province)	His long and extensive program of building has caused a huge advance in the quality of life of the people and to his own prosperity. +10 Happiness, +2 Loyalty.
Magnificent Builder (Kingdom)	His long and extensive program of building has caused a huge advance in the quality of life of the people and the prosperity of the nobility. +10 Happiness in all provinces, +2 Loyalty to all generals.
Magnificent Steward (Kingdom)	His extraordinary program of developing farmlands has brought prosperity to the countryside and his farming policies have vastly increased agricultural output across the realm. +10 Happiness in all provinces, +30% to all agricultural production.
Magnificent Steward (Province)	His extraordinary program of developing local farmlands and his agricultural policies have vastly increased local agricultural output. +10 Happiness, +30% to agricultural production.
Magnificent Trader (Province)	His policies have created a local trading boom, bringing wealth to the towns and greatly increasing trade income. +10 Happiness, +30% to trade income.

NAME OF VICE/VIRTUE	EFFECTS
Magnificent Trader (Kingdom)	His policies have created a trading boom, bringing wealth to many towns and greatly increasing trade income across the realm. +10 Happiness in all provinces, +30% to all trade income.
Man of Abiding Belief	Faith in God is a central feature of his life, and this informs his every choice. All other matters are secondary to his proper desire to help and support religious authorities. -15% agricultural output, -15% trade income.
Man of Deep Devotion	His deep faith in the rightness of religious authority has no boundaries. Quite rightly, it guides and moulds his every action, making him regard secular matters with proper disdain. -20% agricultural output, -20% trade income.
Man of Heartfelt Faith	His religion is important to him, perhaps more important than any secular duty, and properly takes precedence over other matters. -10% agricultural output, -10% trade income.
Man of Honor	He believes in loyalty and honor, and is very unlikely to accept any but the most outrageous of bribes. +100% to cost of bribe.
Man of Principle	He is not easily tempted to betray his principles for money. But everyone has their price. +50% to cost of bribe.
Man of the Law	He follows the law to the letter, meeting out just but harsh punishment to any lawbreakers. He is especially adept at dealing with banditry. +3 Dread
Mass Murderer	It has become widely known that he believes all men with bald heads and brown beards to be assassins, and has tortured and executed many men of that appearance, possibly unjustly. +4 dread -5 piety
Master of Numbers	Numbers hold no mystery for this man, making him a paragon with account books and monetary matters. +3 Acumen
Materialist	He is motivated by material wealth, spending much of his efforts on acquiring more of it. +1 acumen.
Mean	Daylight has never fallen on the contents of this man's purse. His few servants have given up any expectations of consideration or payment. +3 Acumen, -30 Happiness
Merciful	He is indeed merciful when dealing with captured rebels. +20 Happiness, -2 Dread.
Merciless	He has a reputation for killing prisoners even when there is no danger of losing the battle. His men hate this as a great deal of ransom money has been lost. +2 Dread, -2 Morale.
Mighty Warrior	His reputation for skill at arms is spreading as his fighting skills improve. +10 health, +2 valor.
Monopoly Trader	His need to completely dominate and control all trade is absolute. As far as he is concerned, no one else can be allowed to succeed in a trading enterprise. -40% trade income.

NAME OF VICE/VIRTUE	EFFECTS
Moral Flexibility	He believes loyalty is a relative concept. Relative to the amount of money being offered. -30% to Bribery cost.
Most Charitable	He devotes a large portion of his wealth to good works, and encourages others to do similarly. +20 Happiness, +1 piety.
Most Eloquent	He has a gift for being able to talk himself out of any difficulty, making it almost impossible to fault his religious views, and making him a most persuasive administrator. +2 piety, +2 acumen.
Most Honest	He values honesty above all else, making him a popular leader, but he has scruples when it comes to business matters. +2 loyalty, +1 morale, -1 acumen.
Most Loyal	He values loyalty above all else, but can be violently intolerant of lack of loyalty in others. +3 loyalty, +1 dread.
Most Merciful	He is famous for showing mercy to captured rebels. +20 Happiness, -3 Dread.
Murderer (Killer)	His habit of torturing and killing has become public knowledge. He is feared and hated because of it. +5 Valor, +4 Dread, -5 Piety.
Murderer (Paranoid)	The confession of a visiting nobleman recently tortured and killed has been proved to be false, after the man's son successfully underwent a grueling ordeal. +3 dread, -3 piety
Murderous Temper	His murderous temper has been exposed. He could not cover up the death of an unarmed holy man who disagreed with his choice of wine with the cheese course. +2 dread, -2 piety.
Natural Born Killer	He is so adept at killing in hand to hand combat that few can match him, and those that are wise fear him. +3 Valor, +2 Dread.
Natural Leader	He leads his men from the front, gaining much respect and inspiring his men to greater efforts. +2 morale, +1 loyalty.
Natural Philosopher	His understanding of classical scholarship and current philosophical discussions is superb. His learning is exceptional, if sometimes impractical to his less erudite contemporaries! -20% agricultural output, -20% trade income.
Nervous	He is constantly worried about being assassinated, causing sleepless nights and troubled days. It is not good for his health. - 5 health.
No Mercy	He shows no mercy and has killed many prisoners, but is possibly too eager to do so, which deprives his men of their share of the ransom. +2 Dread, -1 Morale.
No Principles	He is entirely motivated by money, as his Grandmother's new owner will attest! -50% to Bribery cost.

NAME OF VICE/VIRTUE	EFFECTS
Not So Bold	His reluctance to get directly involved in hand to hand combat has not gone unnoticed, and undermines the morale of his men. This reputation, however undeserved, is difficult to shake. -2 morale.
Numerate	This man's mastery of the arts of addition and subtraction give him a sound grasp of fiscal affairs. +2 Acumen
Occasional Mercy	He has shown mercy to captured rebels which has made him popular. +10 Happiness.
Odd Number of Toes	Prohibitions on the inter-marriage of cousins have rarely been obeyed in this man's family. -2 Acumen, -2 Command
Often Drunk	He drinks too much and is often incoherent with drink, thus neglecting his duties. -1 command, -1 acumen.
Oozes Charm	This man's manner naturally puts people at their ease. -1 Dread
Order out of Chaos	This man's abilities are such that he could bring order to the chaotic depths of Hell itself! +3 Acumen, +30 Happiness
Organized	This man's organizational talents inspire his followers to work harder, knowing that their efforts are truly purposeful. +1 Acumen, +10 Happiness
Outlaw	He abuses his position to rob and cheat honest traders and merchants, taking goods and money with menaces. He has so far managed to hide his involvement in this thievery. -10% agricultural output and -10% trade income.
Paranoid Security	The accidental death of a famous entertainer who was his guest has caused a public outcry. Claims that he fell down a spiked pit are not widely believed. +3 valor, -20 happiness, -3 acumen
Paranoid	After poisoning several guests including a holy man, he is now infamous as a scheming poisoner with little faith. In fact, he is just paranoid about being poisoned himself. -5 health -4 piety +2 dread.
Perversion	His preference for young boys rather than young women has been exposed. -4 piety.
Philosophical Bent	His interests in philosophy go beyond the merely casual. He has studied, and now applies the fruits of his abstract thinking to his practical duties. -10% agricultural output, -10% trade income.
Philosophically Inclined	He has an interest in matters of philosophy, and a desire to apply classical, rational ideas to all things. -5% agricultural output, -5% trade income.
Pious	He applies his strong religious principles to everything he does. +3 piety.

NAME OF VICE/VIRTUE	EFFECTS
Pleasure Seeker	Life's more expensive luxuries - the best of everything - are important to him, and if these are expensive, that's hardly his problem! -15% agricultural output, -15% trade income.
Poor Assault Defender	He lacks the skills and patience required to defend against castle assaults. -2 Command when defending castles.
Poor Assaulter	He lacks the skills and discipline required to conduct castle assaults. -2 Command when assaulting castles.
Poor Attacker	He hates taking risks, and is right to do so as when he does it does not often go well. -2 Command when attacking.
Poor Defender	He is impetuous and impatient, often throwing away the advantage and taking the battle to the enemy. -2 Command when defending.
Poor Last Stand	He seems to always make mistakes when defending against a superior force. -2 Command in this situation.
Poor Risky Attacks	He is not at his best when attacking numerically superior foes. -1 Command in this situation.
Poor Siege Defender	He is poor at organizing effective resistance to sieges. -2 years to siege duration.
Poor Sieger	He lacks the skills and discipline required to make sieges come to a swift conclusion. +2 years to siege length.
Poor Steward	He finds agricultural and estate management matters dull and pays them little attention. It is causing poverty in his estates. -10 Happiness, -10% agricultural output.
Possessor of Books	Many years of reading have given this man superior intellectual abilities, but sapped his taste for action. +3 Acumen, -1 Valor
Pride	His habit of killing staff members who prove him wrong is now widely known, and so he finds it impossible to get anyone to serve him. However, his legendary pride does make him formidable in combat. -2 command, -2 acumen, +3 valor.
Properly Greased Palms	His attitude to his duties is simple: little will happen without the proper payments to grease the wheels of administration. -15% agricultural output, -15% trade income.
Publicly Generous	He has the occasional desire to help his fellow man, always providing that his fellow man is worthy of the help! -5% agricultural output, -5% trade income, +10 happiness.
Quick Learner	Few areas of expertise baffle this man, once he applies his keen intellect to understanding a new concept. +2 Acumen

NAME OF VICE/VIRTUE	EFFECTS
Random Justice	Everyone now knows there is no justice in his rule. His methods for selecting who is accused of treason and executed seem entirely random. The people hate him. +3 Dread, -50 Happiness.
Rapid Understanding	No subject is beyond this man's grasp, and he quickly learns the principles of any activity he chooses to study. +3 Acumen
Recluse	His deep and constant fear of assassins has made him a recluse. He eats and sleeps little, and is rarely seen in public. The lack of exercise is affecting his combat ability. -5 health, +2 acumen, -1 valor.
Religious Compulsions	His Faith is the overwhelming center of his life. He has a driven need to support his beliefs in financial and practical ways, no matter what the cost. -20% agricultural output, -20% trade income.
Religious Leanings	He has deep religious feelings that inform his every decision, regardless of whether or not the matter in hand is one of faith. -10% agricultural output, -10% trade income.
Remarkably Generous	His good works are legendary and his charitable nature makes him carry all such projects to a conclusion, regardless of petty matters like cost! -20% agricultural output, -20% trade income, +30 happiness.
Resilient	His constitution is robust and his vigilance constant making him a difficult man to assassinate. +2 valor vs. assassins.
Retreats often	He seems to always be retreating, perhaps because he's always given impossible positions to defend. -1 Loyalty, -4 Morale.
Retreats Very Often	He retreats very regularly, perhaps because it's the only thing to do, but his men don't think so. -3 Loyalty, -6 Morale.
Right Hand Man	This man's appointment of an able right-hand man was the best day's work he ever did. His lieutenant is an administrative genius! +3 Acumen, +30 Happiness
Rough Justice (1)	After surviving more than one assassination attempt his deeply suspicious nature often manifests as harsh and summary justice. +2 dread
Rough Justice (2)	When suppressing rebellions, he includes otherwise innocent victims of his own petty vendettas in the list of those to be executed. No one dares speak out against this practice. +2 Dread, -10 Happiness.
Scant Mercy	He has killed prisoners without hesitation when it looked like the battle might go against him. +1 Dread.
Scarred	He has been in the thick of things in battle and has some ugly scars as result, making him look quite intimidating. +1 dread.

NAME OF VICE/VIRTUE	EFFECTS
Scholastic	Although this man's love of learning is exceptional, it is not matched by a love of the manly skills of a warrior! +1 Acumen, -1 Valor
Secret Adultery	He has been having an adulterous affair with another noble's wife. They have been fortunate to keep this secret so far.
Secret Assassinator	His spy network includes assassins ready and able to pre-empt any plots against him. He has quietly removed a number of officials and local worthies. +6 valor vs. spies, -4 loyalty, -20 happiness.
Secret Atheist	He just does not believe. He has succeeded in hiding it so far, but his passion for rational debate puts him in danger.
Secret Avarice	In his endless quest for riches, he secretly engages in complex plots to divest his subordinates of some of their wealth. Some would call what he does fraud. +2 acumen, -10 Happiness.
Secret Bad Temper	He cannot control his temper. More than once a minor argument has ended with the red mist descending and his opponent lying on the floor in a pool blood. So far such incidents have been hushed up. +1 dread, +2 valor.
Secret Blackmailer	He has a habit of using blackmail against his political enemies. Only the victims are aware of this, and they're not talking.
Secret Blood Lover	He kills prisoners even when it is not necessary, which causes discontent amongst his men. He indulges his secret passion for blood, personally executing many captives. +3 Dread.
Secret Dubious Accounting	He secretly misappropriates a small portion of local taxes for his own use. -10% agricultural output, -10% trade income.
Secret Embezzler	Given the opportunity he embezzles a significant portion of local taxes. The full extent of his activities is not widely known. -20% agricultural output, -20% trade Income, -10 Happiness.
Secret Envy	He so passionately wants power and glory, he cannot stand to see others enjoying it. He secretly engages spies and assassins to plot against them. +1 dread, -2 loyalty.
Secret Fanatic	He follows religious doctrine to the letter, and when governing secretly misuses his position to eliminate heretics. +30% zeal when governing.
Secret Gambler	His gambling is getting out of hand, although so far he has managed to hide this from others. Few wagers are too trivial or stakes too large for him to resist. -15% agricultural output, -15% trade income.

NAME OF VICE/VIRTUE	EFFECTS
Secret Gluttony	He secretly binges on luxury foods, spending vast fortunes on rare delicacies while his peasants starve. He is becoming vastly overweight, which seriously affects his combat ability. -3 valor.
Secret Heretic	He is a committed heretic, but has managed to conceal this so far.
Secret Incest (1)	He has an incestuous relationship with his daughter. If this were to become known the pious would be outraged.
Secret Incest (2)	He has an incestuous relationship with his sister. If this were to become known the pious would be outraged.
Secret Killer	He enjoys killing too much. He deliberately kills in practice tourneys, and tortures and kills any who offend him. So far he has managed to keep this vice secret. +4 Valor, +3 Dread.
Secret Kleptocracy	When governing his whole administration is geared towards misappropriating as much cash as possible. Everyone is aware of this, but no one realizes its full extent. -30% agricultural output, -30% trade income, -20 Happiness.
Secret Murderer (1)	His irrational fear of assassins has led him to torture and execute a completely innocent visiting nobleman. Fortunately, he has a signed confession of the man's misdeeds. +2 dread
Secret Murderer (2)	His paranoid fantasies about lurking assassins have caused him to torture and execute many men, including one nobleman, for little or no discernable cause. +3 dread -3 piety
Secret Paranoia	His efforts to test his own defenses against potential assassins have caused the deaths of several food tasters and one or two guests. Fortunately he has managed to keep this quiet so far. -5 health, +2 acumen, -1 valor.
Secret Perversion	His preference is for young boys rather than young women. He has managed to keep this a secret so far.
Secret Pride	He cannot admit being wrong, and has killed members of his staff who had the talent to prove him wrong. This trait does, however, give him great confidence in personal combat. -1 command, +3 valor.
Secret Random Justice	He has given up any pretence of justice when dealing with rebels, executing all those captured and randomly selecting other victims by rolling dice. So far no-one has noticed. +3 Dread, -20 Happiness.
Secret Rough Justice	When suppressing rebellions, he secretly includes otherwise innocent petty enemies in the list of those to be arrested and executed. +1 Dread.
Secret Tyrant	He values obedience and his own opinions above all else, and will not tolerate any dissenters, sometimes resorting to assassination to remove them. +2 Dread.

NAME OF VICE/VIRTUE	EFFECTS
Secretly Paranoid and Security Conscious	His efforts to defend against potential assassins go to insane lengths - an important guest was killed by a pit trap while looking for the privy (he has not yet been missed). +3 valor -3 acumen.
Severe Alcoholic	He is a legendary drunk, and his retainers now perform the majority of his duties. -2 command, -2 acumen, -10 health.
Sharp Mind	This man's quick wits and sharp thinking make this a naturally quick study in any subject. +1 Acumen
Silver Tongued	This man can charm the birds from the trees, and nothing he asks is too much trouble for others to do for such a very, very nice man. -3 Dread, +2 Acumen
Skilled Assaulter	He has a talent for assaulting castles. +1 Command when assaulting castles.
Skilled Attacker	He is particularly skilled in directing attacks in the field. +1 Command when attacking.
Skilled Defender	He has a talent for selecting strong defensive positions and exploiting them well. +1 Command when defending.
Skilled Last Stand	He is a specialist in defending when outnumbered more than 2 to 1. +1 to Command in this situation.
Skilled Risky Attacks	He is skilled at attacking when outnumbered. +1 to Command in this situation.
Skilled Siege Defender	He is skilled in siege defense, organizing supplies, maintaining morale, and harrying the enemy. +2 years to siege duration.
Skilled Sieger	He is skilled in the art of taking castles by siege without resorting to an assault. -1 year to siege duration.
Smuggler	He has little regard for the need to formally control trade, preferring instead to fill his own purse with the taxes that would be paid by more honest merchants. -10% agricultural output, -20% trade income.
Specialist Attacker	He specializes in conducting attacks against defensive positions. +3 Command when attacking.
Specialist Siege Defender	He is a specialist in defending against a prolonged siege, bribing, deceiving and outsmarting his enemy to get supplies in. +4 years to siege duration.
Specialist Sieger	His reputation for relentlessly reducing castles by siege is so great than many castles bow to the inevitable and surrender after token resistance. -3 years to siege duration.

NAME OF VICE/VIRTUE	EFFECTS
Spy Network (1)	Despite the obvious disapproval this causes, he still maintains a comprehensive spy network which occasionally gets out of hand . +4 valor vs. spies, -3 loyalty.
Spy Network (2)	He has placed his agents in positions of power, giving him advanced warning of plots against him, even if they are sponsored by the state. +4 valor vs. spies, -2 loyalty.
Steward (Kingdom)	His extensive program of developing farmlands and his regular attention to farming matters has increased agricultural output across the realm. +10 Happiness in all provinces, +10% to all agricultural production.
Steward (Province)	His program of developing local farmlands has brought prosperity to provinces and his regular attention to farming matters has increased agricultural output across the realm. +10 Happiness, +10% to agricultural production.
Strange	This man's strange habits of talking to invisible servants are not normal, but they are certainly disturbing to those around him. -1 Morale, -10 Happiness
Strong Security	Repeated assassination attempts have led him to make personal security a high priority, with extra guards, constant training and incessant drills. It leaves little time for administration. +2 valor -2 acumen.
Stupidly Charitable	His need to do good works is a compulsion, and one that allows scant attention to fiscal reality! -20% agricultural output, -20% trade income, +20 happiness.
Superb Assault Defender	He superb at defending castles against assaults. +3 Command when in this situation.
Superb Last Stand	He is a specialist in defending when outnumbered more than 2 to 1. +3 to Command in this situation.
Superb Risky Attacks	He is a specialist in attacking when outnumbered. +3 to Command in this situation.
Survivor	Having survived an assassination attempt by killing the assassin with a cooking spit, he is very keen to practice combat with a wide variety of weapons and kitchen implements, to the detriment of his other duties. +1 valor -1 acumen.
Suspicious	After surviving an assassination attempt he is suspicious of all around him, and his justice is swifter and harsher than most. +1 dread
Swift Justice	He has been known to execute every last rebel captured as an example to others. +1 Dread.
Sybarite	He enjoys luxury. Good food, fine wine, and fairly outrageous displays of wealth take their toll on his fitness. -2 valor.
Thinker	While his love of abstract thought has made this man clever, it has also made him question matters of faith. -2 Piety, +2 Acumen

NAME OF VICE/VIRTUE	EFFECTS
Timorous	He has fought many battles but seldom gets into combat himself. His men joke about this, but it also lurks in their minds as they are placed in harm's way. -4 morale, -1 valor.
Tortured	Having been captured and tortured, he is obsessed with avoiding capture. This makes his army harder to break, but seriously affects his judgement on the battlefield. +6 morale, -2 command.
Tough Justice	He is draconian in his measures when suppressing rebellions, executing everyone involved and many innocents around him. No one is safe. +3 Dread, -10 Happiness.
Trader (Province)	His policies have encouraged local trade, bringing prosperity to the townsfolk and increasing trade income. +10 Happiness, +10% to trade income.
Trader (Kingdom)	His policies have encouraged trade, bringing prosperity to the townsfolk and increasing trade income across the realm. +10 Happiness in all provinces, +10% to all trade income.
Traumatized	His experiences as a prisoner have left this man traumatized. He will kill anyone who even considers surrender, and he avoids danger in battle. Paradoxically this makes his capture more likely. +9 morale, -3 command.
True Zealot	He follows religious doctrine to the letter, and uses his position to force others to do likewise. +30% zeal when governing.
Truly Pious	He applies his strong religious principles to everything he does, and surrounds himself with like-minded people. +4 piety.
Tyrant	He insists on complete obedience and has been known to have people who oppose him killed. Not a man to be argued with. +3 Dread -20 Happiness.
Unbribable	He is that rarest of things, an honest man. He cannot be bribed for less than a king's ransom. +200% to cost of bribe.
Unhinged Loon	Convinced that he has been made pregnant by an elephant, this man inspires nothing except pity and contempt in equal measures among his followers. -3 Morale, -30 Happiness
Utter Sybarite	His quest for luxury, pleasure and sensual gratification drives his entire being. Only the very best, at whatever price, will do for his refined - or jaded - tastes. -25% agricultural output, -25% trade income.
Utterly Corrupt	He sees extra payments for doing his duties as his proper right and due for the responsibility he carries. He will do nothing without money going into his purse. -20% agricultural output, -20% trade income.

NAME OF VICE/VIRTUE	EFFECTS
Utterly Fearless	This man wouldn't even know how to spell 'fear', let alone feel any when confronting his enemies. +2 Valor, +2 Morale
Vacillator	He often finds himself ordered to abort attacks at the last minute. He hates this, but his men hate it more. -3 Loyalty, -6 Morale.
Venal	He sees money, especially other people's money, as the essential lubricant in getting things done. Wealth rightly flows into his purse merely for carrying out his duties. -20% agricultural output, -20% trade income.
Very Charitable	He devotes some of his wealth to helping the poor. +10 Happiness, +1 piety.
Very Honest	He is an honest man, and this makes him a popular leader. +1 loyalty, +1 morale.
Very Lazy	He is a master of sloth and procrastination, being most creative in devising excuses for putting off hard work. -2 command, -2 acumen.
Very Loyal	He is very loyal, putting duty before personal gain. +2 loyalty.
Very Nervous	His fear of assassins is so great he does not eat well, sleeps little, and rarely goes out in public. This does give him plenty of time for administrative duties. -5 health, +1 acumen.
Voluptuary	His existence is largely given over to the pursuit of his personal pleasures. There are few limits on the amount of money he will spend in this pursuit. -20% agricultural output, -20% trade income.
Weak Assault Defender	He lacks the patience required to defend against castle assaults. -1 Command when defending castles.
Weak Assaulter	He lacks the discipline required to conduct castle assaults. -1 Command when assaulting castles.
Weak Attacker	He does not like taking risks, which make his attacks predictable. -1 Command when attacking.
Weak Defender	The rigid discipline and attention to detail required to effectively defend on the battlefield are not his strong points. -1 Command when defending.
Weak Last Stand	He does not perform well when defending against a superior force. -1 Command in this situation.
Weak Principles	He is not a man of strong principles and is easy to tempt. -20% to Bribery cost.
Weak Siege Defender	He is not good at organizing effective resistance to sieges. -1 year to siege duration.

NAME OF VICE/VIRTUE	EFFECTS
Weak Sieger	He lacks the discipline required to conduct a siege well. +1 year to siege length.
Well Educated	His good education makes him open-minded and adaptable. +1 acumen, +1 command.
Zealot	He follows religious doctrine to the letter, and encourages those under his control to do likewise. +20% zeal when governing.

APPENDIX 4: ARTILLERY AND SHIPS

Here are all the stats and info you need about the boats and artillery pieces in *Medieval: Total War*.

ARTILLERY

BALLISTA

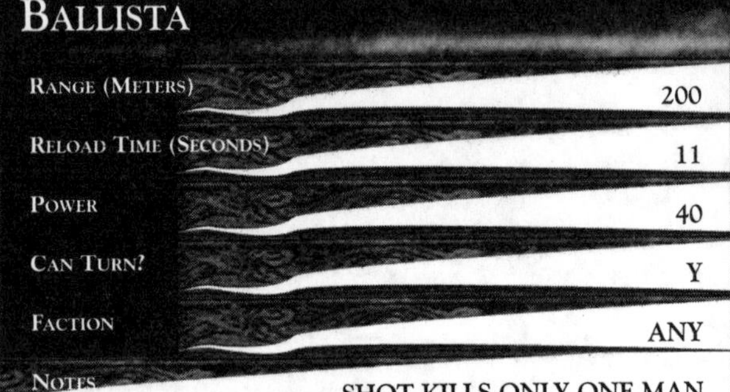

BALLISTA	
RANGE (METERS)	200
RELOAD TIME (SECONDS)	11
POWER	40
CAN TURN?	Y
FACTION	ANY
NOTES	SHOT KILLS ONLY ONE MAN

The ballista's design goes back to the ancient Greeks. It can fire a spear-like bolt or stone missile hundreds of meters with killing force. Although crossbow-like, a ballista uses twisted, spring-like bundles of animal sinew for its power and range.

BOMBARD

BOMBARD	
RANGE (METERS)	320
RELOAD TIME (SECONDS)	20
POWER	150
CAN TURN?	N
FACTION	CHRISTIAN
NOTES	PRONE TO EXPLODE

The bombard, an early gunpowder weapon, is made of wrought iron hoops and mounted on an immobile stand. Bombards are primarily siege weapons and fire stone balls that shatter on impact rather than piercing the target. Although prone to explosions, bombards easily unnerve enemies not used to gunpowder!

CATAPULT

RANGE (METERS)	240
RELOAD TIME (SECONDS)	16
POWER	80
CAN TURN?	Y
FACTION	ANY
NOTES	BOUNCING SHOT, BUT LESS EFFECTIVE THAN CANNONBALLS

The basic design of the catapult goes back to the Romans. The throwing arm is driven by twisted ropes or sinews, and it can hurl missiles quite a long way. The small wheels help to absorb the shock of firing. Although easy to operate and quite powerful, soon the catapult will be outclassed by guns.

CULVERIN

RANGE (METERS)	480
RELOAD TIME (SECONDS)	16
POWER	250
CAN TURN?	Y
FACTION	CHRISTIAN

A culverin is a long-barreled gun on a light carriages. The slim barrel gives a good range and allows the use of less gun-powder per shot, making it safer to fire. Culverins can fire balls up to 45kg, but most generals prefer lighter pieces that are easier to transport to a battlefield.

Demi-Cannon

Range (Meters)	320
Reload Time (Seconds)	20
Power	150
Can Turn?	N
Faction	MUSLIM

A demi-cannon is a small siege weapon. "Small" is a relative term, because demi-cannons are often very heavy! Thanks to the need to mount demi-cannons on sturdy carriages, they aren't moved once they're in place. A demi-cannon might fire shot that weighs up to 30kg and can do substantial damage.

Demi-Culverin

Range (Meters)	320
Reload Time (Seconds)	16
Power	100
Can Turn?	Y
Faction	CHRISTIAN

As the name suggests, a demi-culverin is half the size of a long-barreled culverin. It's a small-bore weapon and usually fires a ball that weighs 3-4kg. Demi-culverins are usually well made and not too expensive, making them useful all-around weapons. Given that they are small, they can be emplaced easily.

Mangonel

Range (Meters)	240
Reload Time (Seconds)	20
Power	250
Can Turn?	N
Faction	ANY

The basic idea of a mangonel, or small catapult, goes back to Classical Greek times. The throwing arm, driven by twisted ropes or sinews, hurls small missiles quite a long way. The frame isn't wheeled, and once it's in place, a mangonel doesn't move. Mangonels are outclassed by gunpowder weaponry.

Mortar

Range (Meters)	240
Reload Time (Seconds)	14
Power	100
Can Turn?	N
Faction	MUSLIM
Notes	HIGH/WIDE ANGLES OF FIRE

A mortar is a short-barreled gun that throws shots on a high trajectory (over fortifications) to plunge down on enemies. Firing mortars can be quite complex. The angle of fire, the amount of gunpowder, and even the wind all affect accuracy. They can be used to great effect in sieges.

Serpentine

Range (Meters)	320
Reload Time (Seconds)	11
Power	40
Can Turn?	Y
Faction	ANY
Notes	MORE OF AN ANTI-PERSONNEL WEAPON

A serpentine is a light cannon with a very long barrel—the name comes from its snake-like proportions—that fires a 1kg ball. It is light, transportable, and quite accurate. It has a good range, and a single shot can kill more than one man.

Siege Cannon

Range (Meters)	560
Reload Time (Seconds)	20
Power	450
Can Turn?	N
Faction	MUSLIM

Siege Cannons are status symbols, and all kings want them in their arsenals! Gunnery is a science rather than a matter of luck. Big guns become practical. Over time, gunsmiths become more skilled and gunpowder improves in quality, so these cannons won't explode and kill the crew rather than the enemy.

Trebuchet

Range (Meters)	240
Reload Time (Seconds)	20
Power	150
Can Turn?	N
Faction	ANY

The Trebuchet is a huge weapon—so big that it is usually built on the battlefield! The throwing arm uses a counterweight to hurl missiles tremendous distances. Missiles can be heavy boulders, fire pots, diseased animals, prisoners, captured spies, or corpses to demoralize the enemy!

SHIPS

Baggala

Range	2
Attack	2
Defense	2
Speed	2
Strength	0

The baggala has the same basic design as a dhow but carries a catapult. This can be used to throw pots of Greek fire (an incendiary mixture of chemicals) at enemy ships. Pirates also use the baggala, but with rock missiles because they lack access to Greek fire.

Barque

Range	1
Attack	1
Defense	2
Speed	3
Strength	0

The barque is a small, single-masted sailing vessel. It's suitable only for short voyages across shallow waters, but it is cheap and easy to build. Away from land, a heavy swell could sink a barque. The crew is few in number and unlikely to mount a very effective boarding action.

Boom

Range	2
Attack	4
Defense	3
Speed	2
Strength	0

The boom is a dhow-like warship. It carries a small cannon as armament to bombard targets, and it has sufficient crew to allow boarding attacks as well. It is strong enough to meet galleys on better-than-equal terms and handy enough under sail to attack from most quarters.

Caravel

Range	1
Attack	3
Defense	3
Speed	1
Strength	0

The caravel is a deep-sea ship, capable of surviving some storms. Originally used in the Mediterranean, it is now used everywhere. It is capable in a fight—rather than exceptional—because it has small catapults to bombard enemy ships but it is not handy in light winds.

Carrack

Range	3
Attack	6
Defense	3
Speed	3
Strength	0

The carrack is a sleek, refined derivative of the cog, able to withstand rough seas and carry a substantial tonnage. It also carries cannons, culverins, and demi-culverins, a contingent of soldiers, and a large crew. Generally, a carrack can be relied on to defeat any other ship.

Cog

Range	2
Attack	4
Defense	2
Speed	2
Strength	0

The cog came about thanks to shipwrights' experiments and gradual improvements in shipbuilding and rigging. It's a sturdy vessel with a deep draft so it can carry a large crew and troops. With demi-cannons as well, it is a handy all-rounder in combat.

Dhow

Range	1
Attack	1
Defense	1
Speed	3
Strength	0

The dhow is a small trading and military ship found throughout the Arab world. It is fast and maneuverable, able to use light winds to enter any fight and also stay out of reach of more powerful enemies. Dhows carry no weapons; their crews attack by grappling and boarding.

Dromon

Range	1
Attack	1
Defense	0
Speed	4
Strength	0

The dromon is a small galley, with both a sail and oars. It is used as a scout and for coastal work, thanks to its shallow draught. It isn't a battleship, but in calm weather a dromon can outmaneuver and outfight smaller ships and still have the speed to escape!

Firegalley

Range	1
Attack	3
Defense	1
Speed	2
Strength	0

The firegalley is an improvement on the galley of old, equipped with a catapult to rain Greek fire upon an enemy. Add soldiers and a ram, and the firegalley is a potent ship. Greek fire is a fearsome concoction that burns when wet—the perfect naval weapon!

Galley

Range	1
Attack	1
Defense	1
Speed	2
Strength	0

The galley is tried, tested, and ancient. With oars and sail, it is suited to Mediterranean waters. The crew is mostly rowers, with a small fighting contingent of archers and soldiers. A galley has grappling irons and a ram to break an enemy's hull and oars.

Gungalley

Range	1
Attack	5
Defense	3
Speed	1
Strength	0

Cannons are the main armament of a gungalley, although it still has a ram and troops who can board enemy vessels. It is a formidable ship by any standard, with both sails and oars. However, it does have blind spots and is not very handy in a close fight.

Longboat

Range	1
Attack	1
Defense	1
Speed	3
Strength	0

The Viking longboat appears to be a simple vessel, but actually it's the end result of many generations of careful improvement. It is capable of long ocean voyages, can be easily beached, and can carry large cargoes, but as a fighting vessel it is only suitable for boarding attacks.

Wargalley

Range	1
Attack	3
Defense	3
Speed	1
Strength	0

A wargalley is a large vessel equipped with several powerful catapults, each capable of throwing Greek fire pots. If one catapult is good, more must be better! Although it also has a ram, it is relatively unwieldy under oars or sail.

Appendix 5: How Offices of State Differ by Faction

Remember that factions cannot change their basic religion. So, Islamic factions can't construct explicitly Christian buildings, and vice versa. For example, the Islamic factions can't build Cathedrals, which is why you won't find a Cathedral entry in the tables for the Almohads, the Egyptians, and the Turkish.

Several of the buildings in *Medieval: Total War* produce Offices of State, which you can confer on your generals. While the buildings produce roughly the same rank of office from faction to faction, the official titles of these ranks have different names and sometimes slightly different effects. The tables below show the Offices of State produced by the buildings for each faction. Yes, it is possible to give a general the Office of Archbishop!

BUILDING	TITLE OF OFFICE
Royal Palace	Qadi al-Quda
Constable's Palace	Master of the Kalifah's Horses
Marshal's Palace	Vizier of the Army
Chancellery	Grand Vizier
Admiralty	Amir al-Bahr

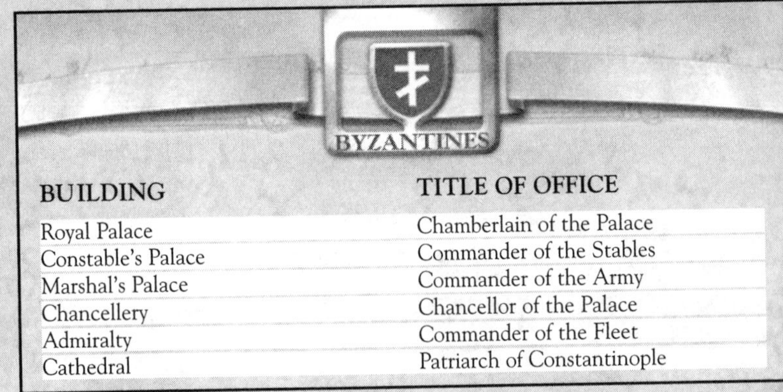

BUILDING	TITLE OF OFFICE
Royal Palace	Chamberlain of the Palace
Constable's Palace	Commander of the Stables
Marshal's Palace	Commander of the Army
Chancellery	Chancellor of the Palace
Admiralty	Commander of the Fleet
Cathedral	Patriarch of Constantinople

BUILDING	TITLE OF OFFICE
Royal Palace	Qadi al-Quda
Constable's Palace	Master of the Stables
Marshal's Palace	Commander of a Thousand
Chancellery	Grand Vizier of the Palace
Admiralty	Amir al-Bahr

BUILDING	TITLE OF OFFICE
Royal Palace	Lord Great Chamberlain
Constable's Palace	Constable of the Tower
Marshal's Palace	Warden of the Northern Marches
Chancellery	Chancellor of the Exchequer
Admiralty	Warden of the Cinque Ports
Cathedral	Archbishop of Canterbury

BUILDING	TITLE OF OFFICE
Royal Palace	Grand Chamberlain
Constable's Palace	Constable of France
Marshal's Palace	Marshal of France
Chancellery	Chancellor
Admiralty	Admiral of France
Cathedral	Archbishop of Reims

BUILDING	TITLE OF OFFICE
Royal Palace	Imperial Chamberlain
Constable's Palace	Grand Constable of the Empire
Marshal's Palace	Grand Marshal of the Empire
Chancellery	Imperial Chancellor
Admiralty	Grand Admiral of the Fleet
Cathedral	Archbishop of Worms

BUILDING	TITLE OF OFFICE
Royal Palace	Chamberlain of the Major Council
Constable's Palace	Constable of the Army
Marshal's Palace	Captain-General of Mercenaries
Chancellery	Chancellor of the Major Council
Admiralty	Admiral of the Arsenale
Cathedral	Archbishop of Milan

BUILDING	TITLE OF OFFICE
Royal Palace	Chamberlain of Poland
Constable's Palace	Master of the King's Horse
Marshal's Palace	Grand Marshal of Poland
Chancellery	High Chancellor of Poland
Admiralty	Admiral
Cathedral	Archbishop of Kraków

BUILDING	TITLE OF OFFICE
Royal Palace	Lord Chamberlain
Constable's Palace	Captain of the Stables
Marshal's Palace	Captain-General
Chancellery	Keeper of the Privy Seal
Admiralty	Lord High Admiral
Cathedral	Archbishop of Toledo

BUILDING	TITLE OF OFFICE
Royal Palace	Chief Eunuch
Constable's Palace	Master of the Sultan's Horse
Marshal's Palace	General of the Divan
Chancellery	Grand Vizier
Admiralty	Admiral of the Fleet

BUILDING	TITLE OF OFFICE
Royal Palace	Earl Chamberlain of Denmark
Constable's Palace	Master of the Stables
Marshal's Palace	Earl Marshal of Denmark
Chancellery	Chancellor of Denmark
Admiralty	Admiral of the North
Cathedral	Archbishop of Lund

BUILDING	TITLE OF OFFICE
Royal Palace	Chamberlain of the Great Palace
Constable's Palace	Grand Warder of the Kremlin
Marshal's Palace	Grand Marshal
Chancellery	Chancellor of All The Russias
Admiralty	Grand Admiral of the Fleet
Cathedral	Metropolitan of Moscow